MENTAL HEALTH STATUS AND COUNSELLING OF "CHILDREN IN CONFLICT WITH THE LAW"

KALPANA PURUSHOTHAMAN

Contents

CHAPTER I

I INTRODUCTION

India has a huge population of children in need of care and protection. Providing mental health services to this population remains a challenge for the State, the mental health community and civil society organizations. Children in conflict with the law also most often belong to this category of children in need of care and protection. When a child is alleged to have committed an offence and comes into conflict with the law, he comes into contact with the juvenile justice system, which is his first real opportunity to be screened for any mental health risks, referred for any specialized mental health service – including counselling, psychiatric services, life skills education and so on. There is a need for all children, and especially growing children and adolescents, including CICL, to be taught that there are consequences for their actions, for they which will be held accountable. However, the means for ensuring such accountability must be grounded in developmentally appropriate correctional mechanisms, the human rights of children and a deeper understanding of the circumstances that led to such behavior or actions.

Adolescence is a developmental phase of tremendous growth; development and changes, and hence amenable to reform and learning positive, socially and legally acceptable behaviours. If at this age, children coming into conflict with the law have access to an array of mental health services including screening and identification of mental illness and risks, treatment and care of any mental health conditions, education and rehabilitative services, life skills and re-socialization – it is more likely to result in reformation and prevent reoffending than simply incarcerating them in the juvenile justice system or sending them to prison and exposing them to adult criminals and further crime.

Mental health of children in conflict with the law is not a very well researched subject in India. The risk factors for the mental health of children in conflict with the law include, but may not be limited to domestic violence, physical and sexual abuse, substance dependence, emotional neglect, homelessness, poverty, lack of parental care and supervision, lack of access or affordability of education, undetected and untreated mental illness. Having empirical data to understand the risk factors that impinge on the mental health of children in conflict with the law will enable in designing and implementing effective treatment, care, prevention, remedial and / or rehabilitative services. At present, there is no empirical data available about the number of children in conflict with the law affected by mental illness, the nature of mental health conditions or the presence of risk factors predisposing them to mental health problems. Hence, the nature and the magnitude of the problem are not known and understood adequately. Consequently, the mental health of children in conflict with the law in India has not been understood or addressed adequately or effectively.

1.1 Concept of Mental Health

Health is regarded as a fundamental human right by all countries around the world. Health has been defined by the World Health Organization as not merely the absence of disease or infirmity, but as "a state of complete physical, social and mental wellbeing of an individual ". (WHO 1948). Further, health is also considered a resource for everyday life and a positive concept that highlights personal and social resources as well as physical capabilities. (Ottawa Charter for Health Promotion, 1986). **Mental health**, more specifically, is defined by the WHO as "***a state of well-being in which every individual realizes his or her own potential, can cope with the normal stresses of life, can work productively and fruitfully, and is able to make a contribution to her or his community***. Mental health explanations also often include psychological well-being, emotional, behavioural and social maturity, balance of work and relationships, and the presence or absence of mental illness. However, mental health is not merely the absence of mental illness but also includes other aspects of emotional and social wellbeing like emotional stability, clear thinking, ability to relate to oneself and to others, to deal with change and cope with the demands of various life situations.

Mental Health services refers to a broad array of activities directly or indirectly related to the mental well-being components included in the WHO's definition of health, the prevention of mental disorders, the promotion of well-being and the treatment and rehabilitation of people affected by mental disorders. Mental health services used to be traditionally thought of as the medical and clinical services provided by physicians and other licensed health professionals, particularly psychologists, counsellors, social workers, psychiatric nurses, etc. However, in addition to the traditional 'disease management' and pharmacological services, mental health services also include rehabilitative services focused on promoting higher levels of functioning and preventing regression or relapse, educational services, life skills training, preparing for future relationships and employment, vocational / job training, family-focussed programs support services needed to compensate for deficits or to modify unsafe / unhealthy behaviour that may be a result of the child's illness, disability, institutionalization, separation from family, addiction to drugs/alcohol, exposure to violence/abuse and so on.

In the context of children in conflict with the law, mental health services may include, but not be limited to appropriate facilities, services, programs, trained personnel, protections and opportunities for these children to heal and recover from abusive or traumatic pasts or environments, negotiate the challenges of the juvenile justice system and participate, contribute and thrive in the community.

1.1.2. The "Child", the "child in need of care and protection" and the "child in conflict with the law"

A "child" is defined under the United Nations Convention on the Rights of the Child, as '*a child means every human being below the age of eighteen years unless under the law applicable to the child, majority is attained earlier*.' (UNCRC, 1989). In the present study, the definitions of "child' and "child in conflict with the law" and "child in need of care and protection", as provided under the Juvenile Justice (Care and Protection of Children) Act, 2015, have been considered as the definition of a "child in conflict with the law."

According to Section 2 (12) of the Juvenile Justice, (Care & Protection of Children) Act, 2015, "child" means a person who has not completed ***eighteen years of age***. "Child in conflict with law" means **a child who is alleged or found to have committed an offence and who has not completed eighteen years of age on the date of commission of such offence** (Section 2 (13), Juvenile Justice, Care & Protection of Children Act, 2015). "Child in need of care and protection" has been defined under (Section 2 (14)) and includes children in distress, neglected, destitute, abandoned, abused, orphaned, trafficked, child labour, child marriage, and other vulnerable circumstances. Therefore, a child alleged or found to be in conflict with the law may also be a ***child in need of care and protection.***

It is essential, to note that not all children who are alleged to have committed an offence are found guilty of it. There are children in the juvenile justice system, who may be actually innocent of the crimes that they have been charged with, but due to a combination of various reasons including caste, class, religion and socioeconomic factors, they find themselves charged with or punished for offences that they have not committed. Such children are often also susceptible to a range of mental health problems like depression, attempting suicide and violence; all of which could lead them to get further sucked into a life of crime and pose a risk to their mental health.

1.1.3 Mental Health problems of children and adolescents in general

The mental health of a person is determined by several biological, social, and psychological and even socio-economic factors at any given point of time. Further, persistent financial pressures, low levels of education, stressful work conditions, social exclusion, exposure to violence, gender discrimination, human rights violations are recognized risks to the mental health of individuals and communities. In addition, there are also some biological causes as well as psychological and personality factors that may make some people vulnerable to mental disorders. (WHO2019)

According to WHO's Adolescent Mental Health Factsheet (2018), 10-20% of children and adolescents around the world suffer from some type of mental health problems which remain underdiagnosed and undertreated. Most of the mental health disorders begin by the age of 14 years and include conditions like depression, anxiety, eating disorders, risk taking and self-harming behaviours, and disorders that include symptoms of psychosis which often have their onset in late adolescence or early adulthood. If untreated, these conditions have a seriously detrimental effect on children's development, academic progress, and their potential to live fulfilling and productive lives. Such children also face major challenges battling social stigma, exclusion and even discrimination with no access to health care and education facilities, in violation of their fundamental human rights.

Research in the area of Adverse Childhood Experiences (ACE) confirms that children carry the effects of childhood experiences into adulthood and that adverse childhood experiences in the first 18 years of life are strongly related to the development of risk factors for disease and well-being throughout the life course of an individual. The challenges that children face in their home or school environment often affect their life and their health, creating symptoms of what are described as "toxic stress". Toxic stress, is different from manageable stress and involves the long-term changes in brain architecture and organ systems that develop when extreme, prolonged and repeated stress is left untreated. Though there are no specific studies on the prevalence of Adverse Childhood Experiences among children in conflict with the law in India, it would be a reasonable assumption to make that most of the children in the Indian juvenile justice system would have experienced a combination of Adverse Childhood Experiences in their lives already.

1.1.4 Mental health problems of children in "conflict with the law" in general and in India

Research findings in the US show that there is a strong correlation between mental illnesses and children in conflict with the law. It is seen that the prevalence rate of mental disorders of youth within the justice system is consistently higher than that of those within the general population of adolescents (Grisso 2000). Out of the 2 million youth who enter the juvenile justice system in the US, approximately 50 to 75 percent meet the criteria for a mental health disorder. Affective disorders, psychotic disorders, anxiety disorders, post-traumatic stress, substance use disorders and disruptive behaviour disorders are some of the common mental health disorders found among youth in the juvenile justice system (Grisso 2008). However, no such information is available either about the prevalence or the nature of mental health problems of children in conflict with law in India.

1.1.4.1 Girls in conflict with the law

Not only in India, but worldwide, the juvenile justice system is primarily one that is a system designed for boys and girls are often neglected. Historically, the focus has been on protecting society from out-of-control adolescents, mainly boys. The juvenile justice system therefore, is also almost totally built on male models. The Indian system is no different. It is important to understand the socio-cultural context of girls in conflict with law to understand the mental health needs of girls in conflict with the law. There is a common perception in India that all children in conflict with the law are always male and that there are no girl children in conflict with the law. While it is true that the majority of offences committed by children in conflict with the law are by males, a small percentage of girls also do come into conflict with the law. But this population of girls in conflict with the law is rather invisible and often left out of all mental health interventions and rehabilitation initiatives.

1.1.5 Counsellor and counselling for children in conflict with the law in India

The role of the counsellor in the juvenile justice system is very crucial and demanding. It calls for a combination of professional competence and personal compassion in the counsellor to provide effective counselling services in the given correctional settings, expecting reform in the face of limited resources, striving for rehabilitation often without access to rehabilitative services and attempting social reintegration even as families and communities struggle to include children in conflict with the law in their regular lives and communities. At the same time, despite the challenges, the counsellor at any correctional institution is in the unique position of making a very valuable contribution to the mental health of children and families facing very challenging circumstances in their lives.

Section 18 of the Juvenile Justice Act, 2015, mentions counselling services (including individual, group and family counselling) as part of the orders that can be passed for a juvenile in conflict with the law, while the JJ Rules 2016 mention requirement of a Mental Health Care Plan and Individual care Plan, referral services of a medical or psychiatric nature, etc. However, the actual implementation of these legislations for a child in conflict with the law rests on the shoulders of a number of key stakeholders including the JJB, the probationary officer, and most importantly, the **counsellor** at the Observation Home or Special Home, who is entrusted with this task of ensuring that mental health services are made available to every child entering the juvenile justice system.

A professionally trained counsellor can play a key part in facilitating access to a range of mental health services to the CICL and his/her family. However, while every CICL is guaranteed the right to legal aid as per the Constitution of India and the Legal Services Authority Act, unlike free legal aid panels set up by various State Legal Services Authorities providing free legal aid to juveniles in conflict with the law, there are no professional or statutory agencies set up to provide mental health services to juveniles and / or their families. It is known fact that there is a severe lack of qualified personnel to identify and respond to the mental health needs in children in the juvenile justice system in India. Many children who urgently need clinical intervention may not be generally referred for mental health services unless the child's presenting problem is very visible and/or poses challenges in managing the child in the child care institution.

While some of the mental health needs could be catered to by the counsellor being appointed under the ICPS in the OH / SH, some children might need specialized mental health treatment and care. Especially children suffering from mental disorders, physical or mental disabilities, emotional disturbances, congenital conditions, behavioural disorders, etc. need a level and standard of clinical intervention which would be beyond what a counsellor or social worker can or should provide. These children would need the services of a child psychiatrist, special educator, etc. for clinical assessment, accurate diagnosis, treatment and management, rehabilitation planning, follow ups, etc. Psychosocial care services needed include emergency treatment, ambulatory service, hospital care, community-based family counselling, psychotherapy, vocational rehabilitation, etc. Referral services may also include services outpatient psychiatric clinics in general hospitals and clinics, rehabilitation services for children after their discharge from a psychiatric facility, supervised care and support at home (at the institution or at the child's home), etc – none of which are currently available. Without mental health and psychological wellbeing, reform, rehabilitation and social reintegration are simply not possible. Therefore, every single child who comes in contact with the juvenile justice system should receive the services of a trained, experienced and competent counsellor; not only children who might be suffering from clinically classified mental illness, disorders or conditions.

Appointing a single counsellor to service groups of children is impractical, unrealistic and not in the interests of the child. The effectiveness of any counselling process is dependent upon the quality of counsellor–client relationships (therapeutic alliance) and this requires both time and application from both. Counselling children and adolescents in contact and conflict with the law requires a special and unique set of skills. Poorly trained, inexperienced and unskilled counsellors appointed for these high-risk children is inadequate to meet the urgent and critical mental health needs of the children in conflict with the law in the juvenile justice system.

1.2 "Children in conflict with the law " in the history of juvenile justice legislation in India

During the British rule in India, children believed or found to be indulging in illegal or antisocial activities were sent to residential institutions, for reform and punishment. Some of these institutions also focussed on teaching these young children, mostly boys, some skill or trade that they could use to find employment once they went out of these homes. Apprentice training and vocational training were the main focus of these institutions. In India, these homes were called Borstal Homes; which was a place where youth suspected of antisocial behaviour were sent for punishments and reform. As of December 31, 2016, there were 20 functioning borstal schools spread across 9 states in India, having an inmate population of 969. (NCRB,2016).

The foundation for the modern juvenile justice system in India was laid by the Indian Jail Committee (1919-1920) which recommended that children who commit crimes must be treated differently from adult offenders and that detention of 'juvenile offenders' must be prohibited. The Indian Jail Committee also recommended the constitution of juvenile courts with informal procedures and reformatory schools. One of the earliest legislations in the area of juvenile justice in India was the Madras Children's Act, in 1920, through which a juvenile court was established for inquiry into offences by children. Following this, many states enacted their own laws regarding children caught in crime and established a variety of reformatory schools and remand homes with the aim of correcting, reforming and rehabilitating these 'young offenders', under a welfare approach.

1.2.1 Juvenile Justice Board

The Juvenile Justice (Care and Protection) Act, 2015 is the prevailing legislation with respect to children in conflict with the law and places the responsibility for adjudicating the cases relating to children in conflict with the law on the Juvenile Justice Board (JJB). The JJB is a three–member, multi-disciplinary team, headed by a Chairperson who is a Principal Magistrate, while the other two members are Social Work Members, with backgrounds in child psychology, education, social work, and related disciplines. One of the social work members must mandatorily be a woman. The purpose of this unique composition of the Board is to adjudicate cases based on an understanding of not just the offence that has been allegedly committed and the child's role in it, but also the circumstances that lead the child into coming into conflict with the law, in order to enable his/her reform, rehabilitation and social reintegration.

1.2.1 Correctional Institutions in India for CICL

Three types of correctional institutions have been established for CICL in India under the JJ Act, 2015.

1.2.1.1 Observation Home

This is for housing children alleged to be in conflict with the law. " (Section 2 (40), Juvenile Justice (Care and Protection of Children) Act, 2015).

1.2.1.2 Special Home

A Special Home is an institution for housing and providing rehabilitative services for children found to be in conflict with the law. (Section 2 (56), Juvenile Justice (Care and Protection of Children) Act, 2015).

1.2.1.3 Place of Safety

A place of safety is an institution or a place, other than a police lockup or jail, where children alleged or found to be in conflict with the law may be housed. (Section 2 (46), Juvenile Justice (Care and Protection of Children) Act, 2015).

1.3. Child Rights and CICL: The Indian scenario

India is a signatory to the United Nations Convention the Rights of the Child UNCRC), which lays down that children are entitled to special care and assistance. For children in conflict with the law, it is crucial to recognize the legal as well as psychosocial contexts in which such care and assistance is provided.

Article 3 of the UNCRC directs that when any action is taken concerning children, the primary concern is their 'best interests'. For children in conflict with the law, any decision that is taken by any stakeholder or functionary, the **'best interest' principle** is the guiding principle to arrive at legal as well as psychosocial outcomes taken with respect to the child. Drawing from this, the JJ, 2015 Act – Chapter II (iv) relating to General principles of Care and Protection of Children highlights the Principle of Best interest directing that all decisions regarding the child must be based on the primary consideration that they are in the best interest of the child and aimed at helping the child to develop to his / her full potential.

Article 3 (1) of the UNCRC places an obligation on public and private social welfare institutions, courts of law, administrative authorities and legislative bodies to ensure that the best interests of the child are assessed and taken as a primary consideration in all actions affecting children. This principle must be observed in all health – related decisions concerning individual children or children as a group.

General Comment No. 4 (in 2003), the Committee highlights the best interests of the child in the context of having access to appropriate information on health issues and highlighting the need for special attention to certain categories of children, including children and adolescents with psychosocial disabilities. Children in conflict with the law are quite likely to suffer from various kinds of psychosocial disabilities requiring support in institutional as well as community settings and hence are included in the interpretation of this General Comment.

Article 12 of the UNCRC refers to another important principle which is the **Right to Participation**, which has significance for children in conflict with the law. The JJ Act , 2015, refers to this key tenet as the Principle of Participation, in Section 3 (iii), Chapter II General Principles of Care and Protection of Children, Juvenile Justice (Care and Protection of Children) Act, 2015, which instructs that every child must have the right to be heard and participate in decisions and processes that affect his interest, and that the child's views must be taken into consideration keeping in mind his / her age and maturity. However, due to a combination of complex social, cultural and systemic reasons, it is doubtful that the 'voice' of the child is actually heard in the Indian juvenile justice system or whether he is able to or enabled to participate in matters and decisions which have such a significant bearing on his life and future. The CICL in India is more likely to be a passive recipient or silent bystander rather than an active, informed and empowered participant in his case before the juvenile justice system.

Specifically, **Article 24** of the UNCRC provides that children have the right to the enjoyment of the highest attainable standard of health and to access health and medical services, and particularly primary and preventative healthcare and to health education.

The Committee on the Rights of the Child, General Comment No. 15 (2013) interprets children's right to health as defined in Article 24 as an inclusive right which includes the right to grow and develop to one's full potential and live in conditions that enable them to attain the highest standards of health though the implementation of programs that address the underlying determinants of health. This also includes health promotion, timely and appropriate prevention, curative, rehabilitative and palliative services.

A holistic and integrative approach to health places the realization of children's right to health within the broader framework of international human rights obligations. This is the manner in which the right to health of children in conflict with the law also needs to be understood, implemented and advocated. However, frequent media reports of abuse in custodial institutions across India and the increased involvement of children and adolescents in offences indicate that despite all the legislative intent and statutory obligations to protect the rights of these vulnerable children, the rights of children in conflict with the law India, especially with regard to mental health appear to be poorly protected.

1.4. Legal provisions in the JJ Act, 2015 and JJ Model Rules, 2016 governing Mental Health Services for Children alleged and found to be in Conflict with Law

The Preamble of the JJ Act, 2015, highlights the legislative goals of care, protection, development, treatment, and social re-integration, and other substantive provisions provide for the State to provide rehabilitation, reformation and restoration services. The Act is based on the idea of **entitlement of all children** to care, protection, treatment and development as reflected in provisions dealing with rehabilitation and social integration, mental health, etc.

The law specifically requires the State to provide **rehabilitation and re-integration services** to all children residing in all institutions registered under the JJ Act, 2015, which includes children residing in the OH and SH as well. These services include mental health interventions, such as individual counselling, and other kinds of counselling services. (Section 53(1)(vi), JJ Act, 2015). The Act also urges for a process of rehabilitation and social integration based on an Individual Care Plan giving options for family-based care, sponsorship, adoption and foster care, placement with a fit person or in a fit facility. (Section 39(1), JJ Act, 2015)

The JJBs are entrusted with the responsibility of ensuring the mental health rights of the CICLs brought before them by basing their orders on the Social Investigation Reports and Individual Care Plans which are required to be prepared for each and every child appearing before the Board. Based on this, the JJB passes interim and final orders for the care, protection, development, treatment, social re-integration, and rehabilitation.

Mental Health practitioners are required to provide a range of mental health services to children and their families as per the provisions of the JJ Act 2015, (Section 2(14), Section 53 (1) (vii), Section 53 (1)(ii) , Section 92 , Sec 93(1)), and the JJ Model Rules 2016 (Rule 8 (3) (iv), Rule 26-26(7)(3)(6)(7), Rule 29(6)(iii)(xii), Rule 33(8)(ii)(iii), Rule 34 (3)(i)(ii), (Rule 34 (3)(xi)(xii), Rule 35 (1)(4)(5) ,

The law recognizes that, for counselling for children to be effective, the ambience and milieu in which such a service is provided should naturally be child friendly and therapeutic. Milieu-based interventions and individual therapy is therefore compulsory for every child and shall be provided in all institutions, including the OH and SH. (Rule 35 (3)). A child-friendly environment is an essential element of the fundamental principles enshrined in the JJ Model Rules and has a powerful effect and impact on the psychological well-being of the child. Having an environment that stimulates growth, promotes healing, provides opportunities for introspection and reflection, strengthens positive beliefs about oneself and the world, builds resilience in the face of hardship and respects the child's right to be safe, protected, healthy, nurtured, educated and live with dignity, is integral to the mental and emotional wellbeing of children in the juvenile justice system.

Mental health needs of institutional staff, caregivers, functionaries in the police, JJBs and District Child Protection Units, also need urgent and close attention, given the extremely challenging conditions in which they work. Unless they are supported and their mental health needs are taken care of, they will not be able to effectively discharge their duties under the law. However, this is one area that appears to have been overlooked and does not find mention in the law.

1.5 Experience of a child "coming into conflict with the law" and entry to the Observation Home

A child who comes into conflict with the law goes through a wide range of experiences which can have a huge impact on his/her emotional wellbeing. It may begin with contact with the police upon being charged with committing an offence, which, even in adults is an anxiety-inducing experience. Preliminary questioning at the police station includes the police preparing a First Information Report and a brief background report giving some basic details about the child, followed by production of the child before the Juvenile Justice Board. There is a formal case registered against the child and the legal process is formally initiated. The JJB then issues instructions for the child in conflict with the law to be remanded to custody at the Observation Home. The Observation Homes all over India, like most correctional institutions housing children in conflict with the law in most parts of the world, is an environment that does not have the care, comfort, emotional assurance or familiarity of a family or home setting.

Once in the Observation Home, the child is expected to follow a bewildering number of rules and regulations with regard to every aspect of his /her life – eating, sleeping, bathing, etc. While at the OH, the child would also be produced before the Juvenile Justice Board at regular intervals (as per date of hearing) and questioned about various aspects of his/her life including the circumstances which brought him into contact / conflict with the law. This puts the child in a position of having to defend / explain himself/herself, which is, in itself an extremely stressful experience for most children. The child further lives in a state of constant stress and prolonged anxiety till he is granted bail and continues to stay in detention at the OH. This state of uncertainty continues till the child's legal case is brought to completion, which could be weeks, months or years.

In addition, the process of coming into conflict with the law may result in the child being exposed to the police, older peers or adults in the system who may subject him to bullying, violence, abuse – physical, verbal or sexual, and other traumatic experiences usually associated with custodial settings. This results in many children living in a state of perpetual fear, anger, anxiety and continuous hypervigilance during their stay at the OH /SH and even after they are released on bail or after the case is legally over.

This is the general experience for a child who comes in contact or conflict with the juvenile justice system in India, which disrupts and impacts a child's mental and emotional wellbeing. Rarely do children in conflict with the law in India experience the juvenile justice system as a child-friendly and child-rights friendly system giving them either justice or dignity.

1.5.1 Effects of institutional settings and its impact on mental health of CICL

Lack of a familiar environment, separation from family, absence or lack of attentive, loving caregivers, constant fear about physical and sexual safety, lack of positive learning opportunities and formal education, lack of positive life experiences that shape emotional and moral character, fear of being sent and sentenced to 'jail'(even though Indian laws forbid children from being jailed), fear of being abandoned by family for having come into conflict with the law, absence of close, loving relationships, lack of adequate or appropriate means for emotional expression, social stigma, exclusion and lack of community, absence of positive role models, uncertainty about the future, are a few factors that have lasting impact on the mental health and emotional wellbeing of children in institutional care.

The mental health risks to children in institutional care include, and may not be limited to, re-traumatisation, secondary victimization, possibility of developing chronic mental illnesses if left untreated, recidivism as they might resort to illegal or inappropriate behaviour when earlier issues remain unresolved, difficulty in reintegrating with the family and acquiring antisocial behaviours as a result of exposure to negative peers. In addition, many of these children may often suffer from physical health problems including injuries, infections, repeated illness and malnutrition. These children often have poor life skills, struggle with emotional regulation, low self-esteem, lack the ability to make socially appropriate choices, engage in high risk behaviours, do not fully understand the connection between behaviour and consequences, have poor impulse control, have academic difficulties resulting in truancy or disruption in education.

1.6 Psychosocial variables and mental health of CICL

1.6.1 CICL and Indian society

A child coming into conflict with the law in India goes through social and emotional consequences as well as legal consequences on account of his brush with the law. The family of the child faces social stigma with relatives and community members often excluding them from social events as well as practical difficulties like landlords refusing to rent them a house on account of their child having had some contact with the law. The child in conflict with the law also faces considerable difficulties in social and educational reintegration as schools and colleges often refuse to allow them to continue their education. There is also a labelling by the police, the functionaries and sometimes even by some of the JJBs of the child as a 'habitual', 'repeater', 'delinquent' etc. which acts as a 'self-fulfilling prophecy' for the child and he takes on a career of crime to fulfil the expectation of the adults around him. When an individual behaves in a manner that others consider socially or legally inappropriate or deviant, and the individual is socially labelled for it, that individual is likely to eventually internalize and accept this label and further behave in the socially labelled manner.

Some experts and activists advocating for children in conflict with the law argue that no child is born a criminal and therefore, offences by children must be treated not only as a legal issue but as a social, psychological and public health issue. Children violating the boundaries of law or developing behaviours that bring them into contact and /or conflict with the law have to be understood in the **social context** of their developmental history, family history, quality of parenting and care received, access to positive experiences and individuals in life that help them imbibe socially and legally appropriate behaviour as well as the social circumstances under which they exist in the community. Hence, offences by children must be understood not only in legal terms but also as social and public health problems which have long term consequences for the child and the family as well as the community at large.

1.6.2 Violence and Children in conflict with the law

It is well established that exposure to violence in childhood – whether as a recipient, bystander, participant or initiator, can have far reaching and detrimental consequences on the psychological make up as well as coping strategies of the individual well into adolescence and adulthood. The link between early exposure to violence and antisocial behaviour in adolescence and adulthood is also well established. There is a social and cultural sanction given to parents, family and teachers to use violence as a means of disciplining and raising children. Children in conflict with the law in India may have almost certainly experienced or been exposed to violence in one or more setting – either at home or at school as many parents and teachers in India believe that violence is an acceptable and often necessary means of disciplining their children. Violence by peers and gangs in school and neighbourhood as part of bullying or harassment or as witnesses (or even participants) of social and community violence seen frequently in riots, mobs and crowd violence is also a fairly common childhood experience for most CICL. In addition, despite laws prohibiting any use of force on the child by the Indian police, apprehension of a CICL is almost always accompanied by some element and different degrees of violence.

However, any empirical evidence on the nature of violence suffered by children in India is almost impossible to gather given the high social value placed on family honour, respect for teachers and impunity granted to the police ; all of which, make it impossible for children to report or even speak about the pervasiveness of violence in their lives. Speaking against one's family would be perceived as bringing disrepute to the family, speaking against teachers would be showing disrespect for them and speaking against the police would invite reprisals and run the risk of false cases being foisted on vulnerable children and adolescents. Speaking against the violence in custodial settings in the juvenile justice system would lead to harsher punishment, withdrawal of privileges and perhaps more violence. All of this leads to a conspiracy of silence against violence suffered by children which is not acknowledged by the State, families, education system or the juvenile justice system. Lack of data on this issue in turn, often leads to a denial of the existence of the problem itself by policy makers in India.

1.6.3 Substance Abuse and children in conflict with the law

Substance abuse in adolescents as a risk factor for mental illness as well as involvement in illegal activities has long been established. When combined with other risk factors like family neglect or substance abuse within the family (commonly alcoholic father), peer pressure to experiment, it can lead adolescents to become entangled with law breaking behaviour that often brings them into conflict with the law. "The early onset of substance use is often associated with comorbid psychiatric or behavioural psychopathology, including hyperactivity, inattention or conduct symptoms, which may make this age group more vulnerable to engage in high-risk behaviours. There is also a greater likelihood of later development of non-communicable and lifestyle diseases among early-onset substance users." (Dhawan, A., et al. (2017)

1.6.4 Family and children in conflict with the law

Family is one of the main influencers of behaviour for most individuals. Family's size and composition, history of substance addiction, mental illness, child's exposure to domestic violence, parental neglect, lack of involvement and monitoring of the child by the parents, and so on, are all factors relating to family that have been known to affect a child's coming into contact and conflict with the law. The nature of relationship between family and the child, quality of parenting, association with deviant peers, all contribute to creating situations and behaviours that put the child at risk of coming into conflict with the law.

1.6.5 Poverty and children in conflict with the law

Even though there are no official statistics about the socioeconomic status of children alleged and found to be in conflict with the law in India, it is common knowledge that the poor and marginalized (in terms of caste, class and religion) are over represented in the juvenile justice system. Poverty often results in children, who are actually in need of care and protection, like orphans, street children, children from broken families, migrant children, child labourers, etc. to come into contact and conflict with the law in their struggle for survival and sustenance. "Poverty and delinquency are related. Children who experience long periods of poverty between birth and age 5 or in the early teenage years (ages 11-15) are more likely to engage in both property and violent offending. Growing up in a chronically poor household is clearly associated with youthful offending. These results are consistent with other research showing a relationship between welfare rates and crime" (Jarjoura, Triplett, and Brinker, 2002)

1.6.6. Suicide and depression and children in conflict with the law

Suicide is the third leading cause of death among individuals aged 15 to 24 years, according to the Centres for Disease Control and Prevention, US. (2012). However, compared to the general population, suicides are more common among youth in the juvenile justice system. (Gray et al., 2002; Hayes, 2009).

According to the Centres for Disease Control and Prevention (Crosby, Ortega, & Melanson, 2011), "*Suicidal ideation* is defined as thoughts of engaging in behaviour intended to end one's life. *Suicide attempt* refers to a nonfatal, self-directed, potentially injurious behaviour with intent to die as a result of the behaviour. A suicide attempt may or may not result in injury". Children in conflict with the law are known to have suicidal ideation as well as a history of suicide attempt(s). There is no empirical data on the prevalence of depression or the rate of completed suicides or attempted suicides among the children in conflict with the law in India.

1.7. Rationale for the study

The stated aims of the Juvenile Justice Act are reform, rehabilitation and reintegration into the community of the child in conflict with the law. However, it is not possible to reform, rehabilitate or socially reintegrate children in conflict with the law by incarcerating children charged with and found guilty of offences in Observation Homes or Special Homes, without understanding the nature of some of the mental health conditions that put them at risk of getting into conflict with the law in the first place.

1.7.1 Research questions

a. Is it true that most of the children coming into conflict with the law are from socio-economically backwards sections of the society?
b. Do many of the children in conflict with the law have a history of substance abuse, exposure to violence and history of attempted self-harm or suicide as part of their mental health history?
c. Is it true that many children in conflict with the law face violence and violation of rights at the hands of the police?
d. Is it true that most children in conflict with the law are cold, remorseless and without any regret for the harm caused by their behaviour and actions towards their victims?

e. Is it true that counsellors in the juvenile justice system are not adequately trained, skilled or experienced to provide counselling to children at the OH/SH?

1.7.2 Need for the present study in the context of current challenges in providing mental health services to CICL

Given that there is very little data on the mental health status of children in conflict with the law in India, the findings of the present research study would help to highlight the urgent and critical need or mental health services for this highly vulnerable group of children.

Research findings of this nature would enable lobbying and advocacy for mental health services for EVERY child who comes into contact or conflict with the law as well as recommendations to make suitable amendments to the law, policy and Rule-making.

The greatest challenge in ensuring mental health for children in conflict with the law is that we do not know the size or magnitude of the problem. There is very little reliable statistics on the number of children in conflict with law with mental health problem in India. This is further compounded by the lack of qualified and / or trained professionals to identify, screen or assess mental health conditions of the children in conflict with the law or the access to mental health services for such children. These children often have a very poor medical and health history which is magnified by a lack of documentation at the institutions where they are held in custody. There is an added risk of undetected mental illness as many children may simply be dismissed or labelled as ‘badly behaved’, ‘irresponsible’, ‘rebellious’ or ‘criminal’, without pinpointing the underlying mental illness that may be causing the behaviour.

There are a very miniscule number of child and adolescent psychiatrists in India, who are trained to provide the specialized services needed by these children. Making a distinction between lifetime and current diagnosis is crucial for establishing accurate prevalence rates. Counselling as a professional field is itself at an emerging stage in India, and “correctional counselling’ which is a term that is sometimes used to describe the specialized counselling services provided to children in conflict with the law, is a specialized area within the broader field of counselling, is in a very nascent stage in India. At the present point of time, there is no registration, licensing or accreditation system for counsellors in the country. There is also a lack of a standardized code of professional conduct or practice protocols for counsellors working with children in general, and children in conflict with the law, in particular. In addition, there is a lack of support, involvement and understanding from parents, families, community, law enforcement agencies, functionaries and role holders in the juvenile justice system for the crucial role that is played by the counsellor.

Awareness about 'rights based' counselling is still in the nascent stage in India. So counselling practices which seek to empower the child to exercise agency, be an active participant in his decisions impacting his life, express his views, thoughts and aspirations, etc., may still be seen as radical rather than fundamental, and as a luxury and an obstruction to the legal process, rather than as a right that he is legally entitled to.

The present study is an attempt to understand the mental health status of children in conflict with the law and the nature of counselling in the juvenile justice system in order to design age and developmentally appropriate counselling interventions that address the mental health needs of these highly vulnerable children.

Despite often having similar backgrounds or being charged with similar offences, each child and / his family have very individual and diverse emotional needs and coping mechanisms to deal with the past or current experiences in their lives, for which they need counselling support. Hence, a one-size-fits-all kind of counselling approach would not be very effective while dealing with these different categories of children. For example, children charged with committing violent or sexual offences, irrespective of whether they are found guilty by the JJB or not, would definitely be recommended for and need to be referred to more intensive and specialized counselling in addition to other mental health services, including psychiatric intervention, de-addiction services and so on, if so indicated.

It is equally important to extend counselling services to the families and caregivers of all these categories of children, to help them cope with separation from their child, anxiety of legal proceedings, social stigma of having a child being taken away by the police, loss of earnings in case the child is the breadwinner in the family, and so on.

CONCLUSION:

Rehabilitation of children in conflict with the law is an art and a science. There are no existing, ready-made mental health models that have been known to be effective in India. In the absence of counsellors and counselling in the juvenile justice system, it is difficult to define or describe what model of counselling would work best and result in reform, rehabilitation and social reintegration. Almost nothing is known of the mental health needs of the children in conflict with the law in India and what is being done to address them. What we do know, however, as mental health professionals, is that early intervention and prevention are usually helpful. Therefore, developing age-appropriate, evidence-based, affirmative, context-based mental health practices like mental health screening and assessment, referrals for diagnosis and treatment, psycho-education for the child and family, individual, group and family counselling, home visits and community involvement, remedial education and educational support, vocational training, life skills education, personal safety and sexuality education, strengths-based personal development programs – must be the starting point.

CHAPTER 2

II REVIEW OF LITERATURE

2.1 Mental Health Status and Counseling of 'Children in Conflict with the Law'

There is little research, literature or empirical data available on the mental health Status of "children in conflict with the law" in India and hence, the present research study had to rely heavily on research in other countries. The details about the number of children affected, type of mental illness or condition, presence of risk factors disposing them to mental illness, types of adverse childhood experiences that they have undergone which may have played a role in bringing them into conflict with the law and the services made available to them through the juvenile justice system, are not also known, as the focus of the juvenile justice system in India so far has been mainly only on understanding the number and type of offences committed by children and adolescents (as reported by the National Crime Reports Bureau (NCRB)).

2.1.1 Mental Health Status of "children in conflict with the law": Prevalence and Magnitude

The prevalence rate of youth with mental disorders within the juvenile justice system is found to be consistently higher than those within the general population of adolescents. (Grisso and Barnum, 2000). There are many detailed studies which have shown that there are certain types of mental disorders common among youthful offenders and that some of the symptoms increase these youths' risk of engaging in aggressive behaviors. In addition, the risk of aggression is increased for many specific disorders and co-morbid disorders because the emotional symptoms, like anger, and self-regulatory symptoms, such as impulsivity, tend to increase the risk (Teplin, Abram, McClelland, Dulcan, Mericle, 2002 ;Wasserman, McReynolds, Lucas, Fisher, Santos; 2002). Research studies also demonstrate that youth in the juvenile justice system who have a substance use disorder or have multiple exposure to violence or victimization are at higher risk for behavioral problems, mental health problems and for coming into conflict with the law. Studies also show that children in conflict with the law often have co-morbidity of more than one psychiatric and substance related disorders at the same time making their diagnosis and management very complex.

2.1.2 Mental Health Status of "children in conflict with the law": Nature and Dynamics

Many studies reported that a large number of youths in the juvenile justice system or in correctional facilities suffer from mental health problems that may often be undetected, undiagnosed and untreated. Cocozza (1991) estimated that as many as 60% of detained youths have an emotional or behavioral disorder, a level similar to that found among clinical samples (Atkins et al., 1999; Davis, Bean, Schumacher, & Stringer, 1991). Youth in juvenile correctional facilities were found to have a distressingly high prevalence of emotional and behaviour disorders. (Snyder and Sickmund ,1995) and Bullock and McArthur (1994). Several studies also found that youth with a combination of conduct problems and depressive symptoms are highly vulnerable and at extreme risk of poor academic performance, rejection by peers, violent behavior, drug and alcohol abuse, suicide, adult psychiatric illness and serious criminality. (Capaldi, 1991, 1992; Cole & Carpentieri, 1990; Mc Conaughy& Skiba, 1993; Rapp &Wodarski, 1997; Robinson, Jenson, &Yaffe, 1992).

2.1.3 Mental Health Status of "children in conflict with the law": The Indian Scene

The fact that children in conflict with the law, like all other children, have a right to education and health is overlooked by the juvenile justice system in India, as legal processes linked to establishing guilt or innocence take priority over providing mental health services. Due to the lack of research, inadequate models of care, insufficient policy development, ineffective experience, lack of training of staff, and inadequate practice, juvenile correction personnel are unable or ineffective in being able to provide adequate services to 'children in conflict with the law" with mental health concerns. This is glaringly evident by the acute lack of literature, research and empirical data on the mental health of children in conflict with the law in India. Lack of mental health services for children in conflict with the law is not unique only to India. The U S Federal Advisory Committee on Juvenile Justice (2011) reports that barriers to providing adequate services include, insufficient resources, inadequate administrative capacity, lack of appropriate staffing, and lack of training for staff.

The present law in force is called the Juvenile Justice Act, (Care and Protection of Children) Act, 2015, which is a mostly progressive legislation with aims of reformation, rehabilitation and reintegration into society as the main aims. It is based on sixteen principles of child rights, namely; Principle of presumption of innocence, Principle of dignity and worth, Principle of participation, Principle of best interest, Principle of family responsibility, Principle of safety, Positive measures, Principle of non-stigmatizing semantics; Principle of non-waiver of rights, Principle of equality and non-discrimination, Principle of right to privacy and confidentiality, Principle of institutionalization as a measure of last resort, Principle of repatriation and restoration, Principle of fresh start, Principle of diversion and Principle of natural justice(JJ Act, 2015).

However, despite its stated intentions and lofty principles, the Act often falls short of meeting its goals or fulfilling its principles due to shoddy implementation. In practice, though the caregivers and functionaries in the juvenile justice system receive some training on their roles and responsibilities under various sections of the JJ Act, they often have little or no skills in rights-based approaches, best practices or 'what works' models of rehabilitation or mental health with regard to children in conflict with the law.

2.2 Correlates of mental health problems of "children in conflict with the law"

Adolescents are likely to suffer from a host of mental health conditions that are likely to lead them into situations that bring them into conflict with the law. Poor emotional regulation, peer pressure, impressionability, immature and ongoing neuro-developmental processes (where the prefrontal cortex of the brain is still not fully developed) are all hallmarks of adolescence. Yet, these very characteristics are likely to make adolescents vulnerable to coming into conflict with the law. Many studies indicate that children and adolescents in conflict with the law in the juvenile justice system suffer from a range of health problems.

2.2.1 Socioeconomic status

Studies show that poverty and delinquency are related and that children, especially in early childhood between birth and 5 years or in the early teenage years, who grow up in chronically poor households, are more likely to engage in offences relating to property and violence. These results are consistent with other research showing a relationship between welfare rates and crime. But unfortunately, it is only when the disadvantaged youth commits an offence for the first time that the community becomes aware of the adverse effects of polices that permit chronic poverty. (Jarjoura, Triplett, and Brinker, 2002)

2.2.2 Family Factors

Family structure, family composition, death or separation of parents, quality of family relationships are all found to have a bearing on a child coming into contact or conflict with the law. Single parent families and those where children of such single parents were living in poverty were strongly associated with juvenile delinquency (Steinberg 2008)). The recent appearance of a step parent in the family causing a change in family structure seemed to have an effect on misbehavior in the case of status offences by children. (Rebellon 2002)

Social learning theories explain how children learn by imitating the behavior of others in their environment. In that context, if children are exposed to deviant, antisocial or illegal activities and experiences in their family or social environment, they are likely to adopt such behavior themselves. Incarceration or involvement of family members in illegal activities may bring the child also into contact with negative peers, role models and the justice system; all of which may bring the child into situations that bring him into contact or conflict with the law.

The role of the father in influencing the behavior of their children appears to be strong. Fathers who have stronger emotional bonds with their children were found to be more likely to monitor and discipline their children thereby decreasing their possibility of involvement in delinquent peer groups. (Warr 2005). Parallel to this research, in the research by Henry et al. (2001) it is found that close family relationships lower the juvenile's probability of joining criminal groups and decreases the probability of commitment (Icli et al, 2012).

2.2.3 Institutionalization and incarceration and mental health

The Stanford Prison Experiment by Philip Zimbardo, which is one of the most powerful examples demonstrating the dehumanizing effects of institutionalization on those imprisoned as well as those responsible for their care and safety, showed how the custodial settings itself could make guards and caregivers behave in brutalizing ways and make the 'prisoners' behave in passive, submissive way. (McLeod,2018). In the case of children in conflict with the law, the process of "deindividuation" and "learned helplessness", explained by Zimbardo is very commonly observed. Deindividuation is the behavior shown by an individual who becomes so immersed in the norms of the group or identity of the role that he loses his sense of personal identity and personal responsibility. Learned helplessness refers to the mental state and / or behavior exhibited by an individual, who because of exposure to complex problems for an extended period, believes that a situation is unescapable, unchangeable and beyond his control. Both these phenomena of deindividuation and learned helplessness are commonly observed among the staff, caregivers, functionaries of the state and the children in conflict with the law placed in their care in the custodial settings

A few studies have shown that incarceration causes a profoundly negative impact on the health and wellbeing, education and employment of youth. One study found that for a third of incarcerated youth who were diagnosed with depression, the onset of depression occurred after they were incarcerated. Another study found that poor mental health and conditions of confinement make it more likely for teenagers to engage in self-harm and suicidal behavior. (Holman and Zeidenberg 2006). Incarcerating youth makes it difficult for them to find or sustain stable employment putting them again at risk of reoffending in order to make ends meet. The child in conflict with the law is also likely to have learnt behaviors while under incarceration that may lead him to reoffend, which further endangers public safety as well as his own wellbeing.

2.2.4 Violence

Exposure to violence is childhood has also been seen to have a link with a range of mental health conditions, including the development of conduct and behavior problems. Studies show that children's aggression at a young age is linked to later exposure to violence. (Boyd, Cooley, Lambert & Ialongo 2003). It was also found that lack of social competence is often seen in children who have been exposed to frequent violence. These deficits in social skills may then turn into a risk for later developing conduct problems (Margolin &Gordis 2000). Research studies established the link between child maltreatment and criminal behavior in adulthood, by showing how the risk of crime in adulthood was increased by childhood abuse, by promoting antisocial behavior during childhood and adolescence, which was followed by forming relationships with antisocial romantic partners and peers in adulthood. (Herrenkohl et al. 2017).

The study also found a "cycle of violence" among individuals with child maltreatment histories, wherein victims of childhood violence became perpetrators of violence towards their peers or partners later in the life cycle. Male participants in the study were more likely to show aggression, hostility and delinquency during adolescence which subsequently led to criminal behavior in adulthood (National Institute Justice Report, 2017).

2.2.5 Substance Use

A combination of factors like lack of prevention programs, awareness creation programs at school and community level about the consequences of substance abuse and addiction, peer pressure, easily access and availability of a range and variety of substances, the adolescent urge to explore and experiment the forbidden, lack of life skills to cope with problems of adolescence, using substances as a rebellion against authority, all contribute towards making the adolescent vulnerable to substance abuse and dependence, further putting him at risk for mental illness, sexually risky behavior as well as coming into conflict with the law.

"An estimated 18 million children live and work on streets in India. Use of substances appear to be particularly high in this vulnerable population, with Indian studies reporting that 40-70% of street children use substances." (Sharma & Joshi 2013). "Poverty, urbanization, breakdown of families and domestic violence are the most immediate causes of this growing phenomenon. There is a close relationship between child labour and substance use disorders. Substance use may be even more common in the marginalized population such as trafficked or abused children." (Dhawan, A., et al. (2017)

Children in conflict with the law in India are observed to use, abuse, be addicted to and be dependent on a range of substances including alcohol, tobacco, marijuana, glue, correction fluid, solution liquid (used to fix punctured bicycle tyres), petrol, paint thinner, paint, sedatives, pain killers, injectables and over-the-counter drugs. Most of these substances are cheap, legally and easily available and give a quick high. Many of these vulnerable children are at risk of physical and sexual abuse and substance use is part of their coping mechanism against poverty, hunger, cold weather and physical / sexual abuse. Many of these children who may have dropped out of school may already be working in jobs that bring them into contact with adults who are substance users or may become part of the drug supply chain networks thus further pushing them into criminal environments. Rarely do these children have access to counselling, treatment or de-addiction services which may then result in their resorting to crime to pay for their substance addiction.

2.2.6 Suicide and depression

One is every 33 children and one in every eight adolescents in the US are estimated to be affected by depression. (SAMHSA 2018). Among mental disorders, depression was particularly found to be the most commonly identified predictor for both suicidal ideation and attempts. (Stokes, Marquita L et al. 2015).

Different aspects of crime and criminal justice involvement were identified as being associated with suicidal ideation or attempts by various studies; repeat offending or prior contact with the justice system (Wasserman and McReynolds, 2006 ; Wasserman et al., 2010), detention or secure placement (Mallett et al., 2012; Wasserman et al., 2010) , gang membership (Evans, Hawton and Rodham, 2004; Morris et al., 1995) and current arrest for violence (Nolan et al., 2008; Wasserman and McReynolds, 2006) Almost 47% of youth in juvenile detention were found to have moderate to severe levels of depressive symptoms (Domalanta, Risser, Roberts, & Risser, 2003). Depression has also been found to be associated with increased recidivism thereby highlighting the potential of unrecognized and untreated depression to influence the criminal course of detained youth. (Clark-Jones, 1999; Cocozza, 1992; Whitbeck, Hoyt, & Bao, 2000).

There appears to be clear link between depression and delinquency in adolescents, which may interact with contextual risk factors and create further vulnerability for the development of conduct problems among children at risk for maladjustment (Weaver et al, 2008). However, despite being a significant problem among youth in the juvenile justice system, depression is often overlooked because of the focus on the compelling disruptive behavior exhibited by these children. (McCarty, Stoep, Kuo& McCauley, 2006).

There is no empirical data on the prevalence of depression or the rate of completed suicides or attempted suicides among the children in conflict with the law in India. As of 2019, there are no formal suicide prevention or intervention programs, screening for suicide risk, awareness and training to staff and caregivers on identification of signals of suicidal behaviour, timely and sensitive response to suicide attempts in any juvenile justice institution in India. Poorly trained and ill-informed staff and caregivers often respond to a child's suicide attempt as "attention seeking behavior" instead of a cry for help by a helpless, hopeless and desperate child.

2.2.7 Adverse Childhood Experiences

The social milieu in which children in conflict with the law often come from, include poor living conditions on account of poverty, unsafe and crowded neighborhoods, gang culture with high exposure to violence, being at risk of arrest and apprehension on account of being poor, or marginalized due to caste or religion – both of which play a huge role in the social status in India, have their own influence on the way a child experiences and copes with the adversities of his young life. Studies have shown that members of a juvenile gang show significantly higher rates of mental health problems like anxiety disorders, conduct disorder, antisocial personality disorder, post traumatic stress disorder and attention deficit hyperactivity disorder, in comparison to the general population as well as other children in conflict with the law populations (Madden 2013). However, there are no specific studies in the Indian context to study the link between marginalization and children getting into conflict with the law or adverse childhood experiences and their impact on children coming into in conflict with the law.

Several theories of crime have proven links between childhood factors and adulthood criminality and victimization. The Adverse Childhood Experiences Theory is also consistent with these theories. (eg. Agnew, 1985; Farrington et al, 2006). ACEs have been linked to many 'criminogenic' risks (factors that increase risk of offending) including substance and alcohol abuse, deprivation, poor educational attainment, and mental health problems. (Centers for Disease Control and Prevention, 2015)

2.3 Counseling of children in conflict with the law

Meta-analysis of various studies that examined the effectiveness of different intervention programs for children in conflict with the law, found that that the most effective interventions were interpersonal skills training, individual counseling, and behavior programs for non-institutionalized adolescents who had offended, and interpersonal skills training and community -based, family-type group homes for institutionalized juveniles. (Wilson, Office of Juvenile Justice and Delinquency Prevention, 2000).

Evidence-based therapeutic interventions are increasingly believed to have a greater effectiveness in reducing recidivism rather than the punitive approaches mostly prevalent in many countries worldwide. Different approaches and models of counseling and rehabilitation of children in conflict with the law, involving community based and restorative approaches which involve the family as well as civil society support mechanism and local community involvement are also being explored in different countries, with varying degrees of success in implementation.

Review of literature suggests that there are no pre-existing models of counseling that have been found to be culture and content specific in the context of children in conflict with the law in India. There appears to be no proper mental healthcare system to promote the positive mental health of CICL in India and hence a strong need for a systematic study into the mental health problems of children in conflict with the law in India. In this context, the importance of the present research study in understanding the mental health of "children in conflict with the law" in India is significant and likely to be the first of its kind in India with this population.

CHAPTER 3

III DEVELOPMENT AND ADMINISTRATION OF TOOLS

3.1 Mental Health Status and Counselling of "children in conflict with the law"

It is known experientially and from anecdotal evidence that children in conflict with the law in India suffer from several serious mental health risks. It is also commonly known that the counselling services provided in the juvenile justice system are not adequate to address the mental health needs of children in conflict with the law. However, very little empirical evidence exists to confirm the same. Hence the present study undertook to study the mental health status and counseling of children in conflict with the law.

3.2 Method

3.2.1 Identification of dimensions and sub-dimensions of mental health of CICL

An attempt was made to identify the main dimensions of mental health which would enable the understanding of the mental health status of children in conflict with the law. Five main dimensions were identified, namely, demographic profile, family and self, health status (5 sub dimensions of medical history, substance use, violence, present risk of depression and suicide and contact with the juvenile justice system), reform and rehabilitation and experience of counseling in the juvenile justice system. An attempt was also made to identify the nature of adverse childhood experiences of children in conflict with the law as adverse childhood experiences are known to impact the mental health status and outcomes of vulnerable populations like children in conflict with the law.

3.2.2 Development of appropriate tools for measurement of mental health status and counseling of CICL

An attempt was made to develop tools that would be socially and culturally appropriate as well as legally compliant with the requirements of the various legislations applicable to the sample. Three tools were developed for this purpose. A Mental Health Status Questionnaire for Children in Conflict with the law (MHSQCICL), a Questionnaire for Counsellors of Children in Conflict with the law (QCCICL) and Adverse Childhood Experiences Questionnaire Adapted for Children in Conflict with the Law (ACEQACICL) was developed for data collection.

3.3 Sample

The present study employed the random sampling technique to select three child care institutions i.e, two Observation Homes and one Special Home which housed children in conflict with the law as representative samples from the entire state of Karnataka. As per research design, the counsellors working at these institutions were also selected as subjects for the present study.

3.4 Description of Tools used in the study

In the present study, two self-developed tools and one adapted tool were used as detailed in 3.4.1, 3.4.2 and 3.4.3.

3.4.1 Mental Health Status Questionnaire for Children in Conflict with the Law (MHSQCICL)

Table 3.4.1: MHSQCICL Number of items in each dimension

S.NO.	Sections	No. of Questions (Total = 90)
1.	PART A : Demographic Profile	18 (Q1 to Q18)
2.	PART B : Family & Self	16 (Q19 to Q34)
3.	PART C : Health Status	Sub Total : 42
	I. Medical History	8 (Q35 to Q42)
	II. Substance Use	8 (Q43 to Q 50)
	III. Violence	6 (Q51 to Q56)
	IV. Present Risk : depression & suicide	9 (Q57 to Q65)
	V. Contact with the justice system - police	4 (Q66 to Q69)
4.	PART D : Experience of counselling in the justice system	5 (Q70 to Q74)
5.	PART E : Future Plans	5 (Q75 to Q79)
6.	ACEQACICL	20 questions
7.	PART F : Closure	6 (Q 80 to 85)
8.	PART G: Reform, rehabilitation & restoration (for SH only)	5 (Q 86 to Q90)

The MHSQCICL consists of 8 main parts.

3.4.1.1 Part A

It contains the items related to the Demographic Profile of children in conflict with the law in terms of educational profile, parents occupation and family income, the nature of the alleged offence for which they are presently in custodial settings at the Observation Home or Special Home and whether their right to legal representation has been upheld or not.

3.4.1.2 Part B

It contains the items related to the **Family and Self** in terms of family composition, right to contact with the family while in custody, significant family member and non –familial member for the child, parents cohabiting with the child, treatment of the child by the family, relationship of family members with each other, child's relationship with parents, child's expectations from parents, involvement of parents in child's life and child's self description in terms of perception of self, abilities, potential and resources and whether the child's right to family contact while in custodial care was upheld or not.

3.4.1.3 Part C

It describes the **Health Status** of the child in terms of exposure and access to health services and hospitalization, parental health history, child's health habits relating to substance use, child's history of exposure to violence, child's present risks relating to depression and suicide and experience of the police.

3.4.1.4 Part D

It describes the child's **Experience of counselling in the juvenile justice system** in terms of access to a counsellor, impact of counselling and qualities expected in a counsellor

3.4.1.5 Part E

It describes the **Future Plans** of the child in terms of goals post release from the institution, accountability for one's behaviour, support and resources required by the child for reform and rehabilitation,

3.4.1.6 Part F

It describes **Reform, Rehabilitation and Restoration** in terms of regret for past behaviour, perceived harm caused, empathy for victim and making amends for harmful behaviour.

3.4.1.7 Part G

It describes the **Closure process** of the research procedure in terms of present emotional status check, distress due to research, experience of participation in the research, perceived usefulness of participation in the research, willingness to participate in future research and an opportunity to seek any clarifications or make some final comments and to also ensure that the child's rights have been protected throughout the research study – especially in the process of data collection and related processes.

3.4.2 Questionnaire for Counsellors of Children in Conflict with the Law (QCCICL)

A self-developed questionnaire for understanding the status of counselling in the juvenile justice system. The QCCICL has 47 items covering areas of educational background, work experience, training received and required, understanding of role, contribution to the role, beliefs around reform, rehabilitation and social reintegration, support and resources required to effectively perform the role of the counsellor, work satisfaction and challenges, contribution to the legal requirements, impact of gender on role, self-care and professional supervision and examples of success stories.

3.4.3 Adverse Childhood Experiences Questionnaire Adapted for Children in Conflict with the Law (ACEQACICL)

The ACEQACICL is a self-developed questionnaire adapted from the Adverse Childhood Experiences International Questionnaire (ACE-IQ), with permission from the World Health Organization (WHO). The original CDC – Kaiser Permanente Adverse Childhood Experiences Study was one of the largest investigations into the link between chronic stress caused by early adversity (like childhood physical and emotional abuse and neglect, domestic violence, parental mental illness, substance abuse and separation or divorce and later-life health and wellbeing. WHO endorses the ACE-IQ which was produced by the International ACE Research Network and aims to enable the measurement of childhood adversities in all countries and comparisons of such adversities between them; the drawing of associations between childhood adversities and health risk behaviors and health outcomes in later life; advocacy for increased investments to reduce childhood adversities, and scientific information to inform the design of prevention programmers.

WHO recommends that the ACE – IQ should be always integrated into broader health surveys, which is what has been done in the present study as well. Although data about adversities on their own may be useful for some purposes, the real value of the ACE-IQ lies in demonstrating the associations between early exposures to ACEs and subsequent risk behaviors and health outcomes. It is only by integrating ACE-IQ into broader health surveys that such associations can be measured. Also, ACE-IQ was designed for adults above 18 years, so it became imperative to adapt the questionnaire for administration to children in conflict with the law, who were mostly less than 18 years of age. Further, it is important to contextualize adverse childhood experiences as an ongoing experience for this population of children in conflict with the law. For this reason, the ACE-IQ has been adapted into the ACEQACICL to make it specific to the needs of this particular population.

The 10 ACEs studied in the original ACE study were:

1. Childhood abuse-Emotional-Physical-Sexual
2. Neglect-Emotional-Physical
3. Growing up in a seriously dysfunctional household as evidenced by:
    a. Witnessing domestic violence
    b. Alcohol or other substance abuse in the home
    c. Mentally ill or suicidal household members
    d. Parental marital discord (as evidenced by separation or divorce)
    e. Crime in the home (as evidenced by having a household member imprisoned)

The present study listed each of these experiences as individual adverse childhood experiences and added 4 ACEs in addition for the purposes of this study. These additional ACEs are: Poverty, disruption in education, family history of poor health, poor family relationships. The additional adverse childhood experiences chosen for inclusion in this study were based on prior research that has shown such childhood experiences to have significant adverse health implications. Child sexual abuse was excluded even though it is known to be a significant ACE that affects mental health, due to reasons of legal reporting mandated by Indian law. Further, the present study checked for the presence of the 20 following ACEs in the research sample. The 20 ACEs thus listed for inclusion were:

1. Poverty. Non–fulfilment of basic needs, education, inability to pay / hire a lawyer as the child's narration of his experience of poverty
2. Disruption in education.
3. Death of a parent
4. Divorce/ separation of parents
5. Neglect – non fulfilment of basic needs, emotional neglect
6. Lack of parental involvement and poor relationship with and among family members
7. Family history of poor health

8. Child's history poor health – hospitalization, illness, accident, violence, attempted suicide, etc.
9. Family history of substance use
10. Child's history of substance use
11. Family history of mental illness
12. Family history of suicide / attempts at suicide
13. Child's history of suicide / attempts at suicide / self harm
14. Exposure of child to violence in the family
15. Exposure of child to violence towards himself
16. Contact of family with justice system
17. Contact of child with justice system
18. Incarceration
19. Experience with police
20. Charged with sexual offence (sexual encounter of any kind before the age of 18 years is considered" child sexual abuse" and irrespective of consent or victim or offender status as per law, the CICL would be considered as having undergone CSA and hence an adverse childhood experience.

3.5 Procedure for Data Collection

The present study was completed in two consecutive phases which was competed with the help of two self–developed tools. The procedure followed for conducting the data-collection with the children in conflict with the law was as follows:

3.5.1 Pre-Visit Procedures

A written permission to visit Child Care Institutions for children in conflict with the law – Observation Homes and Special Homes, was obtained from the Department of Women and Child Development (DWCD), Government of Karnataka (GoK). The purpose and objectives of the research were mentioned and guidelines laid down by the government relating to disclosure of research data, media protocols, etc. were agreed upon.

The DWCD, GoK had given permission to visit, interview children and collect data from 16 Observation Homes in 15 locations (Bangalore has 2 – Urban & Rural) and 1 Special

Home at Bangalore. However, the researcher visited only 2 Observation Homes (one in Bangalore and 1 in Mysore and 1 Special Home at Bangalore.

A similar written permission and information to the Additional Director General of Police, (Crime and Technical Services) giving details of the nature and purpose of the research study was also submitted. This is required as part of the protocol to be followed in case of disclosure of child sexual abuse during the course of the research study. (Mandatory Reporting under Section 19, chapter V of the Protection of Children from Sexual Offences Act, 2012). A time table of the researcher's travel schedule to the OHs and SH was submitted to the ADGP's office as per police protocol requirements.

A copy of the permission letter from DWCD was mailed to the Superintendent of the Observation Home in the districts of Bangalore and Mysore and the Special Home for Boys, Bangalore well in advance along with the request letter from the researcher requesting and confirming the date of the visit – after telephonically ensuring mutual convenience and availability.

3.5.2 Duration of visits for data collection

The researcher spent approximately 4 days at Mysore Observation Home, 4 days at Special Home Bangalore and 15 days at Observation Home, Bangalore, to interview children and Counsellor respectively.

3.5.3 Language for communication with research participants

The questionnaire was in English, however, many of the participants were not able to read, write or speak English. Since the researcher was fluent in some of the south Indian languages spoken by the participants, she offered to conduct the sessions (individual and group) in any language preferred by the participant(s). The choice of languages offered to the participants were English, Hindi, Kannada and Tamil.

3.5.4 Room for personal interviews

The researcher requested a designated room to conduct the personal interviews which was provided at all the data collection centres.

3.5.5 Process followed for Data Collection

3.5.5.1 Introductory Group Session - Day I

The researcher used an Introductory Group Session with the children to establish rapport and give information about the research study. This session was used to provide basic information about the research study, explain the ground rules for the individual counselling and the data collection process to be followed. Since this group discussion session was for children and adolescents in a custodial setting, games and exercises were included to make it participative and interesting. The time taken for the group discussion session was approximately 30 minutes. The group sessions were followed by an individual one-on-one session with each of the children who volunteered and consented to be interviewed for data collection. The details of the group discussion are described along with the day-wise program activities.

The Day 1 session was aimed at :

1. Communicating information about the research study, topic, objectives and purpose of the research, plan and schedule relating to the data collection process, group session (s) and individual interview process, possible benefits from the program and benefits of learning in a group environment
2. Establishing a positive rapport with the children and giving them an opportunity to ask questions, clarify doubts, raise concerns
3. Laying out the ground rules for the data collection process in consultation and participation with the children
4. Seeking consent for the data collection process from the children and giving them the opportunity to decide whether to participate or not.
5. Preparing the children (who communicate willingness) for the individual interview session that was to follow.
6. Drawing up the list of children who were willing to participate in the individual sessions with time slots for each child.

3.5.5.2 Description of Group Activity

Self-Introduction & awareness creation about counselling and the research study

Step 1 : **Prior Permission to meet the children in a group** : The superintendent was requested (in advance) for permission for the researcher to address the children as a group at a time convenient to them and as mutually agreed in advance.

Step 2 : **Room for the session** : Researcher ensured that the group session was conducted in a room where there was enough space for all children to sit comfortably in a circle.

Step 3 : **Seating arrangement** : Once children had assembled, researcher requested the children to be seated in a circle

Step 4 : **Introduction of Researcher by head of the institution** : The superintendent was requested to introduce the researcher to the children by stating the name of the researcher, topic of the research study and brief purpose of the study.

Step 5 : **Self Introduction of Researcher** : Researcher introduced herself by saying her name clearly and slowly in the following words :

Hello. My name is Kalpana and I work with children. Thank you for agreeing to speak to me. I would like to know about you and your life, specifically some things related to your health - for which I would be asking some questions. I am very interested and concerned that all children should be healthy – physically, mentally as well as emotionally. By talking to you and other children like you, I hope to understand what are the different factors and (some significant life events) that affect the health of a child in conflict with the law. This information may be of help to counsellors and other functionaries who work with children in institutional settings.

Step 6 : Awareness about counselling – through a group activity described below

Researcher asked if participants knew who a counsellor was. With a simple show of hands, she tried to find out how many children in the group knew what a counsellor was.

Do you know what a counsellor is? Yes / No. (Observed the response. How many children said they know what a counsellor is/ say they don't know who a counsellor is)

Researcher then asked the group about what was the information about a counsellor or counselling that they had?

So what can you tell me about who is a counsellor or what is counselling? This is not an exam so you can say whatever you know or comes to your mind.

Researcher then explained the work she does as a counsellor (in the exact words given in italics below) and that information about the child's life, specifically aspects related to his health would help the researcher to put together some recommendations which the researcher hoped, may be helpful in understanding and improving the conditions of mental health for children in conflict with the law.

When we have a stomach ache or a fracture, we go to a doctor and they give us medicines to help us get well. But when we feel angry, hurt or sad, we may sometimes not know whom to go to and ask for medicines or help. We often wish we had someone who could talk to us, listen to us and comfort us. A counsellor is a person who is trained to help you understand your feelings and thoughts and make sense of what has happened or is going on in your life. Counsellors don't give medicines like doctors do, but often just talking to a kind and compassionate person can make us feel understood and better.

I am a counsellor who works with children and I hope talking to me and sharing about yourself will make you feel listened to and understood too. You will also be helping me to learn a lot by sharing about your life. I am mainly interested in the health of children – physical, mental and emotional – like I shared with you earlier, so I would be asking you some questions about your health and growing up. I would be writing down your responses.

However, I assure you that I would not be sharing your name or any other details of whatever you are sharing with me with anyone else. The reason and purpose for my asking you to share information about yourself is to understand children better and learn how to help them in the work that I do.

Researcher then explained that she would be visiting or staying with them for a few days and requested their help and cooperation in her work.

I will be visiting or staying with you all for the next few days and interacting with you to collect this information. I request you to kindly help me with the same.

Step 7: About the Research study

Now that we know each other a little better, I would like to talk a little more about the work that I plan to do with you.

As I shared earlier, I have been working with children for some years now and am interested in understanding about the health of children – especially those in conflict with the law. For this purpose, I am doing a research study in which I will be having an interview with each one of you (based on your willingness) and asking some questions about your life, your family and your health. I will need about 60-90 minutes per person for this.

I would like to know who are the people who would be interested in participating in this interview with me. Kindly raise your hands and tell me your names.

This is entirely voluntary, so if you don't wish to participate that is also alright. In case you want to take some time and tell me tomorrow, that is also fine with me.

Researcher then listed down all the names of those who expressed willingness.

Step 8: Explaining details of the process and procedure of data collection

There are a few things about my research study and the process of data collection that I wanted to share with you.

1. ***Consent***

Participating in this study is entirely voluntary. I invite you to participate, but the decision to participate is entirely yours. In case someone does not want to participate, that is also fine. Please do not force others who may not be willing to participate as each person has a reason for wanting to participate or not participate.

2. ***Active Participation***

I invite you to freely and openly share whatever you wish to in response to the questions I would be asking. However, in case you don't feel comfortable answering some question(s), you can always refuse to answer.

3. ***Confidentiality and the limits of confidentiality***

Whatever you share as part of the interview as well as group sessions will not be shared with anyone – either at the Observation Home / Special Home or outside of it.

However, if there is something relating to your health which I feel needs to be brought to the attention of the authorities in order to help you with treatment or counselling, I may be reporting it to the Superintendent / JJB. But I will do this only after consulting with and informing you.

4. ***Punctuality and respect for time***

I would really appreciate if you turn up for your individual interviews on the time agreed to by you. Please try not to plan other activities during the time you have committed to meet the researcher. We will most likely complete our interview within 45-60 minutes. We also have to remember that everyone has to get their turn so please try to not to exceed the maximum time limit of 90 minutes.

5. **Documenting and recording of interview**

I will be writing down your answers and responses to the questions I ask. I will be masking all the identifying information by assigning a code number to each interview so that no one other than me would be able to make out who said what. The information from the interviews would be accessible only to me and it will be stored in my computer.

Step 9: Preparing the list of children who want to participate in the research study

A list of all the children who consented to participate in the research study was prepared and a time table for individual sessions prepared. This list and schedule were shared with the children to check if they were agreeable to it and in case anyone wanted a change in schedule, it was incorporated. Once they consented and committed, they were encouraged to stick to the schedule.

Step 10: Thanking and acknowledging participation

Researcher thanked all the participants and acknowledged their contribution and gave information about the next day schedule.

Thank you all for participating in the group sessions. I look forward to meeting you tomorrow for the individual interviews.

We will start after breakfast at the .... Room (specified location) at 9.00 a.m sharp.

Step 11: Individual Consent Form

Before commencing the individual interviews, the purpose and procedure of the research study was once again explained and a written consent obtained from the participant. The right to withdraw from the study at this or any stage, to remain silent, to refuse to respond to some or any questions, to ask for clarifications, was also explained to the participant

3.5.6 Individual Session for Data Collection

Based on the list and time table, the participants were interviewed in individual face to face sessions. The time taken for every participant was noted.

3.5.6.1 Description of Individual Session - Day 2

A maximum of 5 or 6 children were interviewed per day with each session lasting approximately 75 to 90 minutes. I**nterview** technique using the structured and semi-structured questionnaire were used. This is not a diagnostic, therapeutic or forensic interview. However, counselling skills and rights-based approaches were used in the tone, language and manner in which questions were framed and asked, responses were listened to, and relationship with the participant was established and built for the interview

3.5.6.2 Procedure for Individual Session

The following format and steps were followed by the researcher for individual session:

3.5.6.2.1 Goals for the individual session

1. **Psycho education** about who is a counsellor and what she does – in simple language that can be understood by a child.
2. **Acknowledging** that the sharing of information and feelings by the child is important and valuable to the researcher and her work and that the process of interaction would hopefully be mutually enriching and learning.
3. **Thanking** the child for agreeing to share personal details.
4. **Assuring** the child about **confidentiality** of the information shared and clearly explaining the limits of confidentiality
5. **Encouraging and empowering** the child to exercise the **right to say no** by asserting himself to stop sharing if he feels discomfort in any way and at any point of the interaction.

6. **Information collection** – as per the interview questionnaire

3.5.6.2.2 Process of Self Introduction, rapport building and context setting

The researcher began by seating the child and introduced herself by name. She thanked the child for agreeing to participate in the research study and told him that his sharing of his life is a very critical and important part of the researcher's work. (Exact words given in italics below were repeated for every child for uniformity). *Hello ..... child's name. I am Kalpana. Thank you for meeting me and agreeing to talk to me. Whatever you share is just fine, if you have any questions or something that is bothering you about our meeting, please feel free to ask me.*

Researcher sought the child's consent and asked if he was willing to talk/ take the interview. She asked if there were any concerns he had and clarified the same. Any concerns raised were documented clearly along with clarifications given and signature on the consent form taken. *Yesterday/ on day 1, we had a brief meeting and got introduced to each other, but today we will get an opportunity to talk a little more in detail about your life and I hope to get to know you a little better. Is that alright with you? (*This was an opportunity for the child to withdraw consent even at this stage if he was not feeling comfortable)

Researcher explained that some parts of the interview may be personal and the child could choose to stop at any time if he felt unable or unwilling to go on. *When we speak about our life, sometimes we may feel very emotional about some things. It is very important for me that you are comfortable sharing your story with me. However, if at any point of our discussion, if you feel uncomfortable about anything or don't want to share, it is totally alright not to share, please let me know and we will stop. We can come back and discuss it at a later time if you wish or may not discuss it all if you don't feel like it.*

3.5.6.2.3. Consent for documenting

Researcher asked for consent for documenting the participant's responses. *I will be writing down your responses as well as some portions of our conversations to ensure I don't miss out on any important details. Also, since I would be meeting many children, it may be difficult for me to remember all the details accurately. I would not be using your name or identifying details in any manner. So would you mind if I took notes while you are speaking and documented our conversations? The child could choose to terminate the interview even at this stage.*

3.6 Ethical Principles followed during data collection

1. **Right of participation** : It was the right of the chid to decide at all points in time whether he wanted to participate or not in the research study.
2. **Confidentiality:** No information shared by the child was shared with any of the staff from the institution or with anyone else. All identifying information pertaining to the child was used strictly for research purposes only.
3. **Respect as a person:** The researcher expressed unconditional positive regard for the personhood of the child at all times and in all interactions. The best interests of the child was paramount at all times – during data collection as well as in analysis, presentation of findings. The researcher demonstrated respect by showing appreciation and empathy for sharing, acknowledging the difficulty that each person had shown in sharing their life stories.
4. **Prevention of re-traumatization:** Each of the procedures were carefully designed and structured to ensure the child was not subjected to further distress in the process of data collection for research. The researcher was clear that she would terminate the interview if necessary and if and when necessary, at any stage of the interview if she perceived that the child was in any distress or in need of any support. The well-being of the child took precedence over data collection at all points of time and in all interactions with the child.
5. **Fairness and transparency in communication:** The researcher remained sensitive to communicate in a language familiar to the child. As the researcher could speak English, Hindi, Tamil and Kannada fluently, she offered the child the choice of the language in which the child preferred the interview to be conducted.
6. **Verification of accuracy of communication:** All responses were recorded in English by the researcher and read back to the subject in both English and the vernacular to ensure and cross check for errors and authenticity of translation. This was done at the end of the interview so the participant could get another opportunity to also clarify, modify and voice out objections to any of the information that had been recorded. The child could ask for any of the data to be withheld if he so wished.

3.7 Ethical safeguards followed in data collection process :

The following phases and flow were kept in mind as important steps of the procedure of data collection

1. Rapport building – with functionaries and children
2. Explaining the research topic and process that would be followed – to functionaries and children
3. Obtaining consent for participation, explaining limits of confidentiality, rights of participation, grievance redressal mechanism
4. Administering the questionnaire – interviewing the child
5. Addressing questions, concerns, questions, if any.
6. Closure and termination of process

3.8 Research Data protection : (Digital and paper documents)

All the participants were assured that all the information shared by them would be stored in electronic form in the researcher's computer. Further, all the consent forms signed by the participants were filed and stored all files (both paper and electronic), would not be accessible to anyone other than the researcher. However, participants were informed that the information shared by them might be used by the researcher to write articles, academic papers, books, training material and so on which would be of use to professionals working with children in vulnerable circumstances. Importantly, the privacy of the information from known adults was ensured, especially to protect the child's right to information they wished to keep private from parents or any other adults. The researcher did not find any medical or legal reasons or any special circumstances which necessitated the sharing of such information with anyone known to the child. This is in keeping with Article 17 of the UNCRC on Child's Right to information they wish or need to keep private from parents.

3.9. Administration of Questionnaire for counsellor

The copy of the Questionnaire for Counsellors working at Observation Home / Special Home was given to the professional identified as the counsellor or doing the counselling work at OH and SH.

3.10. Concluding Group Session

After all the participants on the list completed their individual sessions, a group session with all the participants was again convened. Feedback on their experience of participating in the research study was solicited, clarifications if any, were sought and addressed. All the participants were thanked for their participation and contribution to the research study.

CHAPTER 4

IV RESEARCH METHODOLOGY

4.1 Research strategy

Any research study formulated, has two major objectives, i.e., it must have theoretical promise and address the social concerns equally. The present piece of research was formulated with the consideration that very little is known to scholars of psychology and development professionals on the status of mental health of 'children in conflict with law'. On the other hand, what has to be done for such children is also not known; hence, the intervention becomes difficult with regard to their mental health problems in natural life settings when they come out from the OH/ SH. Therefore, the urgent and critical need for mental health services for children in conflict with the law in India and the lack of information about this highly vulnerable group of children made it essential for the researcher to investigate objectively, the mental health status of 'children in conflict with law'. Hence the present study was formulated, following an interdisciplinary approach combining aspects of counselling, psychology, law and child rights, with two main objectives.

4.2 Objectives:

4.2.1 To study the mental health status of 'children in conflict with law'

4.2.2 To study the status of counselling provided to 'children in conflict with the law'

4.3 Sample

In the present study, in accordance with the objectives the number of OH and SH were identified; and, it was found that there is only one special home in the entire state of Karnataka and eighteen observation homes were available run by the State Government directly. Hence, two observation homes and one special home were selected for the purpose of drawing the sample. Furthermore, according to the research design, the counsellors working at these institutions were also selected as subjects for the present study to accomplish the objectives mentioned above. The description of the sample drawn is presented in Table 4.3.1.

Table 4.3.1 Description of the sample

S. No.	JJ Institution	Location	Number of children	Number of Counsellors
1	Observation Home for Boys, Madivala, Bangalore	Bangalore	34	0
2	Observation Home for Boys, Mysore	Mysore	15	1
3	Special Home for Boys	Bangalore	21	1
	Total	3	70	2

4.4 Research Design:

To achieve the objectives stated above, the present study made an in-depth study of the mental health status of the children in conflict with the law detained in the juvenile justice system. In India, legal provision has been made under the JJ Act, 2015,to detain children "**alleged** to have come into contact or conflict with the law" at the Observation Home, while children "**found** to be in conflict with the law" are kept in detention at the Special Home.

India has a total of 316 Observation Homes, 39 Special Homes, 54 Observation-cum-Special Homes, 11 Places of Safety and a total of 420 homes for children in conflict with the law as of 31st March, 2017. In Karnataka, there were a total of 18 Observation Homes and 1 Special Home as of 8th August 2016 (when permission was granted by Department of Women and Child Development, Government of Karnataka for data collection). A preliminary perusal revealed that most of the Observation Homes in Karnataka housed only a few children. Only the districts of Bengaluru (34) and Mysuru (15), had more than 10 children at the time of data collection. Hence, the data was collected only from these two Observation Homes and the Special Home (21) situated at Bengaluru. The data collection was completed for 70 children (Bengaluru OH = 34; Mysuru OH = 15 and Bengaluru Special Home = 21).

Children in conflict with the law are kept in protective judicial custody at the Observation Home and Special Home. For purposes of the study, children residing at 2 OHs (one each in Bangalore and Mysore) and 1 Special Home at Bangalore were included. The Observation Home, Bangalore houses the largest number of children in conflict with the law across the State of Karnataka. Children are detained here till they get bail; a period which could range from a few days, to a few weeks to a few months. The Observation Home Mysore is representative of a typical Observation Home at a district, not as large both in terms of infrastructure as well as number of children.

The Special Home, Bangalore, houses all the children from across the State of Karnataka who are found guilty of the offence(s) they have been charged with. The children at the Special Home are detained for a period ranging from a few weeks to a few months to a maximum of 3 years. Some of the children may be placed in after-care settings which may be institutional, non-institutional, family or community based.

In order to accomplish the second objective, an attempt was made to analyse the counselling services provided to CICL. For this purpose, the available counsellors were interviewed in depth with the help of semi-structured interview schedule. On the other hand, the children residing at the OHs and SH were asked to give their experiences on the counselling services received. The obtained information was then subjected to qualitative analysis and reported accordingly.

4.5 Tools used in the study

In the present study, three following three tools were used

1. **Mental Health Status Questionnaire for Children in Conflict with the Law (MHSQCICL) – a** self-developed questionnaire for assessing mental health status of children in conflict with the law
2. **Questionnaire for Counsellors of Children in Conflict with the Law (QCCICL)** – a self-developed questionnaire for understanding the status of counselling in the juvenile justice system
3. **Adverse Childhood Experiences Questionnaire for CICL (ACEQACICL) -** The ACEQACICL is a self-developed questionnaire adapted from the Adverse

Childhood Experiences International Questionnaire (ACE-IQ), with permission from the World Health Organization (WHO).

4.6 Procedure

The present study required in-depth information gathering from children in conflict with law. Hence it was decided that the children who were present on the visit- day of OH/SH would be taken into the sample. As a result, the number of total sample was found to be very less. However, in order to have divergent information related to mental health and for accomplishment of the objectives, the available children were interviewed in a dyadic situation, after seeking approval from all the concerned government agencies and consent of the children residing in the OH/SH. On an average, one child was interviewed for two to two and a half hours in a day. The entire interview was completed in 2-3 sittings with an exception of a few, who took 4- 5 sittings. The process of entire data collection was completed over a period of six months.

4.7 Plan of Data Analysis

The interview schedule used in the present study was semi- structured and 30- 40% items were open -ended hence the obtained data was treated to qualitative analysis and presented accordingly. The advanced statistical techniques could not be employed on account of non- availability of a standardized test for the assessment of mental health problems of children in conflict with law. Therefore, it was decided that the information will be gathered and analyzed in terms of its occurrence and has been reported in the result section, accordingly. In order to substantiate the result, 10 cases were picked up for detailed assessment, which have been reported in Chapter V – Case Studies.

CHAPTER 5

V RESULTS

RESULT I - CHILDREN IN CONFLICT WITH THE LAW: DEMOGRAPHIC **PROFILE**

1.1 DEMOGRAPHIC PROFILE

5.1.1 Age of children in conflict with the law in the juvenile justice system

The highest number of CICL in the OH were in the age group of 16 to 18 years (77.55%) and similar trend was observed in the Special Home (66.67%) and a total of 74.29% CICL were from this age group. The next highest number of CICL in the OH (14.29%) were in the age group of 14 to 15 years. On the contrary, in the Special Home, the next highest number of CICL (19.05 %) were in the age group of 21 years and above Significantly, 14.29 % of the children in the Special Home were in the age group of 19 and 20 years, followed by 10% in the age group of 14 and 15 years and 8.57 % in the age group of 19 and 20 years (Table 5.1.1). A glance at Fig. 5.1.1 suggested that the children in the age range of 16 to 18 years were more vulnerable to get in conflict with the law followed by slightly younger children (14 to 15 years)

Table 5.1.1 Age of children in conflict with the law in the Juvenile Justice system (N=70)

S. No.	Age	Observation Home		Special Home		TOTAL	
		F	%	F	%	F	%
1	12 and 13 years	1	2.04	0	0	1	1.43
2	14 and 15 years	7	14.29	0	0	7	10
3	16 to 18 years	38	77.55	14	66.67	52	74.29
4	19 and 20 years	3	6.12	3	14.29	6	8.57
5	21 years and above	0	0	4	19.05	4	5.71
	TOTAL	49	100	21	100	70	100

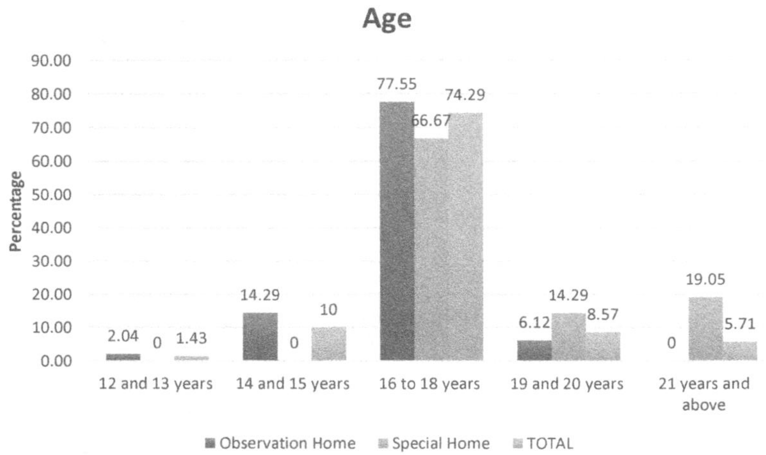

Figure 5.1.1 Age of children in conflict with the law in the Juvenile Justice system (N=70)

5.1.2 Education Status of children in conflict with the law

5.1.2.1 Level of Education of children in conflict with the law

Table 5.1.2.1 showed that highest level of education of CICLs was found to be High School (41.43%), with 42.86% children in the Observation Home and 38.10 % in the Special Home at this level. The next highest educational level of CICL at the Observation Home were those who had studied up to PUC or 12th standard (24.49%) followed by those who have studied up to Middle School (16.33%) and up to the primary only (10.20%). Whereas, at the Special Home, there were an equal number of children with educational levels at PUC or 12th standard, Middle School and Primary school (14.29% each). A total of 41.43% of CICL had studied up to the High School Level (9th and 10th standard), followed by 21.43% who had studied up to PUC or 12th standard, followed by 15.71% having studied up to or studying in Middle School (5th to 8th standard) and 11.43% having studied till Primary school level (1st -5th standard). A close perusal of Fig 2 indicated that majority of the children in Observation Home or Special Home had an education up to high school, followed by middle school. A few had been educated up to PUC level also.

Table 5.1.2.1 Education Status of children in conflict with the law : Level of Education (N= 70)

Education Status	Observation Home		Special Home		Total	
	F	%	F	%	f	%
No Schooling	2	4.08	2	9.52	4	5.71
Upto primary (1-5th Standard)	5	10.20	3	14.29	8	11.43
Upto Middle school (5th to 8th standard)	8	16.33	3	14.29	11	15.71
Upto High School (9th and 10th Standard)	21	42.86	8	38.10	29	41.43
Upto PUC / 12th standard	12	24.49	3	14.29	15	21.43
Upto College / diploma	1	2.04	2	9.52	3	4.29
Total	49	100	21	100	70	100

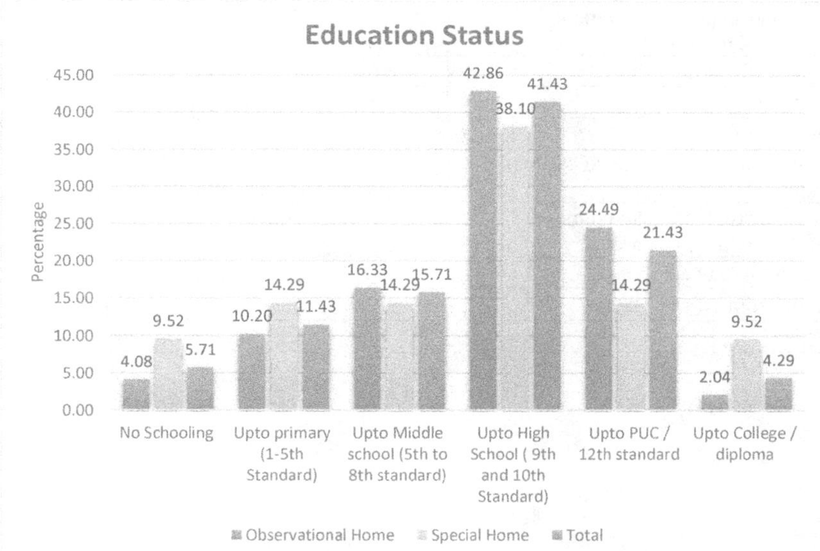

Figure 5.1.2.1 Education Status of children in conflict with the law: Level of Education (N=70)

5.1.2.2 Reason for dropping out from school

Further, an attempt has been made to analyze the detrimental factors (Table 5.1.2.2) associated with disruption in education of CICL. It was evident from the Table that coming into conflict with the law (28.57%), academic failure (18.58 %), and demise of parent (14.29%) and compulsion for earning (14.29%) were the major reasons for disruption. For the children at the SH, the top reason for disruption was stated to negative peer pressure (23.81%), followed by academic failure (19.05%) and a problematic school environment (14.29%) (Fig 5.2.2).

Table 5.1.2.2 Education Status of children in conflict with the law : Reasons for dropping out from school / college (N= 70)

Reasons for disruption of Education	Observation Home		Special Home		Total	
	F	%	F	%		
Lack of money to pay fees	0	0	2	9.52	2	2.86
Was not good at studies	3	6.12	0	0	3	4.29
Failed in exams	6	12.24	4	19.05	10	14.29
Distance of school from home	1	2.04	0	0	1	1.43
Not interested in subject / forced by parents	0	0	1	4.76	1	1.43
Problematic School Environment (teachers and school environment were not good to me)	1	2.04	3	14.29	4	5.71
Illness of self and / or family	2	4.08	0	0	2	2.86
Death of parent	8	16.33	2	9.52	10	14.29
Compulsion to go to work	8	16.33	2	9.52	10	14.29
Discriminated in school due to caste / religion	1	2.04	0	0	1	1.43
Education disrupted due to coming into conflict with law / case	18	36.73	2	9.52	20	28.57
Friends and wrong company	0	0	5	23.81	5	7.14
Migration from village / state	1	2.04	0	0	1	1.43
Total	49	100	21	100	70	100

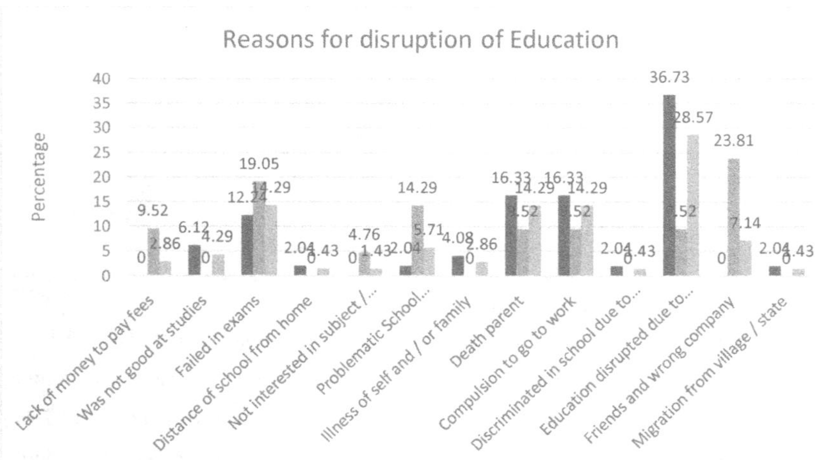

Figure 5.1.2.2 Education Status of children in conflict with the law : Reasons for dropping out from school / college (N= 70)

5.1.3 Socio economic status

5.1.3.1 Father's Occupation

Table 5.1.3.1 depicted the occupation of the fathers of CICLs from the OH and SH. Significantly, a total of 37.14% of the fathers of CICLs were dead, with fathers of 38.78% of CICLs in the OH and fathers of 33.33% of CICLS at the SH were dead. In terms of occupation, a total 17.14% of fathers of CICL were semi-skilled, with 14.29 % fathers of CICLs at the OH and 23.81% of the fathers of CICLs at the SH being semi-skilled. The term 'semi-skilled' refers to jobs like construction labourer, painter, shop keeper's assistant, watchman and labour at garment factories. A group of children's father's occupation were daily wage earners (total of 12.86% and 23.81% at the SH) and agriculture related jobs (19.05% at SH). A few of the fathers of CICL at the OH (12.24%) were in skilled work. The term 'skilled work' refers to the jobs like cable operator, car painter, building contractor and political party worker. (Fig. 5.1.3.1)

Table 5.1.3.1 Father's Occupation (N=70)

Father's Occupation	Observation Home		Special Home		Total	
	F	%	f	%	F	%
Skilled	6	12.24	0	0	6	8.57
Semi-Skilled	7	14.29	5	23.81	12	17.14
Auto driver	2	4.08	0	0	2	2.86
Agriculture	2	4.08	4	19.05	6	8.57
Coolie / daily wages	4	8.16	5	23.81	9	12.86
Factory Worker	2	4.08	0	0	2	2.86
Security Guard	4	8.16	0	0	4	5.71
Father died	19	38.78	7	33.33	26	37.14
Father unemployed	2	4.08	0	0	2	2.86
Don't know	1	2.04	0	0	1	1.43
TOTAL	49	100.00	21	100	70	100

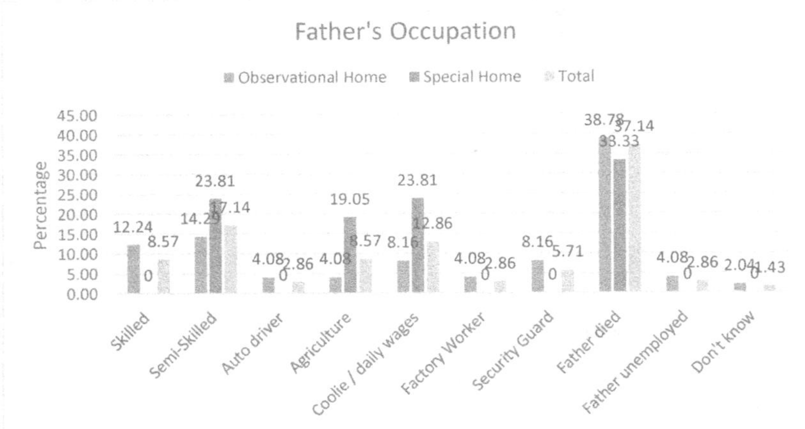

Figure 5.1.3.1 Father's Occupation (N=70)

5.1.3.2 Mother's Occupation

A total of 32.86% (28.57% at OH and 42.86% at SH) of mothers of CICL were housewives and did not have a formal paid job or employment. Against the population trend (49.99%), 53.05% of mothers of CICL at the OH were found to be working and 42.86% of mothers of CICL at the SH were working mothers doing skilled work like housekeeping, shopkeeper, factory worker, cook, canteen worker and tailoring, semi-skilled work like agriculture or labour work, or domestic help, unskilled work – flower or fruit vendor, etc. Meanwhile, 15.71% of mothers CICL were dead and 32.86% were housewives, which meant that 48.57% of mothers of CICL were not employed or earning any income. (Fig. 5.1.3.2)

Table 5.1.3.2 Mother's Occupation (N=70)

Mother's Occupation	Observation Home		Special Home		TOTAL	
	F	%	F	%	f	%
Skilled	10	20.41	3	14.29	13	18.57
Semi-Skilled	5	10.20	0	0	5	7.14
Unskilled	5	10.20	0	0	5	7.14
Agriculture / labour	1	2.04	4	19.05	5	7.14
Housewife	14	28.57	9	42.86	23	32.86
Domestic help	0	0	2	9.52	2	2.86
Factory Worker	5	10.20	0	0	5	7.14
Mother died	8	16.33	3	14.29	11	15.71
Mother unemployed	0	0	0	0	0	0
Don't know	1	2.04	0	0	1	1.43
TOTAL	49	100	21	100	70	100

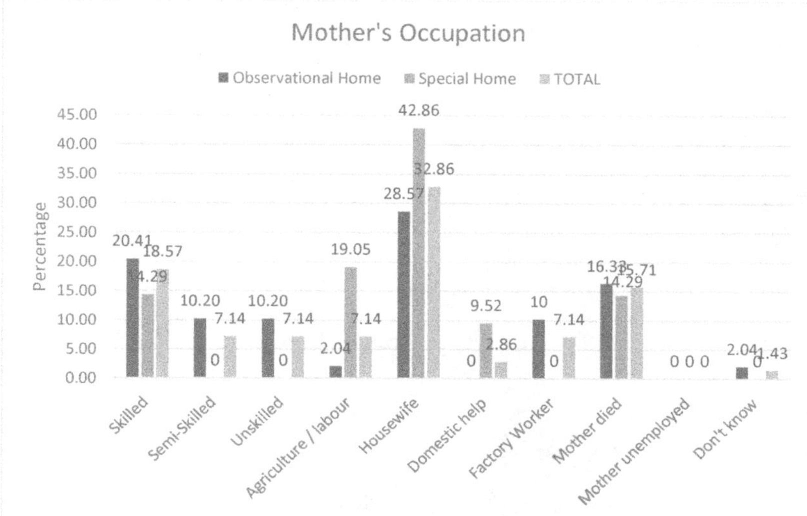

Figure 5.1.3.2 Mother's Occupation (N=70)

5.1.3.3 Family Monthly Income

Table 5.1.3.3 showed that not a single CICL had a family monthly income of above Rs. 30,000/- per month. A total of 44.29% of CICL, (34.69% at the OH and 66.67% at the SH) had a family monthly income of up to Rs.10,000/- per month. Followed by a total of 22.86% of CICL, (28.57% at the OH and 9.52% at the SH) had a family monthly income of up to Rs 30,000/- per month. This was followed by a total of 20% of CICL, (18.37% at the OH and 23.81% at the SH) who had a family monthly income of less than Rs. 5,000/- per month. Significantly, 12.24% of the CICL at the OH had no source of family income and 6.12% of children at the OH, the child was the earning himself with no family income. (Fig. 5.1.3.3)

Table 5.1.3.3 Family Monthly Income (N=70)

Family Monthly Income	Observation Home		Special Home		TOTAL	
	F	%	f	%	f	%
Upto 50,000 per month	0	0	0	0	0	0
Upto 30,000 per month	14	28.57	2	9.52	16	22.86
Upto 10,000 per month	17	34.69	14	66.67	31	44.29
Less than 5,000 per month	9	18.37	5	23.81	14	20
Child earning himself	3	6.12	0	0	3	4.29
No source of family income	6	12.24	0	0	6	8.57
TOTAL	49	100	21	100	70	100

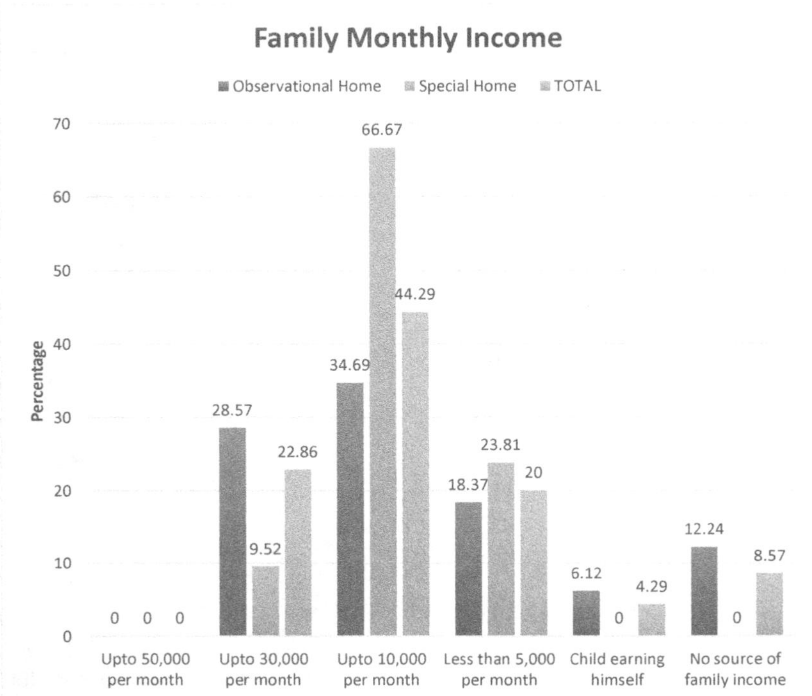

Figure 5.1.3.3 Family Monthly Income (N=70)

RESULT II: CHILDREN IN CONFLICT WITH THE LAW: FAMILY PROFILE

1.2 CHILDREN IN CONFLICT WITH THE LAW: FAMILY PROFILE

5.2.1 Family Composition

Table 5.2.1. described family composition of children in conflict with the law. It was found that 34.69% of the CICL at the OH, 23.81% of the CICL at the SH and a total of 31.43% of CICL had both parents and siblings in their family. However, it is significant to note that 32.65% of CICL at the OH, 38.09% at the SH and a total of 34.29% of the total CICL had a single parent (with or without siblings.) It is also significant that 14.29% of CICL at the SH had grandparents, both parents and siblings. (Fig. 5.2.1)

Table 5.2.1Family Composition (N=70)

Family Composition	Observation Home		Special Home		Total	
	F	%	F	%	F	%
Both parents and child	6	12.24	0	0	6	8.57
Both parents, siblings and child	17	34.69	5	23.81	22	31.43
Single parent and child	6	12.24	2	9.52	8	11.43
Single parent, siblings and child	10	20.41	6	28.57	16	22.86
Grandparents, both parents, siblings and child	0	0	3	14.29	3	4.29
Grandparents, single parent, siblings and child	2	4.08	1	4.76	3	4.29
Grandparents, siblings and child	1	2.04	0	0	1	1.43
Grandparents and child	2	4.08	0	0	2	2.86
Relatives and child	0	0	0	0	0	0
Older siblings and child	2	4.08	2	9.52	4	5.71
Child and younger sibling	0	0	1	4.76	1	1.43
Single step parent, siblings and child	0	0	1	4.76	1	1.43
Child alone	3	6.12	0	0	3	4.29
TOTAL	49	100	21	100	70	100

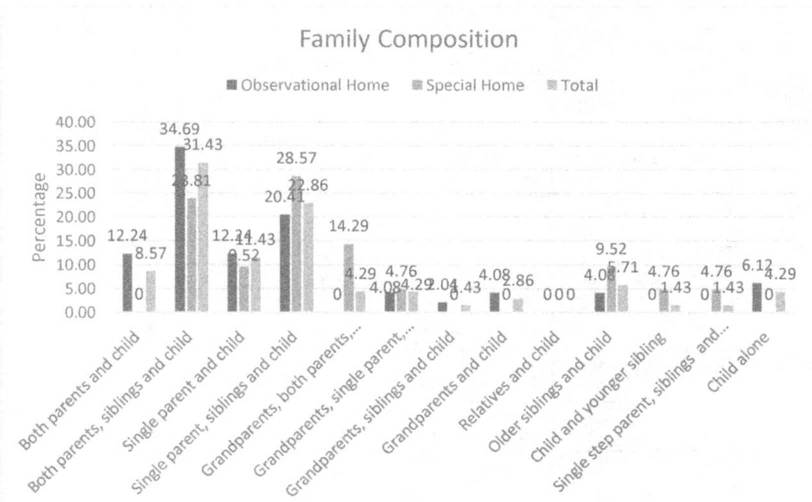

Figure 5.2.1 Family Composition (N=70)

5.2.2 Living arrangements with parents: Father

It was noticed from Table 5.2.2. that fathers of 48.98% of the CICL at the OH, 33.33 % at the SH and a total of 44.29% of the CICL lived with the family. However, very significantly, fathers of 36.73 % of CICL at the OH, 33.33% at the SH and 35.71% of the total CICL were dead. In a significant finding at the SH, it is found that fathers of 14.29% of CICLs at the SH had remarried and moved out, while for 9.52% of the CICL, the whereabouts of the father were not known. Hence, a total of 17.14% of fathers were separated from their children and not parenting them on account of having remarried and moved away (5.71%), refused and did not support in any way (5.71%), were in jail (1.42%) and whereabouts were not known (4.29%) (Fig. 5.2.2). Thus, a total of 52.85% (35.71% dead + 17.14% not parenting) of CICL did not have a father to parent them for various reasons, including death.

Table 5.2.2 Living arrangements with parents (Father N =70)

Living Arrangements : Father	Observation Home		Special Home		Total	
	F	%	F	%	F	%
Father lives with family	24	48.98	7	33.33	31	44.29
Father visits 2 to 3 times a month	1	2.04	0	0	1	1.43
Father visits 2 or 3 times a year	0	0	0	0	0	0
Father does not visit but sends home money regularly	1	2.04	0	0	1	1.43
Father does not visit or support in any way	3	6.12	1	4.76	4	5.71
Father remarried and moved out	1	2.04	3	14.29	4	5.71
Father in jail	0	0	1	4.76	1	1.43
Father died	18	36.73	7	33.33	25	35.71
Father's whereabouts not known	1	2.04	2	9.52	3	4.29
TOTAL	49	100	21	100	70	100

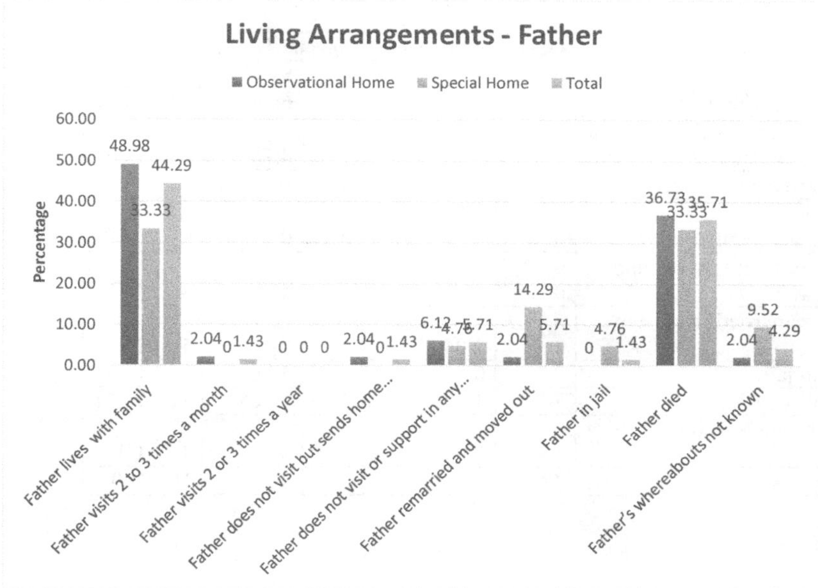

Figure 5.2.2 Living arrangements with parents (Father N =70)

5.2.3 Living arrangements with parents : Mother

It is evident from Table 5.2.3 that an overwhelming majority of mothers of CICL(75.71%), (79.59% at the OH, 66.67% at the SH) lived with their families and children. The main reason for mothers not living with their children appeared to be death. Mothers of 14.29% of the CICL at the OH, 19.05% of CICL at the SH and a total of 15.71% of the CICL are dead. Other conditions (5.72%) where mothers were not parenting their children were separated from husband (2.86), remarriage (1.43%), being in jail (1.43%), whereabouts being unknown (1.43%) or the mother refusing to support in any way (1.43%). Hence, a total of 24.29 of CICLs (15.71% dead + 8.58% other reasons), do not have a mother raising them for various reasons, including death. In this context, a significant finding to be noted was that a total of 51.42% of CICLs had either their father or mother dead (15.71% mothers dead + 37.71% fathers dead). Hence, a staggering total of 77.14% of CICL (52.85% absent father + 24.29% absent mother) did not have a parent in their lives. Fig. 5.2.3. highlighted the finding that such a large number of children did not have a parent.

Table 5.2.3 Living Arrangements with parents : Mother (N=70)

Living Arrangements – Mother	**Observation Home**		**Special Home**		**Total**	
	F	%	F	%	F	%
Mother lives with the family	39	79.59	14	66.67	53	75.71
Mother visits 2 or 3 times a month (separated from husband)	1	2.04	1	4.76	2	2.86
Mother visits 2 or 3 times a year	0	0	0	0	0	0
Mother does not visit but sends home money regularly	0	0	0	0	0	0
Mother does not visit or support in any way	0	0	1	4.76	1	1.43
Mother remarried and moved out	1	2.04	0	0	1	1.43
Mother in jail	0	0	1	4.76	1	1.43
Mother died	7	14.29	4	19.05	11	15.71
Mother's whereabouts not known	1	2.04	0	0	1	1.43
TOTAL	49	100	21	100	70	100

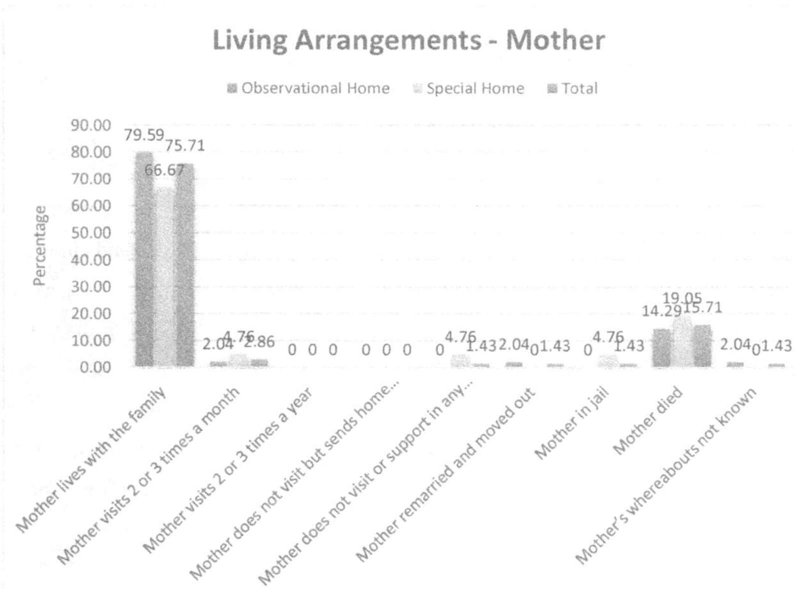

Figure 5.2.3 Living Arrangements with parents: Mother (N=70)

5.2.4 Significant family member as support system to CICL

It was found that for most CICL (61.43%), (71.43% at the OH and 38.10% at the SH), their mother was stated to be the most significant person in their life. After the mother, the younger sibling was stated to be the most significant person in their life for CICLs (10%), (6.12% at the OH and 19.05% at the SH). It was significant that 19.05% of the CICL at the SH stated their father to be the most significant person in their life.

Table 5.2.4 Significant family member as support system to CICL (N = 70)

Significant Family Member	Observation Home		Special Home		Total	
	f	%	F	%	F	%
Father	1	2.04	4	19.05	5	7.14
Mother	35	71.43	8	38.10	43	61.43
Older sibling	3	6.12	1	4.76	4	5.71
Younger sibling	3	6.12	4	19.05	7	10
Grandparents	1	2.04	2	9.52	3	4.29
Don't know / have anyone in my family to call significant	2	4.08	2	9.52	4	5.71
Step mother	0	0	0	0	0	0
Mother's sister	4	8.16	0	0	4	5.71
Total	49	100	21	100	70	100

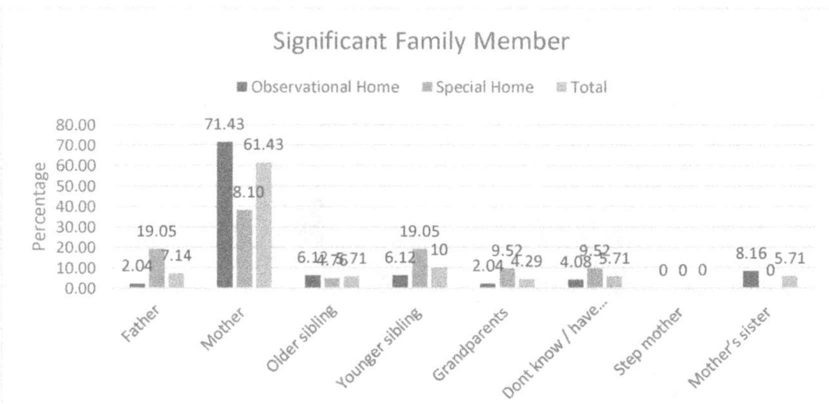

Figure 5.2.4 Significant family member as support system to CICL (N = 70)

5.2.5 Significant non- family member as support system to CICL

Table 5.2.5 revealed that a total of 42.86% of CICL, (53.06% of the CICL at the OH, 19.05% at the SH) stated their friends to be the most significant person in their lives. Importantly, 22.45% of the CICL at the OH, 19.05% at the SH and a total of 21.43% of CICL did not have anyone in their lives that they could call significant. Further, 28.57% of the CICL at the SH and a total of 14.29% of the CICL state their cousin to be the most significant person in their lives. In a significant finding, 19.05% of the CICL at the SH mention the Superintendent of the SH as the significant person (outside of family) in their lives. (Fig.5.2.5)

Table 5.2.5 Significant non- family member as support system to CICL (N=70)

Significant Non- familial member	Observation Home		Special Home		Total	
	F	%	F	%	f	%
Teacher	2	4.08	0	0	2	2.86
Employer	1	2.04	0	0	1	1.43
Relative – uncle / aunt	4	8.16	2	9.52	6	8.57
Cousin	4	8.16	6	28.57	10	14.29
Grandparents who don't live with the child	1	2.04	1	4.76	2	2.86
Superintendent of Special Home	0	0	4	19.05	4	5.71
Friends	26	53.06	4	19.05	30	42.86
Don't know / have anyone outside my family to call significant	11	22.45	4	19.05	15	21.43
Others	0	0	0	0	0	0
Total	49	100	21	100	70	100

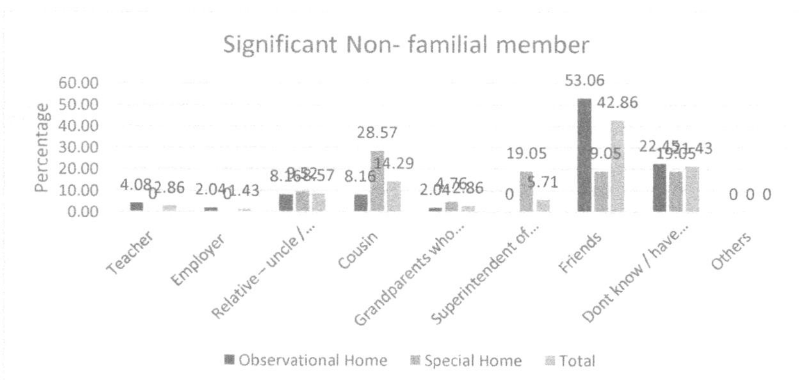

Figure 5.2.5 Significant non- family member as support system to CICL (N=70)

5.2.6 Quality of relationships with family

5.2.6.1 Relationship with father

Table 5.2.6.1 revealed that the fathers of a total of 30% of the CICL, with 26.53% at the OH and 38.10% at the SH were dead. A total of 20% of the CICL, (20.41% at the OH and 19.05% at the SH) stated that their fathers cared for them. However, a total of 12.86% of the CICL, (10.20% at the OH and 19.05% at the SH) stated that their father was not supportive at all. Significantly, 12.24% of CICL at the OH stated that their father was the cause of all their troubles while another 12.24% of CICL at the OH stated that they had never had a father so they did not know how it felt to have a father and were hence unable to describe their relationship with a father.

Table 5.2.6.1 Relationship with Father (N=70)

Relationship with Father	**Observation Home**		**Special Home**		**Total**	
	F	%	F	%	f	%
Father cares for child	10	20.41	4	19.05	14	20
Father fulfils duties but no interaction	3	6.12	0	0	3	4.29
Father helps only in crisis	3	6.12In a	3	14.29	6	8.57
Father is not supportive at all	5	10.20	4	19.05	9	12.86
Father is dead	13	26.53	8	38.10	21	30
Father is in jail	0	0	1	4.76	1	1.43
Father is mentally ill	1	2.04	1	4.76	2	2.86
Don't want to talk about father	2	4.08	0	0	2	2.86
Father is cause of all troubles	6	12.24	0	0	6	8.57
Never had a father so don't know	6	12.24	0	0	6	8.57
TOTAL	49	100	21	100	70	100

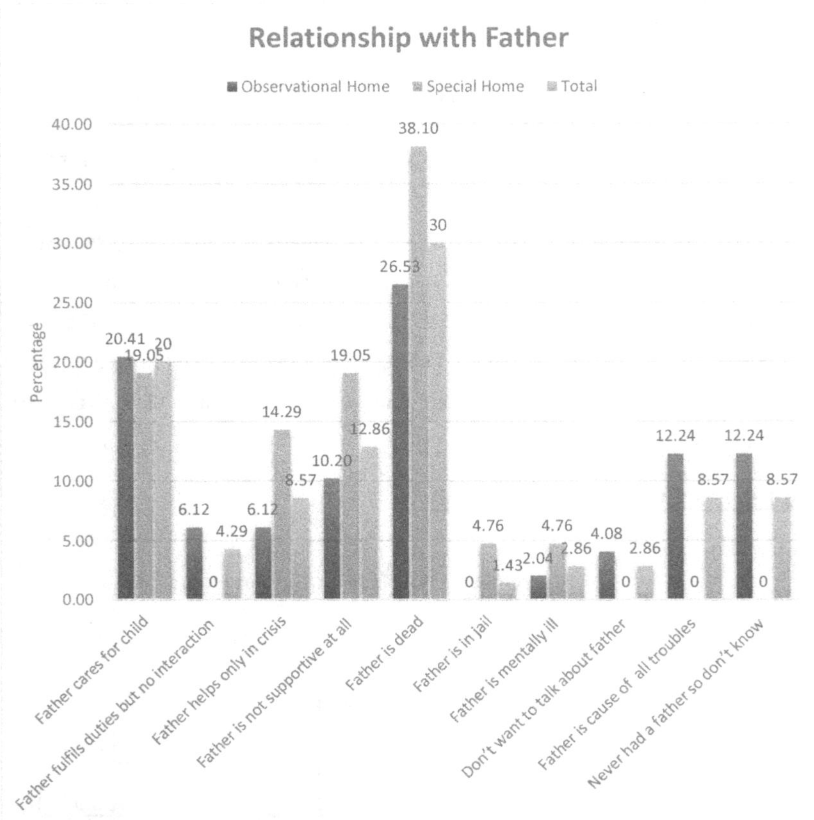

Figure 5.2.6.1 Relationship with Father (N=70)

5.2.6.2 Relationship with Mother

Table 5.2.6.2 revealed that a total of 47.14% of CICL, (53.06% at the OH and 33.33% at the SH) described their relationship with their mother as caring and loving. However, a total of 15.71% of the CICL, (14.29% at the OH and 19.05% at the SH) also stated that their mothers were helpless and therefore, unable to care for them. An equally significant 14.29% of the CICL, (12.24% at the OH and 19.05% at the SH) stated that their mother was dead and therefore, they did not receive any maternal care (Fig.5.2.6.2)

Table 5.2.6.2 Relationship with Mother (N=70)

Relationship with Mother	**Observation Home**		**Special Home**		**Total**	
	F	%	F	%	F	%
Mother cares for child	26	53.06	7	33.33	33	47.14
Mother fulfils duties but no interaction	1	2.04	2	9.52	3	4.29
Mother helps only in crisis	2	4.08	0	0	2	2.86
Mother is not supportive at all	0	0	1	4.76	1	1.43
Mother is helpless	7	14.29	4	19.05	11	15.71
Mother is dead	6	12.24	4	19.05	10	14.29
Mother is in jail	0	0	1	4.76	1	1.43
Mother is mentally ill	0	0	1	4.76	1	1.43
Mother abandoned child / family	1	2.04	1	4.76	2	2.86
Don't want to talk about mother	3	6.12	0	0	3	4.29
Never had a mother so don't know	3	6.12	0	0	3	4.29
TOTAL	49	100	21	100	70	100

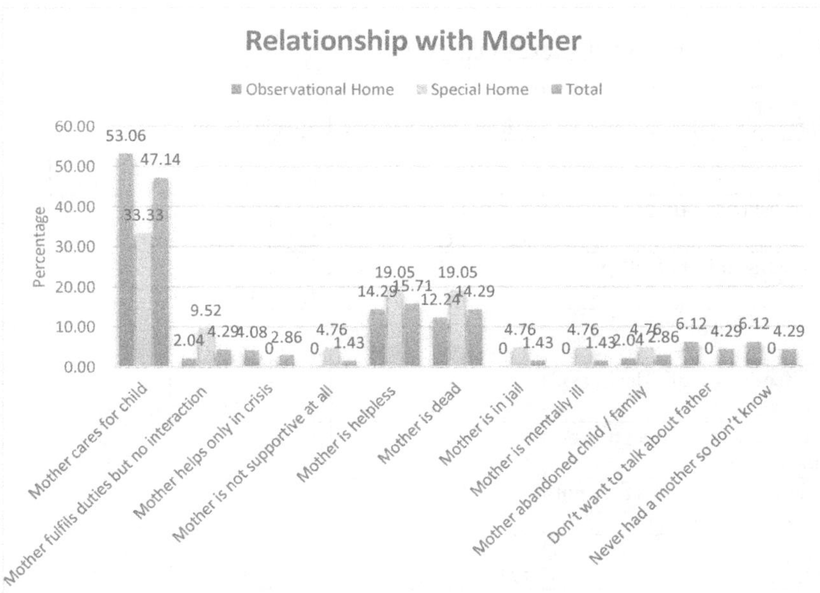

Figure 5.2.6.2 Relationship with Mother (N=70)

5.2.6.3 Treatment of CICL by family

A total of 38.57% of CICL, (46.94% at the OH and 19.05% at the SH) described the treatment of child by family as loving even though they scolded sometimes. However, 18.57% of CICL, (14.29% at the OH and 28.57% at the SH) described their treatment by their family as emotional neglect where they felt that often they were not protected or taken care of. It was encouraging to note that a total of at least 11.43% CICL and 23.81% at the SH described the treatment by their family as loving most of the time. Sadly, 19.05% of CICL at the SH described the treatment by their families as lacking affection while 10.20% described their families as often lacking a feeling of importance and 22.45% at the OH and a total of 17.14% of CICL describe their families as neglectful with often even clothes or food not being provided. A total of 49.99% of the CICL described experiencing some aspect of neglect from their families, 5.71% stated their families lack affection, 8.57% experienced lack of importance, 17.14% stated their families were physically neglectful with even clothes or food not being provided, while 18.57% said their families were emotionally neglectful and did not care or protect them (Fig. 5.2.6.3).

Table 5.2.6.3 Treatment of CICL by family (N=70)

Treatment of Child by Family	**Observation Home**		**Special Home**		**Total**	
	F	%	F	%	F	%
Loving most of the time	3	6.12	5	23.81	8	11.43
Sometimes scolds but otherwise loving	23	46.94	4	19.05	27	38.57
Often lack of affection	0	0	4	19.05	4	5.71
Often feelings of lack of importance	5	10.20	1	4.76	6	8.57
Often Neglect (not enough food or clothes)	11	22.45	1	4.76	12	17.14
Often emotional neglect (not protected or taken care of	7	14.29	6	28.57	13	18.57
TOTAL	49	100	21	100	70	100

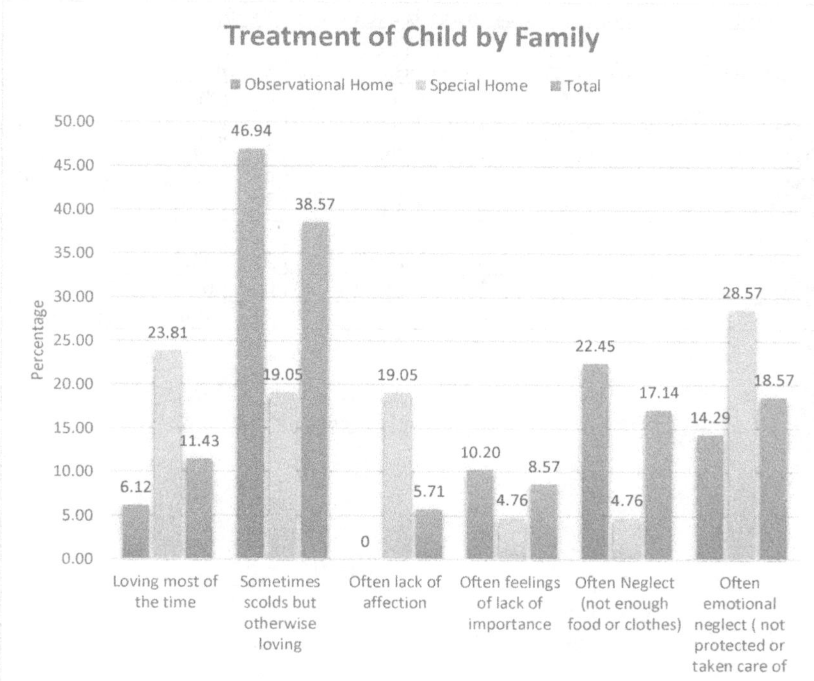

Figure 5.2.6.3 Treatment of CICL by family (N=70)

5.2.6.4 Relationships in the family towards each other

Table 5.2.6.4 showed that a total of 24.29% of CICL, (20.41% at the OH and 33.33% at the SH) described their family's relationship with each other as loving and supportive of each other. This was followed by a total of 22.86% of CICL, (26.53% at the OH and 14.29% at the SH) who described their family as not close but helping each other during crisis times. Another 22.86% of CICL, (18.37% at the OH and 33.33% at the SH) described their families as not caring for or helpful to each other even during difficult times. A total of 12.86% of CICL, (12.24% at the OH and 14.29% at the SH) described their families as not close. Worryingly, a total of 10% of CICL with 14.29% at the OH stated that they had no family to care for them (Fig.5.2.6.4).

Table 5.2.6.4 Relationships in the family towards each other (N=70)

Family's relationships with each other	Observation Home		Special Home		Total	
	F	%	F	%	F	%
Loving and supportive to each other	10	20.41	7	33.33	17	24.29
Not close but help during crisis	13	26.53	3	14.29	16	22.86
Not close	6	12.24	3	14.29	9	12.86
Do not help or support each other	4	8.16	1	4.76	5	7.14
Do not care for each other even in difficult times	9	18.37	7	33.33	16	22.86
No family to care	7	14.29	0	0	7	10
Total	49	100	21	100	70	100

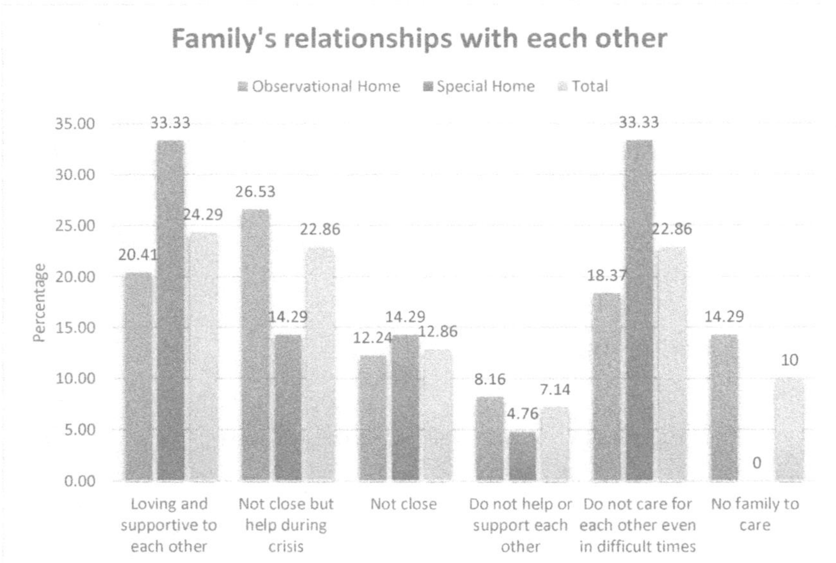

Figure 5.2.6.4 Relationships in the family towards each other (N=70)

5.2.6.5 Parent's understanding of CICL's problems and worries

Table 5.2.6.5 revealed that a total of 27.14% of CICL, (28.57% at the OH and 23.81% at the SH) started that even though parents did not always understand them, they did understand them most of the time. Another 20% of the CICL, (24.49% at the OH) feel that sometimes their parents understand them while 10.20% at the OH stated that their parents very rarely understood them. Significantly, 21.43% of the total CICL, (18.37% at the OH and 28.57% at the SH) stated that they did not have any family or anyone else who could understand them (Fig.5.2.6.5)

Table 5.2.6.5 Parent's understanding of CICL's problems and worries (N=70)

Parents understanding of child's problems	**Observation Home**		**Special Home**		**Total**	
	F	%	F	%	F	%
Yes parents understand the child very well	1	2.04	2	9.52	3	4.29
Not always but parents understand the child most of the time	14	28.57	5	23.81	19	27.14
Sometimes parents understand the child	12	24.49	2	9.52	14	20
Very rarely parents understand the child	5	10.20	1	4.76	6	8.57
Parents don't understand the child at all	8	16.33	5	23.81	13	18.57
There's one there to understand the child	9	18.37	6	28.57	15	21.43
TOTAL	49	100	21	100	70	100

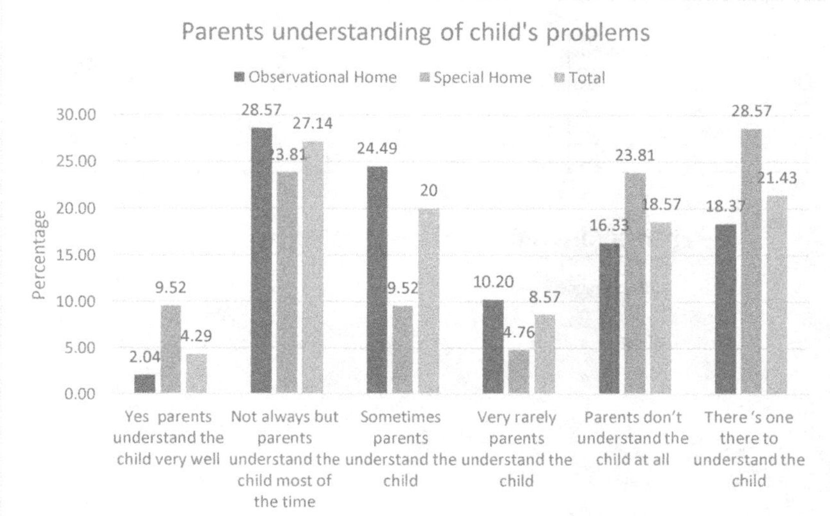

Figure 5.2.6.5 Parent's understanding of CICL's problems and worries (N=70)

5.2.6.6 Parent's involvement in CICL's life

Table 5.2.6.6 revealed that a total of 40% of the CICL, (40.82% at the OH and 38.10% at the SH), described the involvement of their parents in their lives as somewhat involved but somewhat careless also. Significantly, a total of 22.86% CICL, (16.33% at the OH and 38.10% at the SH) stated that did not have any parents to care for or be involved in their lives. Further a total of 14.29% of CICL, (18.37% at the OH) stated that their parents were involved only when there was a crisis, while 11.43% of the CICL stated that their parents were not interested or involved at all in their child's life (Fig. 5.2.6.6).

Table 5.2.6.6 Parent's involvement in CICL's life (N=70)

Parental involvement in child's life	Observation Home		Special Home		Total	
	F	%	F	%	F	%
Parents are very involved in child's life	1	2.04	1	4.76	2	2.86
Involved most of the time	5	10.20	1	4.76	6	8.57
Somewhat involved but somewhat careless also	20	40.82	8	38.10	28	40
Involved only when there is a crisis	9	18.37	1	4.76	10	14.29
Not interested or involved at all in the child's life	6	12.24	2	9.52	8	11.43
No parents to care for or be involved in child's life	8	16.33	8	38.10	16	22.86
TOTAL	49	100	21	100	70	100

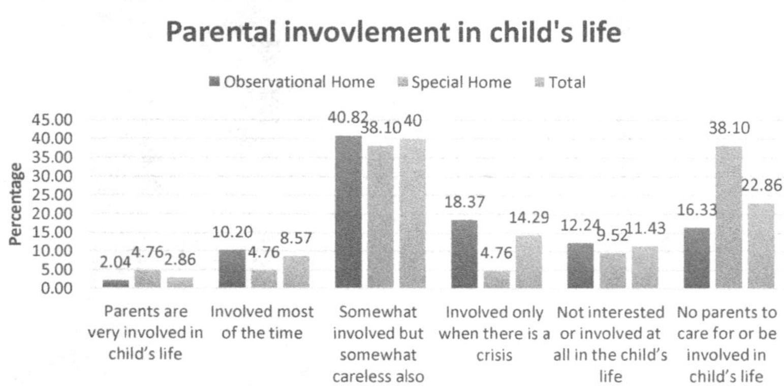

Figure 5.2.6.6 Parent's involvement in CICL's life (N=70)

5.3 RESULT III : HEALTH STATUS

5.3.1 MEDICAL HISTORY

5.3.1.1. Exposure of CICL to Health Services

Table 5.3.1.1 showed that a total of 54.29% of CICL, (51.02% at the OH and 61.90% at the SH) had been exposed to any kind of a medical service only once or twice in their entire life. While a total of 25.71% of the CICL, with 24.49% at the OH and 28.57% at the SH stated that they had been exposed to medical services many times in their lives, a total of 20% of CICL and 24.49% at the OH stated that they had never been to a hospital or seen a doctor ever in their lives. A total of 74.29% (20% never + 54.29% once or twice) indicates that a majority of children do not have adequate exposure or access to medical services (Fig. 5.3.1.1)

Table 5.3.1.1 Exposure of CICL to Health Services (N=70)

Exposure to Health Services	Observation Home		Special Home		Total	
	F	%	F	%	F	%
Yes, many times	12	24.49	6	28.57	18	25.71
Once or twice in entire life	25	51.02	13	61.90	38	54.29
Never	12	24.49	2	9.52	14	20
Total	49	100	21	100	70	100

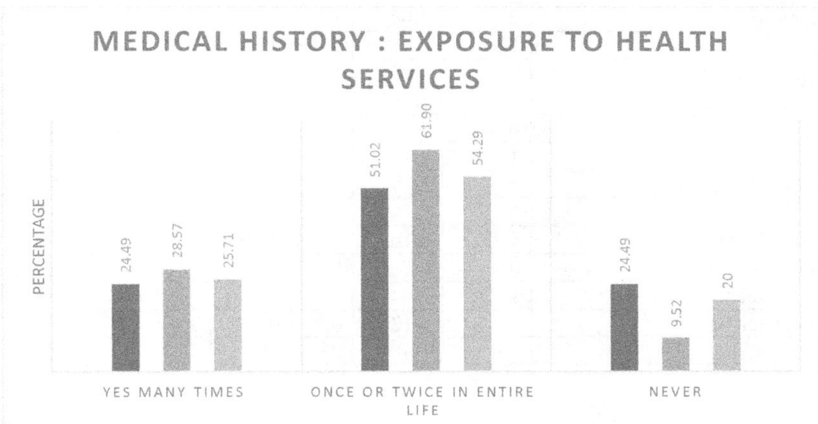

Figure 5.3.1.1 Exposure of CICL to Health Services (N=70)

5.3.1.2 Reason(s) for doctor visit

Table 5.3.1.2 revealed that a total of 30% of the CICL, (24% at the OH and 21% at the SH) stated that illness was their reason for visiting the doctor, while a total of 17.14%, with 14.28% at the OH and 23.81% at the SH stated accident or injury as the reason for visiting a doctor. A total of 12.86%, (18% at the OH and 0% at the SH) stated that they had visited a doctor for a general health check-up. Significantly, a total of 14.29% of CICL, with 18.37 % at OH and 10% at SH stated that they had never visited a doctor in their life. Significantly, many among those stating that they have seen a doctor once or twice in their lives (54.29%) stated that the this exposure to a doctor or a medical service happened only after coming into conflict with the law, when they were taken for a medical or psychiatric consultation from the OH or SH. The reasons stated by CICL for visiting a doctor or a hospital include general check-up, vaccination, illness, injury, accident, loss of weight, age determination ordered by the JJB, drugs, mental illness, violence, malnourishment and check-up ordered by JJB when child was apprehended under POCSO (Fig. 5.3.1.2).

Table 5.3.1.2 Reason (s) for doctor visit (N=70)

Medical History : Reason(s) for visit to doctor	**Observation Home**		**Special Home**		**Total**	
	F	%	F	%	F	%
General Check up	9	18	0	0	9	12.86
Vaccination	2	4.08	1	4.76	3	4.29
Illness	12	24	9	42.86	21	30
Accident / injury	7	14.29	5	23.81	12	17.14
Never seen a doctor	9	18.37	1	4.76	10	14.29
Loss of weight	0	0	1	4.76	1	1.43
Age determination	1	2	1	4.76	2	2.86
Drugs related reasons	1	2	1	4.76	2	2.86
Mental Illness	0	0	1	4.76	1	1.43
Violence related reasons	4	8.16	1	4.76	5	7.14
Attempted suicide related reasons	0	0	0	0	0	0
Malnourishment	1	2	0	0	1	1.43
POCSO check up	3	6.12	0	0	3	4.29
Total	49	100	21	100	70	100

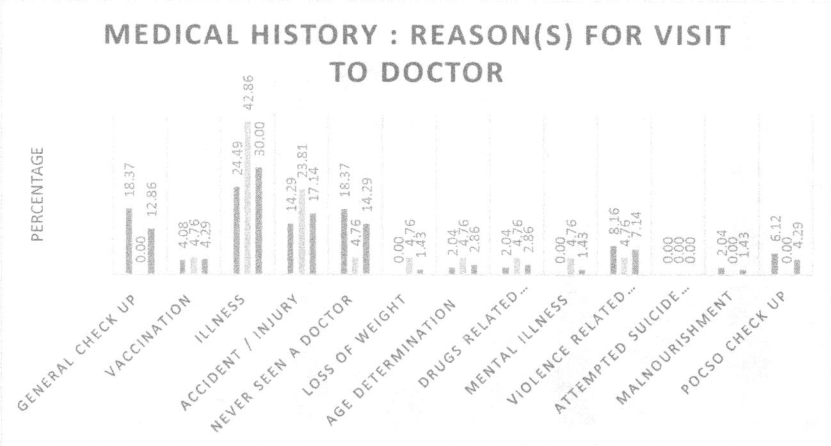

Figure 5.3.1.2 Reason (s) for doctor visit (N=70)

5.3.1.3 History of Hospitalization of CICL

Table 5.3.1.3 revealed a total of 41.43% of CICL, (45% at the OH and 33.33% at the SH) stated that they had never been hospitalized in their entire life. Another 41.43% of CICL, (44.90% at the OH and 33.33% at the SH) stated that they had been hospitalized once or twice in their life. Further, 10% of CICL, (14.29% at the SH) stated that they had been hospitalized up to 3 times, while 19.05% at the SH stated that they had been hospitalized more than 3 times (Fig. 5.3.1.3).

Table 5.3.1.3 History of Hospitalization of CICL (N=70)

Hospitalization History	**Observation Home**		**Special Home**		**Total**	
	F	%	F	%	F	%
Never been hospitalized	22	45	7	33.33	29	41.43
Hospitalized once or twice till now	22	44.90	7	33.33	29	41.43
Hospitalized upto 3 times	4	8.16	3	14.29	7	10
Hospitalized more than 3 times	1	2	4	19.05	5	7.14
Total	49	100	21	100	70	100

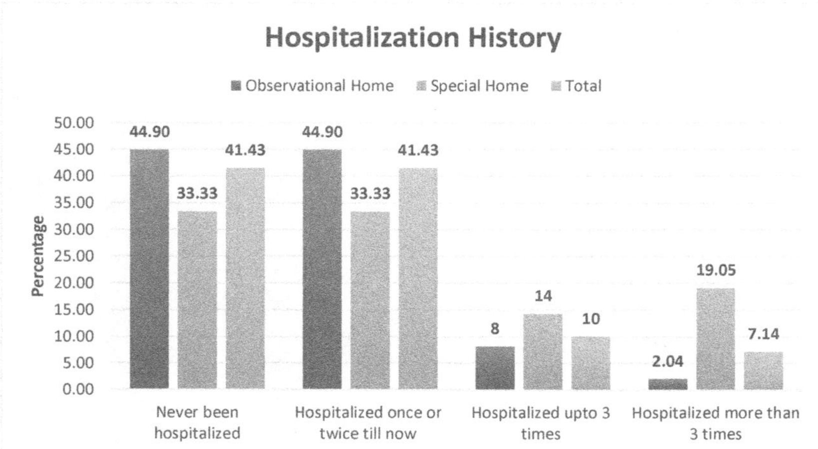

Figure 5.3.1.3 History of Hospitalization of CICL (N=70)

5.3.1.4 Reason(s) for Hospitalization of CICL

A total of 45.71% of CICL, (51.02% at the OH and 33.33% at the SH) stated that they had never been hospitalized. Followed by a total of 17.14% of CICL, (20.41% at the OH) stated that they had been hospitalized due to illness. A total of 11.43% of CICL, (10.20% at the OH and 14.29% at the SH) stated they had been hospitalized due to an accident (Fig. 5.3.1.4).

Table 5.3.1.4 Reason(s) for Hospitalization of CICL (N=70)

Reasons for Hospitalization	**Observation Home**		**Special Home**		**Total**	
	F	%	F	%	F	%
Never been hospitalized	25	51.02	7	33.33	32	45.71
Illness	10	20.41	2	9.52	12	17.14
Injury	1	2.04	2	9.52	3	4.29
Accident	5	10.20	3	14.29	8	11.43
Violence	3	6.12	2	9.52	5	7.14
Tried committing suicide	1	2.04	2	9.52	3	4.29
Drug related	3	6.12	1	4.76	4	5.71
Mental illness	0	0	1	4.76	1	1.43
Police Torture	1	2.04	1	4.76	2	2.86
Total	49	100	21	100	70	100

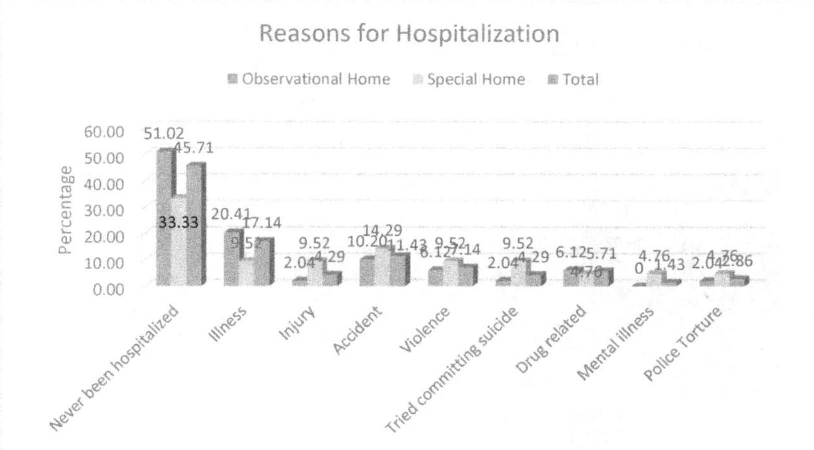

Figure 5.3.1.4 Reason(s) for Hospitalization of CICL (N=70)

5.3.1.5 Duration of Hospitalization of CICL

Table 5.3.1.5 depicted a total of 44.29% of CICL, (48.98 % at the OH and 33.33% at the SH) who stated that they had never been hospitalized. Followed by a total of 20% of CICL, (22.45% at the OH and 14.29% at the SH) who stated that they had been hospitalized for up to 3 days. Another 14.29% of CICL, (16.33% at the OH) stated that they were hospitalized for up to 7 days, while a total of 21.43% of CICL had undergone hospitalization of more than 7 days (Fig. 5.3.1.5).

Table 5.3.1.5 Duration of Hospitalization of CICL (N=70)

Duration of Hospitalization	**Observation Home**	**Special Home**	**Total**
Never been hospitalized	48.98	33.33	44.29
Upto 3 days	22.45	14.29	20
Upto 7 days	16.33	9.52	14.29
Upto 15 days	4.08	14.29	7.14
Beyond 15 days	2	0	1.43
Upto 1 month	4.08	14.29	7.14
Upto 3 months	0	9.52	2.86
Upto 6 months	2	0	1.43
Upto 12 months	0	4.76	1.43
Total	100	100	100

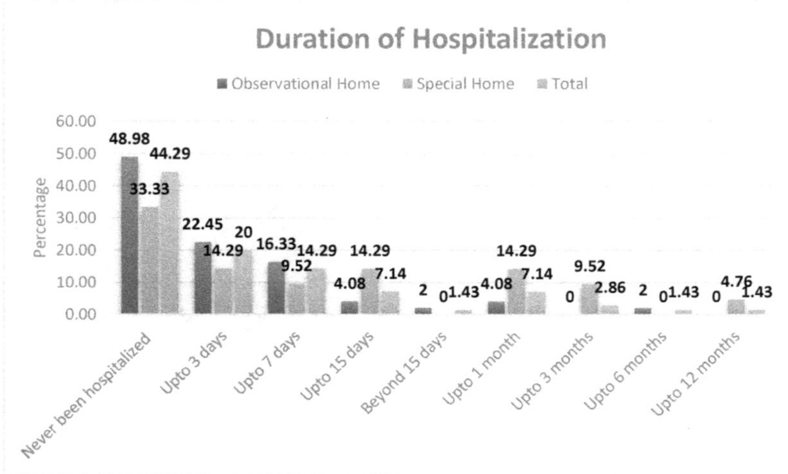

Figure 5.3.1.5 Duration of Hospitalization of CICL (N=70)

5.3.1.6 Check-up of CICL at Child Care Institution

Table 5.3.1.6 showed that a total of 38.57% of CICL, (55 % at the OH) stated that they have not got any check up at the CCI even once. However, a total of 37.41% of CICL, (with 26.53% at the OH and 61.90% at the SH) stated that they had received only a general health check-up since their admission to the CCI. Significantly, 19.05% of the CICL at the SH stated that they had undergone several health check-ups since admission to the SH (Fig. 5.3.1.6).

Table 5.3.1.6 Check-up of CICL at Child Care Institution (N=70)

Check up at CCI	Observation Home		Special Home		Total	
	F	%	F	%	F	%
Yes as soon as admission to the OH / SH	4	8.16	1	4.76	5	7.14
Many times since admission	0	0.00	4	19.05	4	5.71
General health check up only	13	26.53	13	61.90	26	37.14
Dental health check up	0	0.00	2	9.52	2	2.86
Some medical camps at the OH/ SH	1	2	0	0	1	1.43
Police took me for check	4	8.16	1	4.76	5	7.14
No check up	27	55	0	0	27	38.57
Total	49	100	21	100	70	100

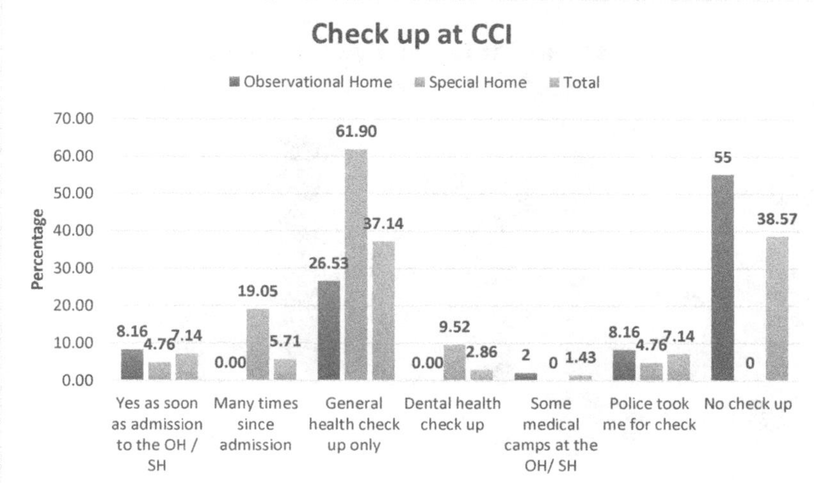

Figure 5.3.1.6 Check-up of CICL at Child Care Institution (N=70)

5.3.2 SUBSTANCE USE

5.3.2.1 Status of Substance use by CICL Usage

Substance abuse usage appeared to be widespread among CICL. Table 5.3.2.1 revealed that a total of 71.43% of CICL, (65.31 % at the OH and 85.71% at the SH) stated that they used some substance. However, a total of 28.57% of CICL, (34.69% at the OH and 14.29% at the SH) stated that they do not use any substance (Fig. 5.3.2.1)

Table 5.3.2.1 Status of Substance use by CICL : Usage (N=70)

Status of substance use by CICL : Usage	**Observation Home**		**Special Home**		**Total**	
	F	%	F	%	F	%
No I don't use any substance	17	34.69	3	14.29	20	28.57
Yes I use	32	65.31	18	85.71	50	71.43
Total	49	100	21	100	70	100

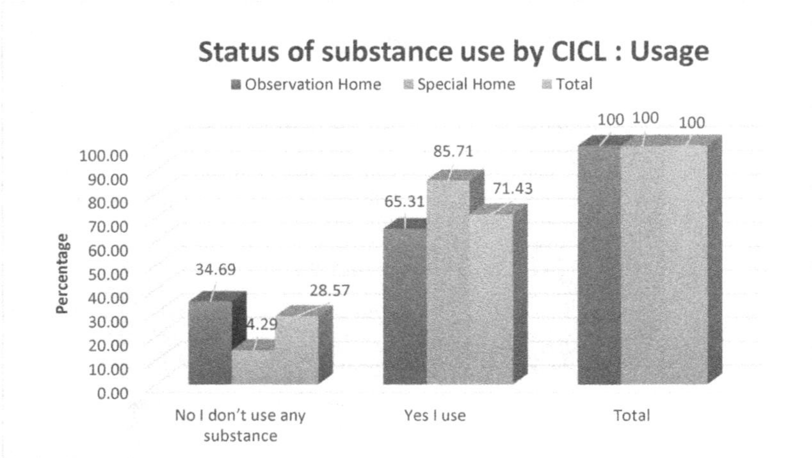

Figure 5.3.2.1 Status of Substance use by CICL Usage (N=70)

5.3.2.2 Status of Substance use by CICL Type of Substance

The type of substance use by CICL appeared to be varied and Table 5.3.2.2 revealed that a total of 48.57% of CICL (36.73 % at the OH and 76.19% at the SH) stated that they used a combination of substances (which includes cigarettes, marijuana, alcohol and inhalants). However, 25.71% of CICL (30.60% at the OH and 14.29% at the SH) stated that they did not use any substance. Around 20% of CICL (24.49% at the OH) stated that they only smoked cigarettes or beedis. Significantly, none of the CICLs stated that they took marijuana only, but admitted to using it in combination with other substances (Fig. 5.3.2.2).

Table 5.3.2.2 Status of Substance use by CICL: Type of substance (N=70)

Status of substance use by CICL : Type of substance	**Observation Home**		**Special Home**		**Total**	
	F	%	F	%	F	%
No substance	15	30.61	3	14.29	18	25.71
Cigarette or beedi / Use of tobacco	12	24.49	2	9.52	14	20
Alcohol	2	4.08	0	0	2	2.86
Cannabis or opium	0	0	0	0	0	0
Solution / glue (inhalants)	2	4	0	0	2	2.86
Combination	18	36.73	16	76.19	34	48.57
Total	49	100	21	100	70	100

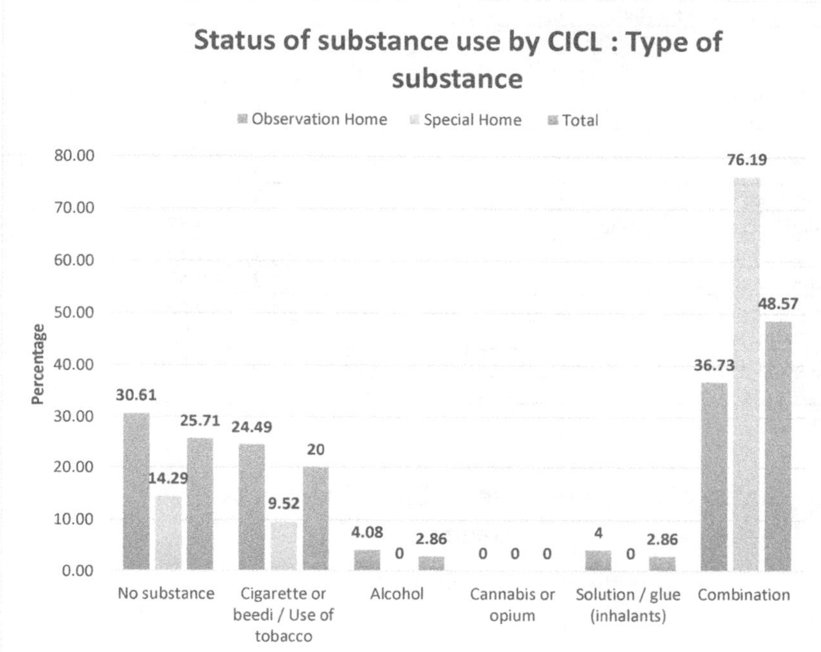

Figure 5.3.2.2 Status of Substance use by CICL: Type of substance (N=70)

5.3.2.3 Status of Substance use by CICL: Frequency of Usage

There appears to be regular frequency of usage of substance use by CICLs. Table 5.3.2.3 revealed that a total of 24.29% of CICL (18.37% at the OH and 38.10% at the SH) stated that they took a combination of substances daily, while 14.29% at the SH took a combination of substances weekly. Followed by a total of 15.71% of CICL (18.37% at the OH and 9.52% at the SH) stated that they took some substance few times in a week. Additionally, a total of 11.43% of CICL, (12% at the OH) stated that they took some substance daily. Further, 12.86% of CICL (12.24% at the OH and 14.29% at the SH) stated that they had experimented once or twice and gave up. Around 17.14% of CICL (24.49% at the OH) stated that they had never taken any substance. Significantly, every single child at the SH had taken a substance at some point with some frequency (Fig. 5.3.2.3).

Table 5.3.2.3 Status of substance use by CICL: Frequency of Usage (N=70)

Status of substance use by CICL : Frequency of usage	**Observation Home**		**Special Home**		**Total**	
	F	%	F	%	F	%
Never	12	24.49	0	0	12	17.14
Experimented once or twice and gave up	6	12.24	3	14.29	9	12.86
On social occasions / festivals	5	10.20	2	9.52	7	10
Few times in a month	1	2	1	4.76	2	2.86
Few times in a week	9	18.37	2	9.52	11	15.71
Daily	6	12	2	9.52	8	11.43
Combination weekly	1	2	3	14.29	4	5.71
Combination daily	9	18.37	8	38.10	17	24.29
Total	49	100	21	100	70	100

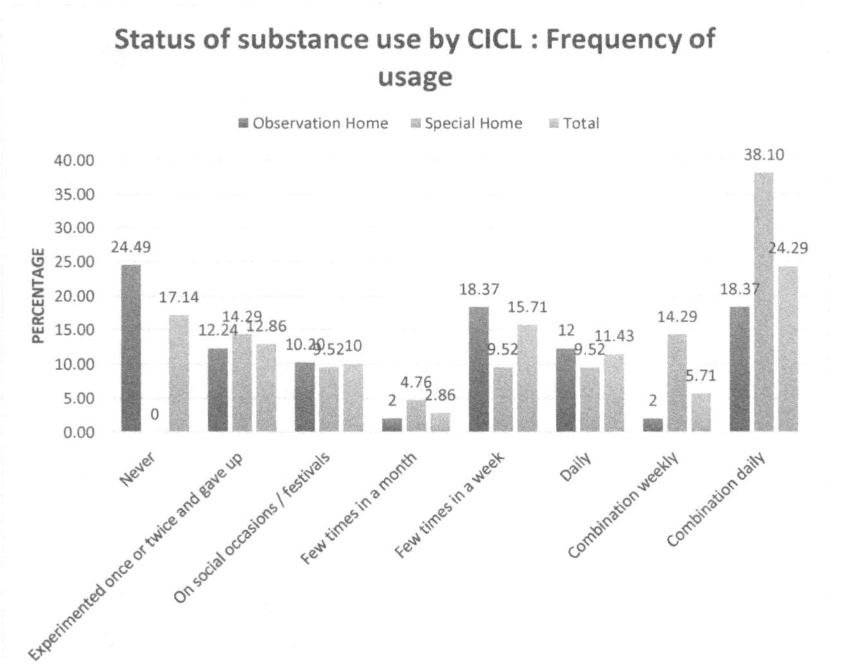

Figure 5.3.2.3 Status of substance use by CICL: Frequency of Usage (N=70)

5.3.2.4 Status of substance use by CICL: Perceived reasons for consumption

Table 5.3.2.4 revealed that a total of 30% of CICL (36.73% at the OH and 14.29% at the SH) stated that they had no history of taking any substance. But a total of 27.14% of CICL (30.61% at the OH and 19.05% at the SH) stated that the consumption of substances made them forget reality for some time. On the other hand, a total of 14.29% of CICL (28.57% at the SH) stated that the consumption of substances made them feel accepted by friends, while another 10% of CICL (12% at the OH) stated that consumption of substances made them feel grown up (Fig. 5.3.2.4).

Table 5.3.2.4 Status of substance use by CICL : Perceived reasons for consumption (N=70)

Status of substance use by CICL : Perceived reasons for consumption	**Observation Home**		**Special Home**		**Total**	
	F	%	F	%	F	%
No history	18	36.73	3	14.29	21	30
Makes me forget reality for sometime	15	30.61	4	19.05	19	27.14
Makes me feel accepted by friends	4	8	6	28.57	10	14.29
Makes me feel grown up	6	12	1	4.76	7	10
Makes me feel smart and capable	3	6	2	9.52	5	7.14
Makes me feel powerful and people scared of me	0	0	1	4.76	1	1.43
Working in pub so exposed to smoking and drinking	0	0	1	4.76	1	1.43
Needed it to do hard work	0	0	1	4.76	1	1.43
Makes me feel sleepy	1	2	0	0	1	1.43
Don't like to talk / socialize so smoke	2	4	2	9.52	4	5.71
Total	49	100	21	100	70	100

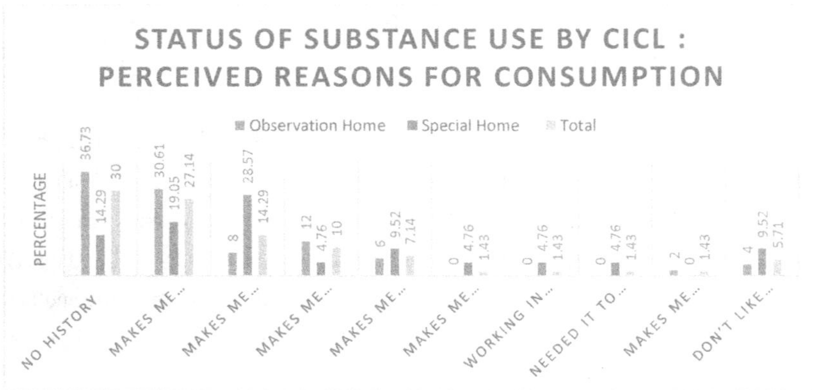

Figure 5.3.2.4 Status of substance use by CICL : Perceived reasons for consumption (N=70)

5.3.2.5 Treatment received by CICL for substance use

Table 5.3.2.5 revealed that a total of 42.86% of CICL, (51.02% at the OH and 23.81% at the SH) stated that they did not have any addiction to any substance and hence had not taken any treatment. A total of 25.71% of CICL, (22.45% at the OH and 33.33% at the SH) stated that though they were addicted they had not received any treatment so far, while 18.57% of CICL, (18.37% at the OH and 19.05% at the SH) stated that they had no access to treatment for their substance addiction.

Table 5.3.2.5 Treatment received by CICL for substance use (N=70)

Treatment received by CICL for substance use	**Observation Home**		**Special Home**		**Total**	
	F	%	F	%	F	%
No addiction no treatment	25	51.02	5	23.81	30	42.86
Treatment received and gave up usage	0	0	2	9.52	2	2.86
Treatment received but discontinued	1	2.04	2	9.52	3	4.29
Treatment received but not given up usage	0	0	0	0	0	0
Addicted but no treatment received	11	22.45	7	33.33	18	25.71
No access to treatment	9	18.37	4	19.05	13	18.57
Treatment received and relapsed	3	6.12	1	4.76	4	5.71
Received hell in the name of treatment	0	0	0	0	0	0
TOTAL	49	100	21	100	70	100

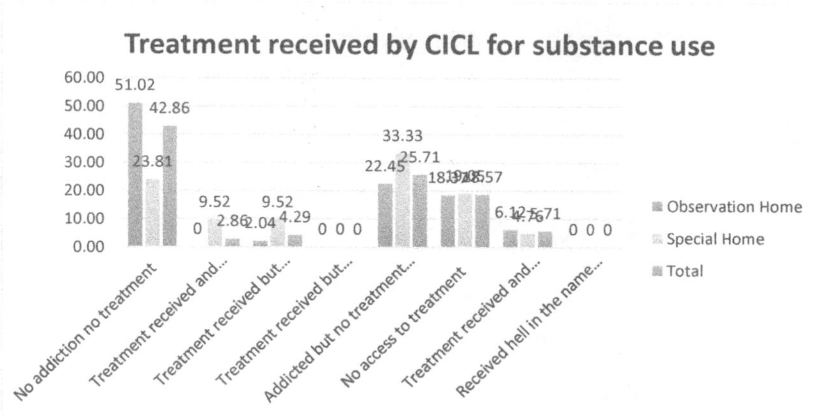

Figure 5.3.2.5 Treatment received by CICL for substance use (N=70)

5.3.2.6 Willingness of CICL to seek treatment

Table 5.3.2.6 showed that a total of 34.29% of CIC (42.86% at the OH and 14.29% at the SH) stated that they had no history of taking any substance and hence no treatment was needed. However, a total of 31.43% of CICL(20.41% at the OH and 57.14% at the SH) stated that they were addicted and that they were willing to receive treatment. Further, a total of 11.43% of CICL (12.24% at the OH) stated that they were willing to receive treatment if their family supported them in the same, while 10.20% at the OH stated that they were willing to receive treatment if the addiction became serious (Fig. 5.3.2.6)

Table 5.3.2.6 Willingness of CICL to seek treatment (N=70)

Willingness to seek treatment	Observation Home		Special Home		Total	
	f	%	f	%	f	%
No addiction no treatment needed	21	42.86	3	14.29	24	34.29
Yes – willing	10	20.41	12	57.14	22	31.43
Denial about need for treatment	1	2.04	1	4.76	2	2.86
Willing if family supports	6	12.24	2	9.52	8	11.43
Would be willing if it becomes serious	5	10.20	0	0	5	7.14
Not willing	4	8.16	2	9.52	6	8.57
Bad earlier experience so not willing	2	4.08	1	4.76	3	4.29
Total	49	100	21	100	70	100

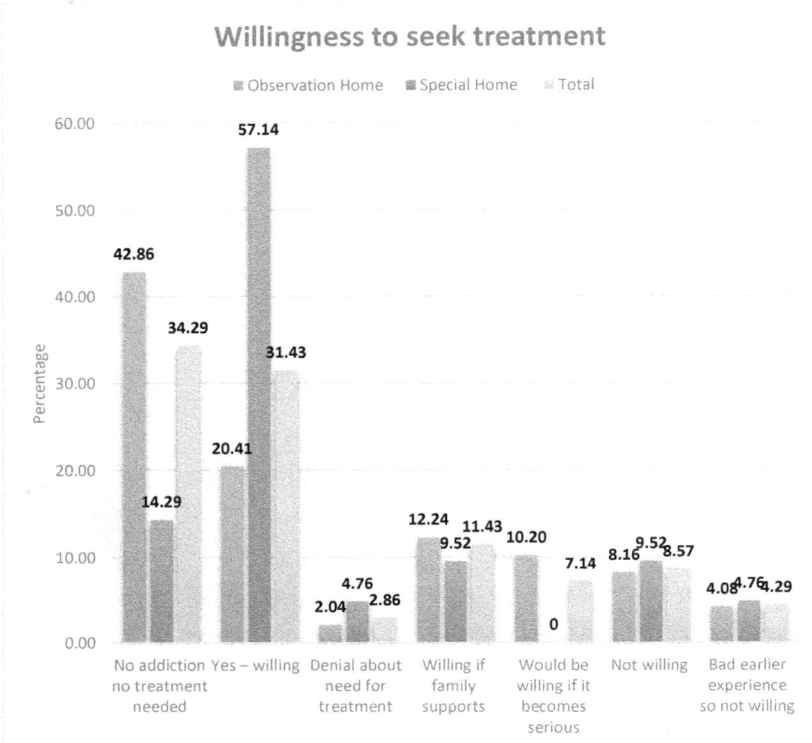

Figure 5.3.2.6 Willingness of CICL to seek treatment (N=70)

5.3.3 VIOLENCE

5.3.3.1 Presence of Violence at CICL's home

In a significant finding, Table 5.3.3.1 highlighted that a total of 68.57% of CICL (63.27% at the OH and 80.95% at the SH) stated that they faced violence at home. An additional 2.86% of CICL stated that they grew up in orphanage and had faced violence there as well. Another 2.86% didn't want to talk about violence indicating that there was something probably disturbing about the topic that they did not wish to speak about. However, a total of 25.71% of CICL (31% at the OH and 14.29% at the SH) said they did not face any violence at home (Fig. 5.3.3.1).

Table 5.3.3.1Presence of Violence at CICL's home (N=70)

Presence of violence at home	Observation Home		Special Home		Total	
	F	%	F	%	F	%
No	15	31	3	14.29	18	25.71
Yes	31	63.27	17	80.95	48	68.57
Don't want to talk about it	1	2	1	4.76	2	2.86
Grew up in orphanage with violence	2	4.08	0	0	2	2.86
Total	49	100	21	100	70	100

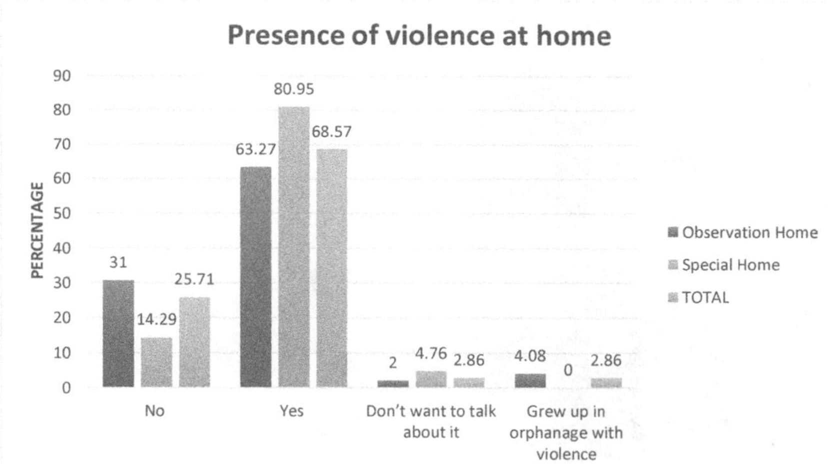

Figure 5.3.3.1 Presence of Violence at CICL's home (N=70)

5.3.3.2 Violence Directed at CICL

It is evident from Table 5.3.3.2 that a majority of CICL (74.29%) including at the OH (73.47%) and at the SH (76.19%) stated that the violence in the family was directed at them. However, a total of 22.86% of CICL (24.49% at the OH and 19.05% at the SH) stated that there was no violence directed at them (Fig. 5.3.3.2).

Table 5.3.3.2 Violence Directed at CICL (N=70)

Violence directed at child	Observation Home		Special Home		Total	
	F	%	F	%	F	%
No	12	24.49	4	19.05	16	22.86
Yes	36	73.47	16	76.19	52	74.29
Don't want to talk about it	1	2	1	4.76	2	2.86
Total	49	100	21	100	70	100

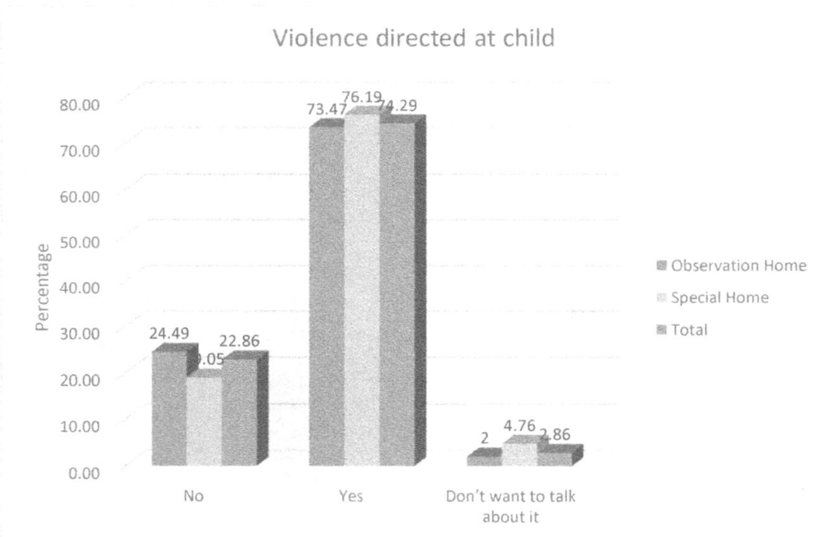

Figure 5.3.3.2 Violence Directed at CICL (N=70)

5.3.3.3 Nature of Violence towards CICL

The nature of violence expressed towards the child was evident in Table 5.3.3.3 which described a total of 18.57% of CICL (18.37% at the OH and 19.05% at the SH) who stated that the way in which violence was inflicted on them was by beating with a stick. Further, a total of 12.86% of CICL (16.33% at the OH) stated that the CICL watched violence on others in the family, extended family or community. Interestingly, 14.29% of CICL at the SH did not want to talk about the type of violence they had faced. Elaborating on the nature of the violence, a total of 11.43% of CICL (23.81% at the SH) stated that the type of violence inflicted on them was by being hit with some household object, while 10.20% at the OH say they were kicked. Additionally, a total of 10% of CICL (with 14.29% at the OH) stated that they were pushed, shoved and hair was pulled. A total of 10% of CICL stated that there was no violence at home (Fig. 5.3.3.3).

Table 5.3.3.3 Nature of violence towards CICL (N=70)

Nature of violence	Observation Home		Special Home		Total	
	F	%	F	%	F	%
No violence at home	4	8.16	3	14.29	7	10
Pushing, shoving, pulling hair	7	14.29	0	0.00	7	10
Slapping	2	4.08	0	0	2	2.86
Kicking	5	10.20	0	0.00	5	7.14
Hitting with object / household things	3	6.12	5	23.81	8	11.43
Beating with hand	3	6.12	0	0.00	3	4.29
Beating with stick	9	18.37	4	19.05	13	18.57
Hitting on head with hand or object	5	10.20	0	0.00	5	7.14
Hitting head or body against wall	0	0	0	0	0	0
Burning, scalding or branding	1	2.04	1	4.76	2	2.86
Attempted strangulation	0	0	0	0	0	0
Stabbing with knife or sharp object	0	0	1	4.76	1	1.43
Combination of multiple forms of violence	1	2.04	1	4.76	2	2.86
Don't want to talk about it	0	0	3	14.29	3	4.29
Child watched violence on others in family / extended family or community	8	16.33	1	4.76	9	12.86
Subjected to violence by police	1	2.04	2	9.52	3	4.29
Total	49	100	21	100	70	100

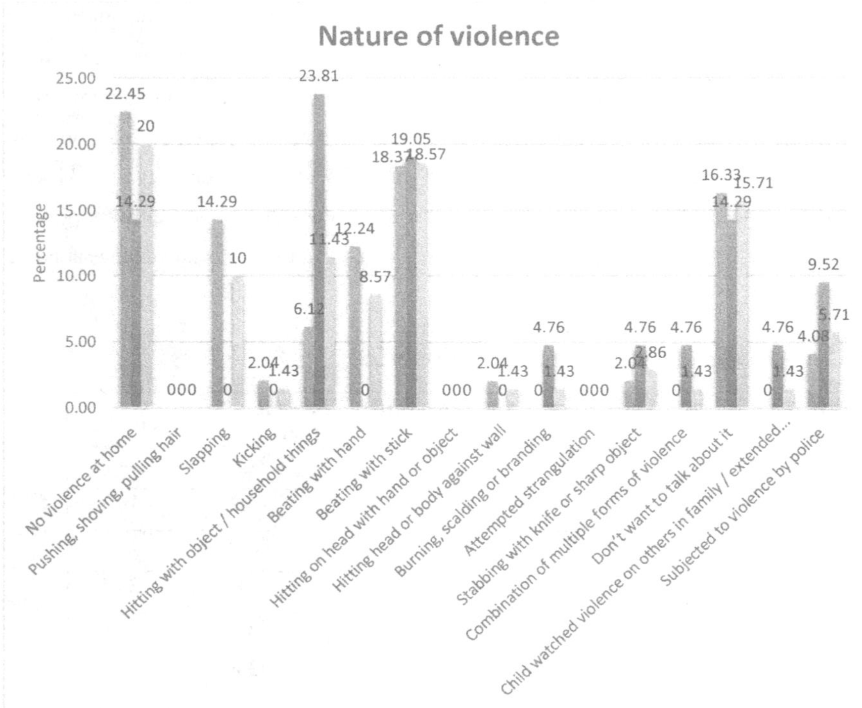

Figure 5.3.3.3 Nature of violence towards CICL (N=70)

5.3.3.4 Violence towards other children at home

It was found that violence was not always restricted only to the CICL and often extended to other family members as well. Table 5.3.3.4 revealed that a total of 40% of CICL (40.82% at the OH and 38.10% at the SH) stated that the CICL, mother and family members were subjected to physical violence by hitting. However, a total of 15.71% of CICL (14.29% at the OH and 19.05% at the SH) stated that only the CICL was singled out for violence, while the other children in the family were not hit. Although, a total of 27.14% of CICL (30.61% at the OH and 19.05% at the SH) stated that there was no violence directed towards anyone at home, an overwhelming majority of 71.42% of CICL had the experience of violence directed towards other children at home, including or excluding himself (Fig. 5.3.3.4).

Table 5.3.3.4 Violence towards other children at home (N=70)

Violence towards other children at home	Observation Home		Special Home		Total	
	F	%	F	%	F	%
No violence at home	15	30.61	4	19.05	19	27.14
Yes	4	8.16	2	9.52	6	8.57
Only child was hit, other children were not hit	7	14.29	4	19.05	11	15.71
Child not hit, but father hit mother	0	0.00	1	4.76	1	1.43
Child, mother and family members were hit	20	40.82	8	38.10	28	40
Don't want to talk about it	0	0.00	1	4.76	1	1.43
Child witnessed violence in extended family	3	6.12	1	4.76	4	5.71
Total	49	100	21	100	70	100

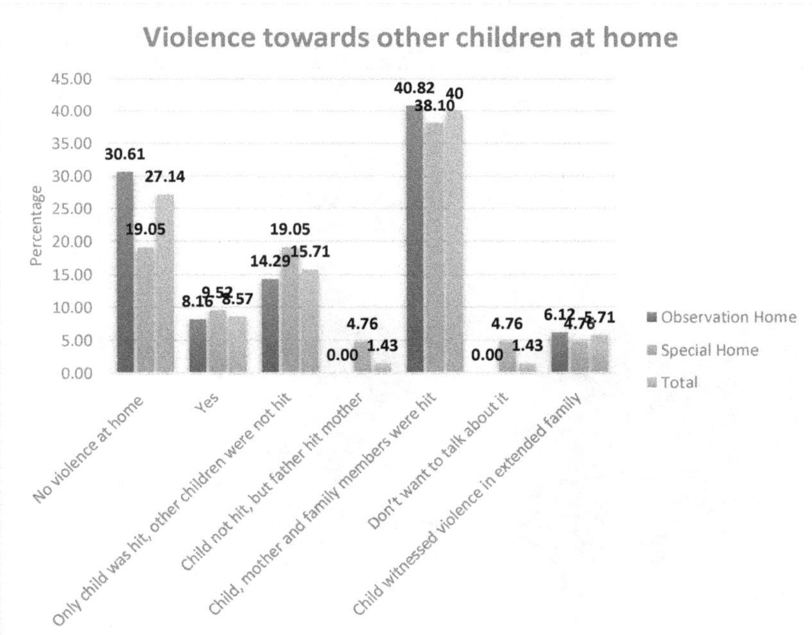

Figure 5.3.3.4 Violence towards other children at home (N=70)

5.3.3.5 Violence by CICL towards others

Table 5.3.3.5 showed that a total of 51.43% of CICL (43% at the OH and 71.43% at the SH) stated that they had shown violence towards others, while a total of 48.57% of CICL (57% at the OH and 28.57% at the SH) stated that they had not shown any violence towards others (Fig. 5.3.3.5).

Table 5.3.3.5 Violence by CICL towards others (N=70)

Violence by child towards others	Observation Home		Special Home		Total	
	F	%	F	%	F	%
No	28	57	6	28.57	34	48.57
Yes	21	43	15	71.43	36	51.43
Total	49	100	21	100	70	100

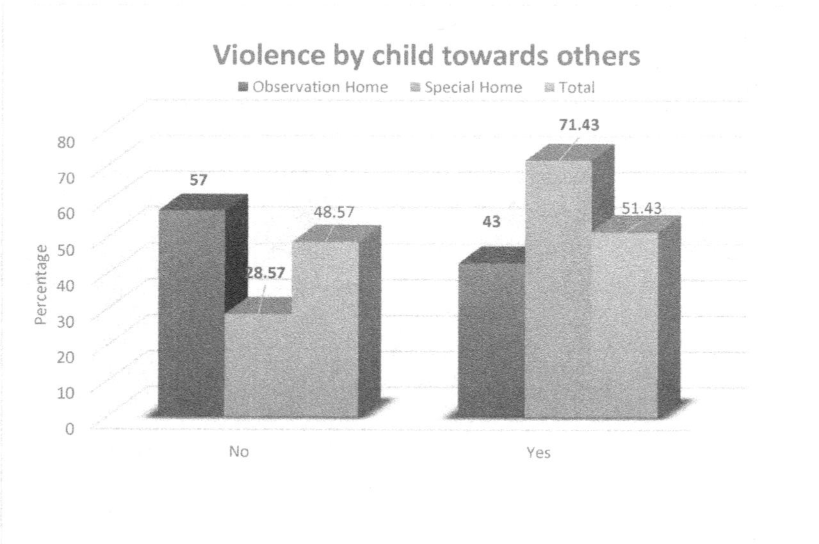

Figure 5.3.3.5 Violence by CICL towards others (N=70)

5.3.3.6 Nature of violence by CICL towards others

Table 5.3.3.6 elaborates on the nature of violence by the CICL towards others. A total of 51.43% of CICL (63% at the OH and 23.81% at the SH) stated that they were not violent towards anyone. At the SH, 23.81% of CICL admit to slapping, while another 19.05% admit to beating with the hand. The CICL describe the nature of their violence towards others to include pushing, shoving, pulling hair, slapping, kicking, beating with hand, stabbing with knife or sharp object, breaking things but not hurting people. Significantly, they also include of murder through violence (7.14%) and the CICL being called upon to beat up others (5.71%) (Fig. 5.3.3.6).

Table 5.3.3.6 Nature of violence by CICL towards othe (N=70)

Nature of violence by child towards others	**Observation Home**		**Special Home**		**Total**	
	F	%	f	%	f	%
Not violent towards anyone	31	63	5	23.81	36	51.43
Pushing/ shoving / pulling hair	4	8.16	1	4.76	5	7.14
Slapping	1	2	5	23.81	6	8.57
Kicking	0	0	2	9.52	2	2.86
Hitting with object / household things	0	0	0	0	0	0
Beating with hand	4	8	4	19.05	8	11.43
Beating with stick	0	0	0	0	0	0
Hitting on head with hand or object	0	0	0	0	0	0
Hitting head or body against wall	0	0	0	0	0	0
Burning, scalding or branding	0	0	0	0	0	0
Attempted strangulation	0	0	0	0	0	0
Stabbing with knife or sharp object	2	4	1	4.76	3	4.29
Child is called upon to beat up others	3	6	1	4.76	4	5.71
Murder through violence	4	8.16	1	4.76	5	7.14
Breaking things but not hurting people	0	0	1	4.76	1	1.43
Total	49	100	21	100	70	100

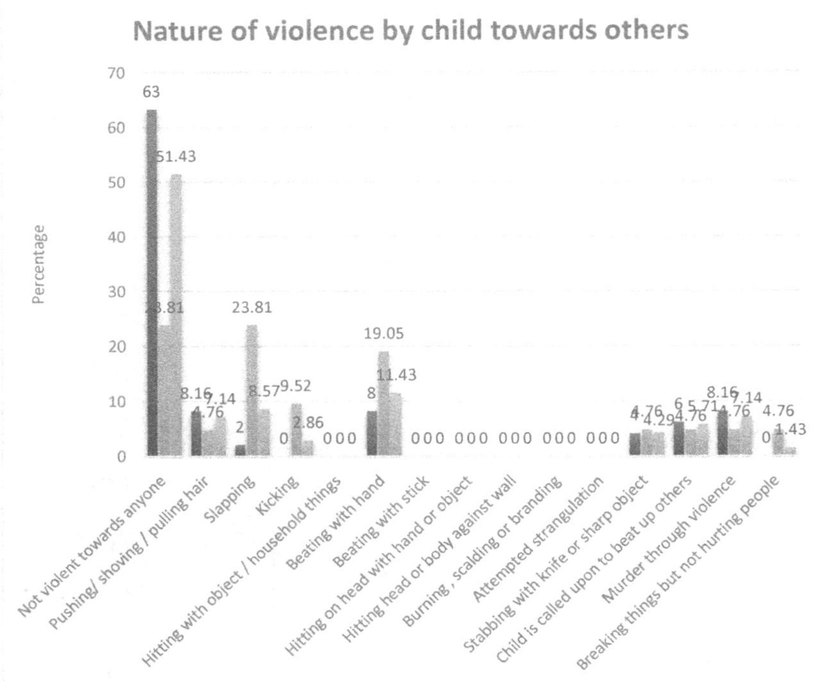

Figure 5.3.3.6 Nature of violence by CICL towards others (N=70)

5.3.4 Concurrent Risk - Depression & Suicide

5.3.4.1: Risk of Depression: Sadness and Weepiness

Table 5.3.4.1 showed that a total of 47.14% of CICL (53.06% at the OH and 33.33% at the SH) stated that they felt very sad and weepy sometimes but that they were able to cope. A total of 18.57% of CICL (14.29% at the OH and 28.57% at the SH) stated that they felt weepy all the time and were unable to cope. A total of 17.14% of CICL (14.29% at the OH and 23.81% at the SH) stated that they felt very sad and weepy sometimes and were unable to cope, while a total of 17.14% of CICL (18.37% at the OH and 14.29% at the SH) stated that they sometimes felt weepy and angry and unable to cope (Fig. 5.3.4.1).

Table 5.3.4.1 Risk of Depression: Sadness and weepiness (N=70)

Risk of Depression : Sadness and weepiness	Observation Home		Special Home		Total	
	f	%	F	%	f	%
No sadness	0	0	0	0	0	0
Sometimes very sad & weepy but able to cope	26	53.06	7	33.33	33	47.14
Sometimes very sad & weepy and unable to cope	7	14.29	5	23.81	12	17.14
Weepy all the time and unable to cope	7	14.29	6	28.57	13	18.57
Sometimes weepy and angry and unable to cope	9	18.37	3	14.29	12	17.14
Total	49	100	21	100	70	100

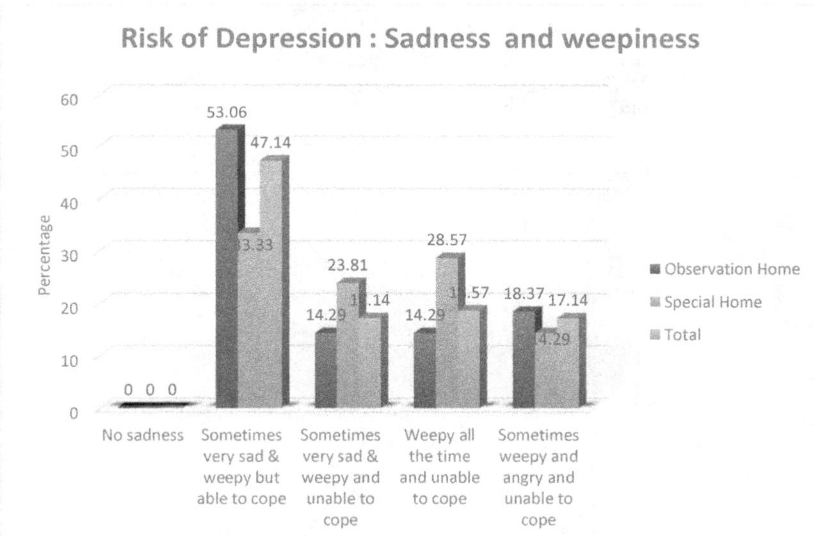

Figure 5.3.4.1 Risk of Depression: Sadness and weepiness (N=70)

5.3.4.2 Risk of Depression: Energy Level and fatigue

Table 5.3.4.2 indicated that 50% of the CICL (53.06% at the OH and 42.86% at the SH) stated that they sometimes felt very tired but that they were still able to cope. However, a total of 27.14% of the CICL (24.49% at the OH and 33.33% at the SH) stated they sometimes felt very tired and unable to cope. Further, a total of 18.57% of the CICL (22.45% at the OH) stated that they were tired all the time and were unable to cope. Interestingly, 14.29% of the CICL at the SH stated that they felt energetic and able to cope. Clearly, there seems to be something that was working at the SH for these 14% of the CICL that was helping them not only cope but feel energetic despite being at the SH (Fig. 5.3.4.2).

Table 5.3.4.2 Risk of Depression: Energy level and fatigue (N=70)

Energy and fatigue	**Observation Home**		**Special Home**		**Total**	
	F	%	F	%	F	%
Energetic, no fatigue	0	0.00	3	14.29	3	4.29
Sometimes very tired but able to cope	26	53.06	9	42.86	35	50
Sometimes very tired and unable to cope	12	24.49	7	33.33	19	27.14
Tired all the time and unable to cope	11	22.45	2	9.52	13	18.57
Sometimes weepy and angry and unable to cope	0	0	0	0	0	0
Total	49	100	21	100	70	100

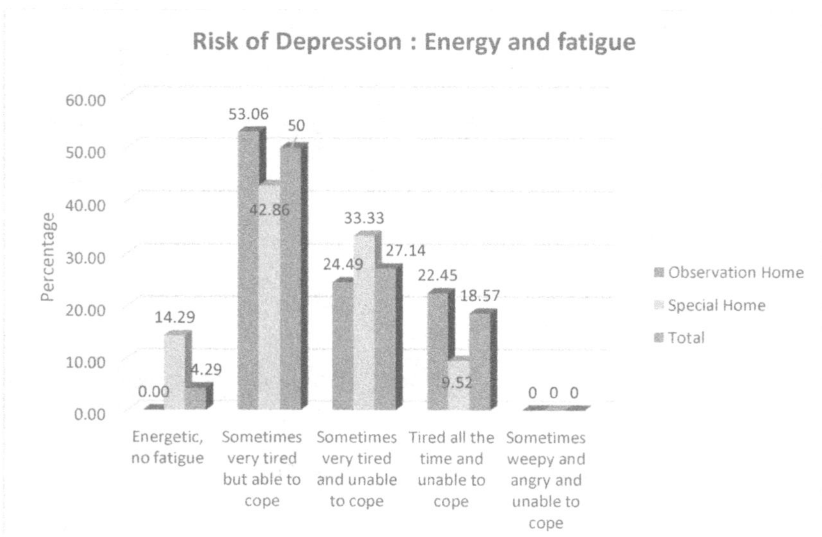

Figure 5.3.4.2 Risk of Depression: Energy level and fatigue (N=70)

5.3.4.3 Risk of Depression: Appetite

Table 5.3.4.3 revealed that a total of 27.14% of CICL (12.24% at the OH and 61.90% at the SH) stated that their appetite was normal as usual, while 31% at the OH stated that they felt hungry all the time and 30.61% at the OH stated they have no interest in eating at all. Further, total of 21.43% of CICL (22.45% at the OH and 19.05% at the SH) stated that they were eating lesser than usual. Overall, a total of 72.86% of the CICL had a change in their appetite – ranging from being hungry all the time, eating more than usual, eating lesser than usual or having no interest in eating at all. Significantly, 61.90% at the SH stated that their appetite is normal as usual.

Table 5.3.4.3 Risk of Depression: Appetite (N=70)

Appetite	**Observation Home**		**Special Home**		**Total**	
	F	%	F	%	F	%
Normal as usual	6	12.24	13	61.90	19	27.14
Hungry all the time	15	31	1	4.76	16	22.86
Eating more than usual	2	4	2	9.52	4	5.71
Eating lesser than usual	11	22.45	4	19.05	15	21.43
No interest in eating at all	15	30.61	1	4.76	16	22.86
Total	49	100	21	100	70	100

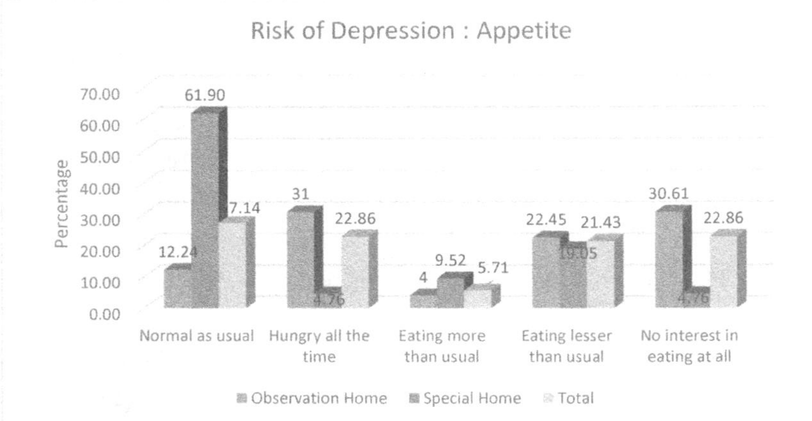

Figure 5.3.4.3 Risk of Depression: Appetite (N=70)

5.3.4.4 Risk of Depression: Sleep

Table 5.3.4.4 revealed that a total of 34.29% of CICL (35% at the OH and 33.33% at the SH) had disturbed sleep with nightmares. A total of 22.86 % of CICL with 29% at the OH felt sleepy all the time. A total of 18.57% of CICL (12.24% at the OH and 33.33% at the SH) found it hard to fall asleep, while a further 12.86% of CICL (14% at the OH) had frequently disturbed sleep. A total of 11.43% of CICL (10.20% at the OH and 14.29% at the SH) stayed awake almost all night. Disturbingly, 100% of the children have different levels of difficulty with sleep (Fig. 5.3.4.4).

Table 5.3.4.4 Risk of Depression: Sleep (N=70)

Sleep	**Observation Home**		**Special Home**		**Total**	
	F	%	F	%	F	%
Hard to fall asleep	6	12.24	7	33.33	13	18.57
Sleepy all the time	14	29	2	9.52	16	22.86
Stay awake almost all night	5	10.20	3	14.29	8	11.43
Frequently disturbed sleep	7	14	2	9.52	9	12.86
Disturbed sleep with nightmares	17	35	7	33.33	24	34.29
Total	49	100	21	100	70	100

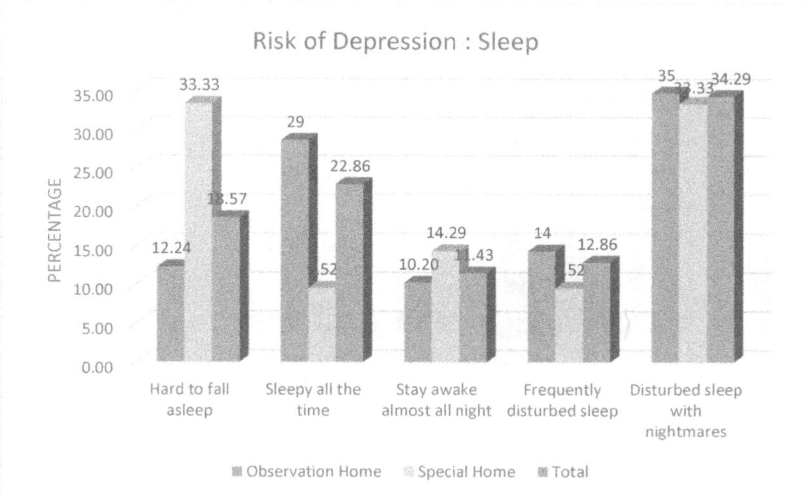

Figure 5.3.4.4 Risk of Depression: Sleep (N=70)

5.3.4.5 Risk of Suicide: Suicidal Ideation

Table 5.3.4.5 revealed that a total of 30% of CICL (28.57% at the OH and 33.33% at the SH) had thought about suicide once or twice in their lives. A total of 25.71% of CICL (16.33% at the OH and 47.62% at the SH) stated that they thought about suicide 'quite often'. Disturbingly, 12.24% of the CICL at the OH stated that they thought about suicide 'almost every day', while 14.29% of the CICL stated that they had thought about suicide three or four times in their life. Very disturbingly, 95.24% of the CICL at the SH stated that they had thought about suicide at some point of their lives. Significantly, 31% of the CICL at the OH stated that they have no suicidal ideation at all (Fig. 5.3.4.5).

Table 5.3.4.5 Risk of Suicide: Suicidal Ideation (N=70)

Risk of Suicide : Suicidal Ideation	Observation Home		Special Home		Total	
	F	%	F	%	F	%
No suicidal ideation at all	15	31	0	0	15	21.43
Once or twice	14	28.57	7	33.33	21	30
Three or four times	3	6.12	3	14.29	6	8.57
Quite often	8	16.33	10	47.62	18	25.71
Almost everyday	6	12.24	0	0	6	8.57
Does not want to reveal	0	0	1	4.76	1	1.43
Only after coming into conflict with the law	3	6	0	0	3	4.29

Total	49	100	21	100	70	100

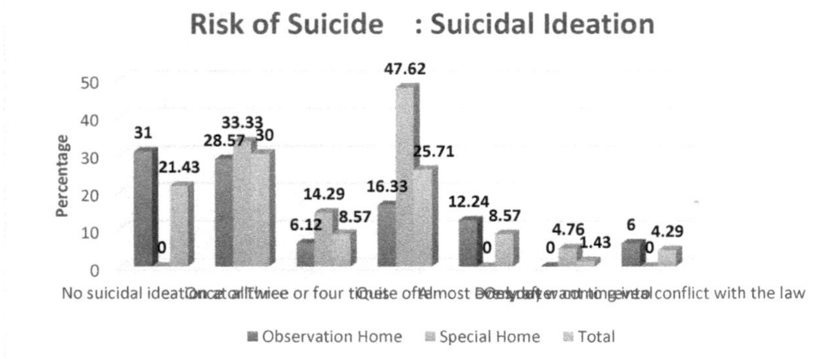

Figure 5.3.4.5 Risk of Suicide: Suicidal Ideation (N=70)

5.3.4.6 Risk of Suicide: Present risk of suicide

Table 5.3.4.6 revealed that a total of 32.86% of CICL (28.57% at the OH and 42.86% at the SH) stated that they had thought about suicide only once or twice in the last 6 to 8 weeks, while a total of 27.14% of the CICL, (35% at the OH) stated that they had not had any thoughts of suicide at all over the last 6-8 weeks. A total of 18.57% of the CICL, (18.37% at the OH and 19.05% at the SH) stated that they had had thoughts of suicide quite often over the last 6-8 weeks. Disturbingly, a staggering total of 71.42% (85.72% of the CICL at the SH and a 65.02% at the OH) stated that they had thought about suicide over the last 6-8 weeks (Fig. 5.3.4.6).

Table 5.3.4.6 Risk of Suicide: Present risk of suicide(N=70)

Present risk of suicide	Observation Home		Special Home		Total	
	F	%	F	%	F	%
Not at all	17	35	2	9.52	19	27.14
yes only or twice	14	28.57	9	42.86	23	32.86
two or three times	2	4.08	4	19.05	6	8.57
quite often	9	18.37	4	19.05	13	18.57
almost everyday	3	6	1	4.76	4	5.71
don't want to tell -	0	0	1	4.76	1	1.43
only after coming into conflict with the law	4	8	0	0	4	5.71
Total	49	100	21	100	70	100

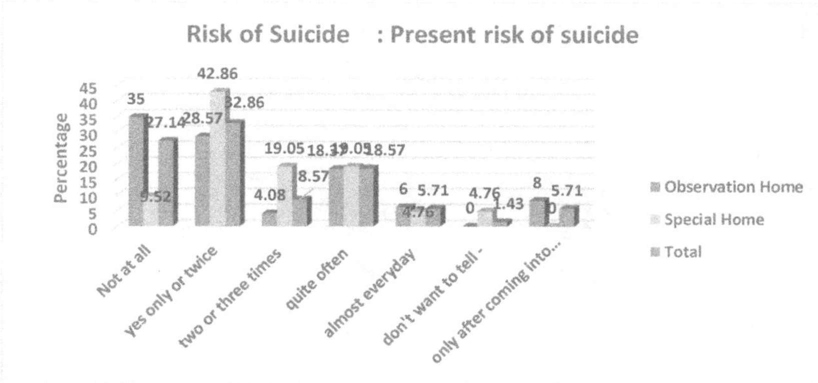

Figure 5.3.4.6 Risk of Suicide: Present risk of suicide(N=70)

5.3.4.7 Risk of Suicide: History of Attempted suicide(s)

Table 5.3.4.7 showed that a total of 34.78% of CICL (39% at the OH and 25% at the SH) stated that they had never ever attempted suicide in their lives. A total of 27.54% of CICL (28.57% at the OH and 25% at the SH) stated that they had thought about committing suicide once or more than once but had never carried it out. A total of 18.84% of CICL (28.57% at the OH and 25% at the SH) stated that they had attempted suicide once but not succeeded, while 10% at the SH stated that they had attempted suicide twice and 15% at the SH stated that they had attempted more than 4 times. A total of 37.69% of CICL (32.49% at the OH and 50% at the SH) stated that they had a history of attempted suicide (Fig. 5.3.4.7).

Table 5.3.4.7 Risk of Suicide: History of Attempted suicide(s) (N=70)

Risk of Suicide : History of Attempted suicide(s)	Observation Home		Special Home		Total	
	F	%	F	%	F	%
Never attempted ever	19	39	5	25	24	34.78
Thought about but never carried out	14	28.57	5	25	19	27.54
Once	8	16.33	5	25	13	18.84
Twice	4	8.16	2	10	6	8.70
Thrice	2	4	0	0	2	2.90
ore than 4 times	2	4	3	15	5	7.25
Does not want to reveal	0	0	0	0	0	0
Total	49	100	20	100	69	100

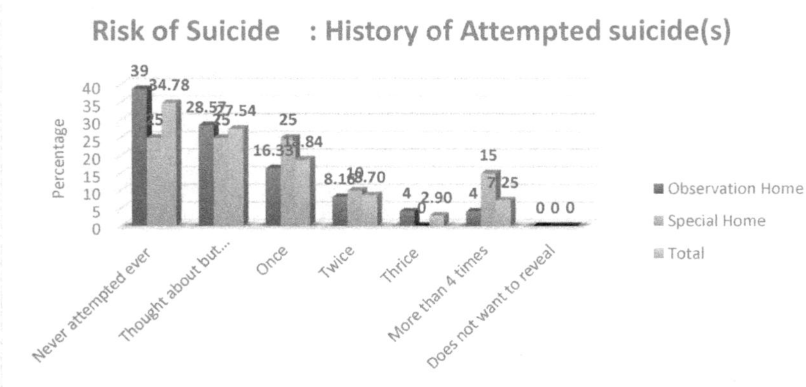

Figure 5.3.4.7 Risk of Suicide: History of Attempted suicide(s) (N=70)

5.3.5 Family Health History

5.3.5.1: Parental Health Status: Father

Table 5.3.5.1 showed that fathers of a total of 28.57% of CICL(24% at the OH and 38.10% at the SH) were reported to be suffering from alcoholism, while fathers of 14.29% of CICL (12% at the OH and 19.05% at the SH) were reported to have died due to drinking. Further, fathers of a total of 11.43% of CICL (12% at the OH and 9.52% at the SH) suffered from a communicable or non-communicable disease; while fathers of a total of 10% of CICL (14.29% at the SH) had died due to illness. Overall, the health status of fathers of CICL appeared to be poor, with a total of 82.87% (78.52% at OH and 90.48% at the SH) fathers of CICL who were either ill or dead (Fig. 5.3.5.1).

Table 5.3.5.1 Parental Health Status: Father (N=70)

Parental Health Status: Father	Observation Home		Special Home		Total	
	F	%	F	%	F	%
Healthy	3	6.12	2	9.52	5	7.14
Mostly healthy but falls ill often	6	12.24	1	4.76	7	10

Suffers from communicable / non-communicable disease	6	12	2	9.52	8	11.43
Suffers from alcoholism	12	24	8	38.10	20	28.57
Died because of illness	4	8.16	3	14.29	7	10
Died due to drinking	6	12	4	19.05	10	14.29
Don't know father's health history	5	10.20	0	0	5	7.14
Suffers from mental illness	1	2	1	4.76	2	2.86
Don't want to talk about father's health history	2	4	0	0	2	2.86
Committed suicide	3	6.12	0	0	3	4.29
Was murdered	1	2	0	0	1	1.43
Total	49	100	21	100	70	100

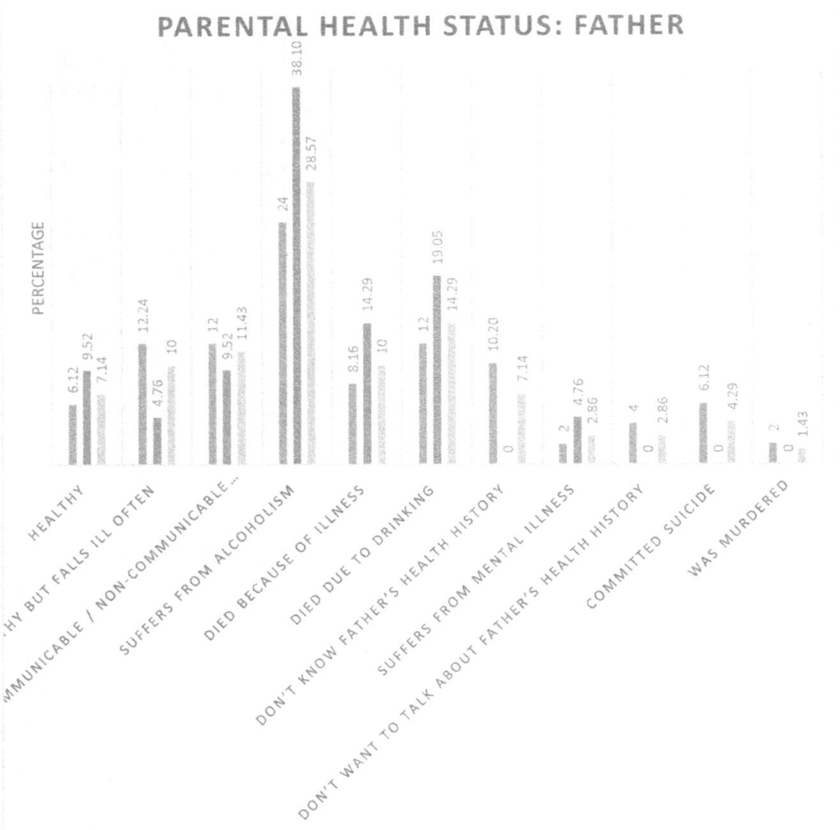

Figure 5.3.5.1 Parental Health Status: Father (N=70)

5.3.5.2 Parental Health Status: Mother

Table 5.3.5.2 revealed that mothers of a total of 55.71% of CICL (61.22% at the OH and 42.86% at the SH) were reported to be mostly healthy but fell ill often. Further, mothers of a total of 15.71% of CICL (16.33% at the OH and 14.29% at the SH) were reported to be suffering from a communicable or non –communicable disease. Overall, the health status of mothers of CICL appeared to be poor, with a total of 88.57 % (89.89% at OH and 85.71% at the SH) mothers of CICL who were either ill or dead (Fig. 5.3.5.2).

Table 5.3.5.2 Parental Health Status: Mother (N=70)

Parental Health Status: Mother	**Observation Home**		**Special Home**		**Total**	
	f	%	F	%	F	%
Healthy	1	2.04	1	4.76	2	2.86
Mostly healthy but falls ill often	30	61.22	9	42.86	39	55.71
Suffers from communicable / non-communicable disease	8	16.32653	3	14.29	11	15.71
Suffers from alcoholism	0	0	1	4.76	1	1.43
Died because of illness	1	2.04	1	4.76	2	2.86
Died due to drinking	0	0	0	0	0	0
Don't know mother's health history	3	6.12	2	9.52	5	7.14
Suffers from mental illness	0	0	2	9.52	2	2.86
Committed suicide	4	8.163265	2	9.52	6	8.57
Don't want to talk about mother's health history	1	2.040816	0	0	1	1.43
Was murdered	1	2.04	0	0	1	1.43
Total	49	100	21	100	70	100

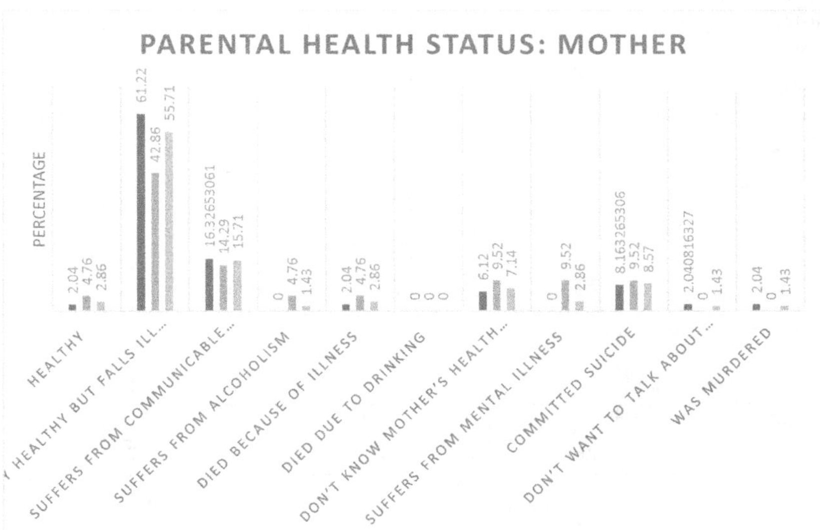

Figure 5.3.5.2 Parental Health Status: Mother (N=70)

5.3.5.3 Family History of Substance Use

The status of substance use in the family was found to be high with the parents of a total of 48.58 % (44.90% at OH and 57.14 % at the SH) were found to be using some substance (smoking, drinking or drugs). Table 5.3.5.3 revealed that the fathers of a total of 21.43% of CICL (18.37% at the OH and 28.57% at the SH) reported that their fathers died due to drinking, while fathers of a total of 20% of CICL (20.41% at the OH and 19.05% at the SH) reported that their father used to consume alcohol. A total of 18.57% CICL (20.41% at the OH and 14.29% at the SH) reported that no one in the family smoked, drank alcohol or consumed drugs. Fathers of a total of 12.86% (23.81% at the SH) were reported to be smoking and drinking, while fathers of a total of 11.43% of CICL (16.33% at the OH) were reported to be smoking (Fig. 5.3.5.3).

Table 5.3.5.3 Family History of Substance Use (N=70)

Status of substance use : Family	**Observation Home**		**Special Home**		**Total**	
	F	%	F	%	F	%
No one in the family smokes, drinks or does drugs	10	20.41	3	14.29	13	18.57
Father smokes	8	16.33	0	0	8	11.43
Father drinks	10	20.41	4	19.05	14	20
Father smokes and drinks	4	8.16	5	23.81	9	12.86
Father smokes, drinks and does drugs	0	0	0	0	0	0
Mother smokes	0	0	0	0	0	0
Mother drinks	0	0	0	0	0	0
Father and mother smoke	0	0	0	0	0	0
Father and mother drink	0	0	2	9.52	2	2.86
Father and mother smoke, drink and do drugs	0	0	1	4.76	1	1.43
Father died due to drinking	9	18.37	6	28.57	15	21.43
Don't want to talk about this	1	2.04	0	0	1	1.43
Don't know about family history	7	14.29	0	0	7	10
Total	49	100	21	100	70	100

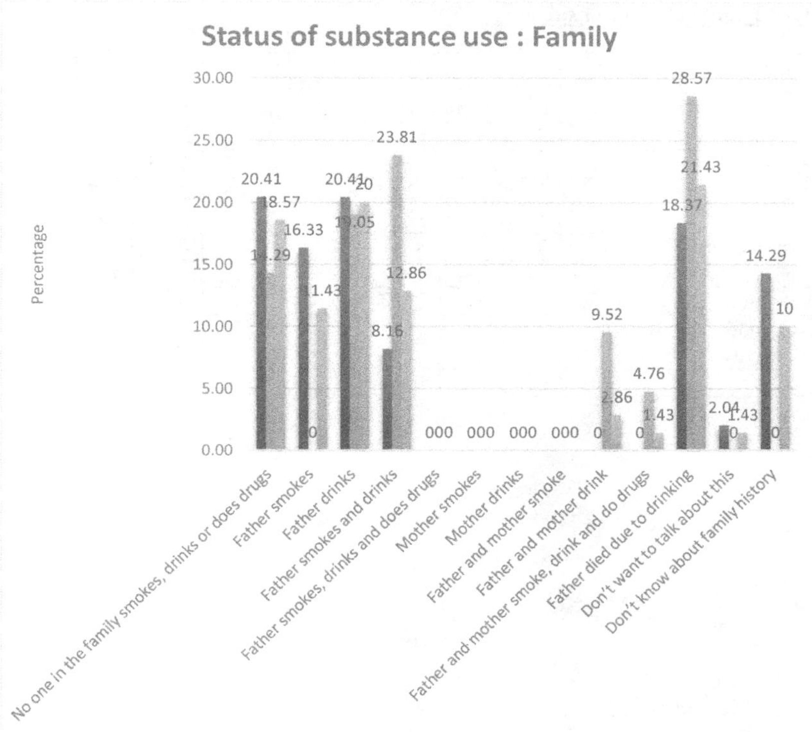

Figure 5.3.5.3 Family History of Substance Use (N=70)

5.3.5.4 Family History of suicide

It was found that there was a significant family history of suicide (34.29) among families of children in conflict with the law. Table 5.3.5.4 showed that a total of 35.71% of CICL (37% in the OH and 33.33% at the SH) reported that there was no history of suicide in the family. Further, a total of 28.57% of CICL (32.65% at the OH and 19.05% at the SH) stated that they did not know whether there had been any suicide in their family or not. However, a total of 22.86% of CICL (22.45% at the OH and 23.81% at the SH) stated that there had been a suicide in their immediate biological family. Overall, a total of 34.29% of CICL (30.45% at the OH and 42.85 % at the SH) stated there was a history of a completed suicide in their family (Fig. 5.3.5.4).

Table 5.3.5.4 Family History of suicide (N=70)

Family History of Suicide (s)	Observation Home		Special Home		Total	
	F	%	F	%	F	%
No family history	18	37	7	33.33	25	35.71
Child does not know	16	32.65	4	19.05	20	28.57
Yes	1	2	2	9.52	3	4.29
More than one family member	3	6	1	4.76	4	5.71
Don't want to reveal	0	0	1	4.76	1	1.43
Immediate biological family	11	22.45	5	23.81	16	22.86
Neighbourhood / community / extended family	0	0	1	4.76	1	1.43
Total	49	100	21	100	70	100

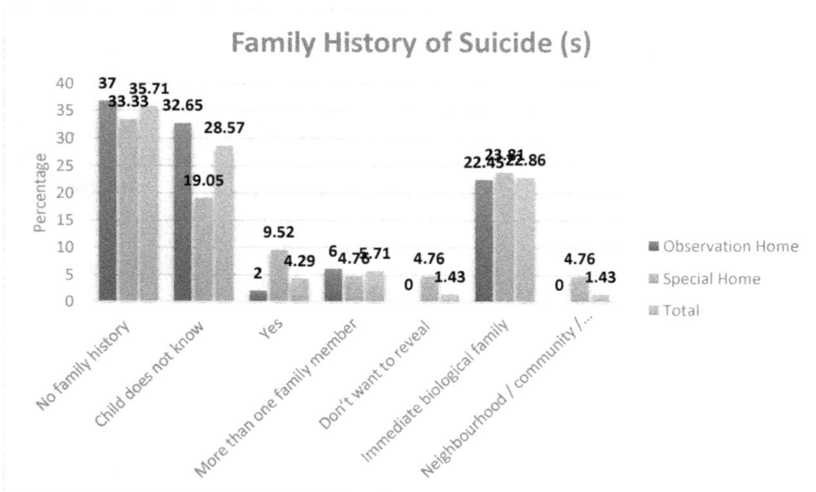

Figure 5.3.5.4 Family History of suicide (N=70)

5.3.5.5 Family History of Mental Illness

Table 5.3.5.5. showed that a total of 30% of the CIC (34.69% at the OH and 19.05% at the SH) stated that there was no history of any mental illness in their family. There was some uncertainty in about 22.86% of CICL (24% at the OH and 19.05 % at the SH) who stated that there might be a possibility of some mental illness in their family but they were not sure as it was not diagnosed as such and because no treatment was taken. Another 21.43% of CICL (27%

at the OH) stated that they did not know about any history of mental illness in their family. However, a total of 18.57% of CICL (14.29% at the OH and 28.57% at the SH) stated that someone in their immediate biological family had a mental illness. Overall, families of a total of 25.72% of the CICL (14.29% at the OH, 52.38% at the SH) were reported to have had a history of some mental illness (Fig. 5.3.5.5).

Table 5.3.5.5 Family History of Mental Illness (N=70)

History of Mental Illness in family	Observation Home		Special Home		Total	
	F	%	F	%	F	%
No mental illness in family	17	34.69	4	19.05	21	30
Does not know about MI history	13	27	2	9.52	15	21.43
Maybe but not sure	12	24	4	19.05	16	22.86
Yes	0	0	2	9.52	2	2.86
Extended family / blood relatives	0	0	3	14.29	3	4.29
Immediate biological family	7	14.29	6	28.57	13	18.57
Total	49	100	21	100	70	100

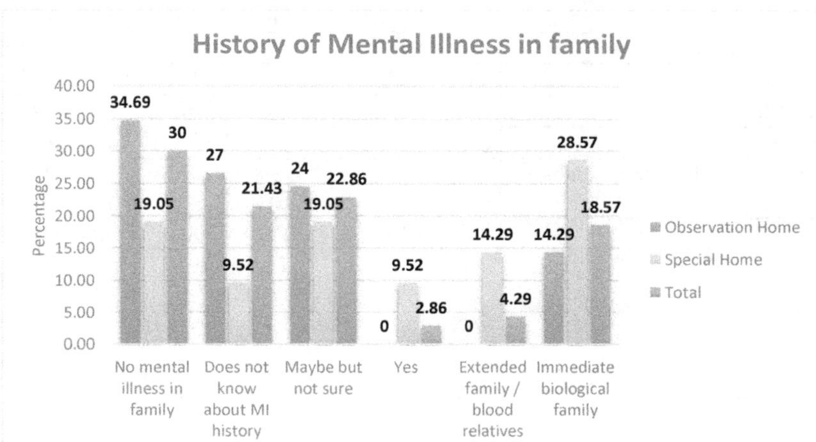

Figure 5.3.5.5 Family History of Mental Illness (N=70)

5.4 RESULT IV - COMING INTO CONFLICT WITH THE LAW

5.4.1 Experience of CICL with police:

5.4.1.1 Duration of detention of CICL in police station

Table 5.4.1.1 revealed that a total of 30% of CICL (43% at the OH) stated that they were produced before the JJB within 12 hours. However, it is found that not a single CICL from the SH reported being produced within 12 hours. Disturbingly, 21.43% of the CICL (22.45% at the OH and 19.05% at the SH) were detained at the police station for up to a week (4 to 7 days). Followed by a total of 18.57% of CICL (12.24% at the OH and 33.33% at the SH) stated that they were detained at the police station for 48 to 72 hours. A total of 18.57% of CICL (14.29% at the OH and 28.57% at the SH) stated that they were produced before the JJB within 24 hours (Fig. 5.4.1.1).

Table 5.4.1.1 Duration of detention of CICL in police station (N=70)

Duration of detention in police station	**Observation Home**		**Special Home**		**Total**	
	F	%	F	%	F	%
Within 12 hours	21	43	0	0	21	30
Within 24 hours	7	14.29	6	28.57	13	18.57
Within 48 to 72 hours	6	12.24	7	33.33	13	18.57
Upto a week	11	22.45	4	19.05	15	21.43
Upto a fortnight	4	8.16	2	9.52	6	8.57
Upto a month	0	0	1	4.76	1	1.43
Detained on and off over 3 months	0	0	1	4.76	1	1.43
Total	49	100	21	100	70	100

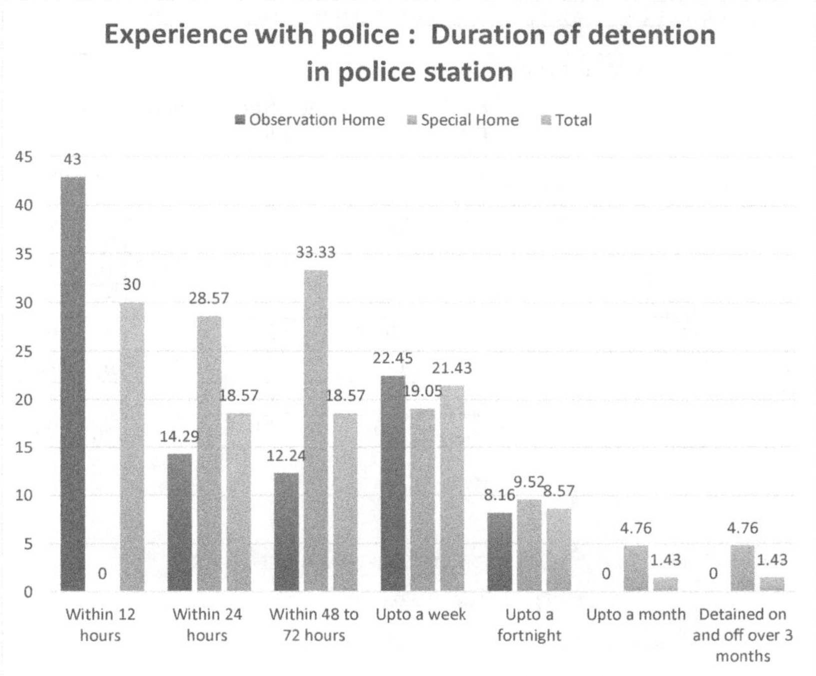

Figure 5.4.1.1 Duration of detention of CICL in police station (N=70)

5.4.1.2 Contact of CICL with parents while in police custody

Table 5.4.1.2 revealed that a total of 30% of CICL (22.45% at the OH and 47.62% at the SH) stated that their parents were contacted and informed while they were in police custody. However, a total of 27.14% (32.65% at the OH and 14.29% at the SH) stated that their families were not informed and that they had no contact with their families while in police custody. Disturbingly, a total of 12.86% of CICL (14.29% at the OH and 9.52% at the SH) stated that their families were contacted only after a week after they had been in police custody. A total of 12.86% of CICL (16.33% at the OH) stated that they were only allowed contact over the phone with their families but not allowed to meet. 10% of the CICL (10.20% at the OH and 9.52% at the SH) stated that they had no family for the police to contact (Fig. 5.4.1.2).

Table 5.4.1.2 Contact of CICL with parents while in police custody (N=70)

Contact with parents while in police custody	Observation Home		Special Home		Total	
	F	%	F	%	F	%
Yes	11	22.45	10	47.62	21	30
Do not remember	1	2.04	2	9.52	3	4.29
Only over phone	8	16.33	1	4.76	9	12.86
No contact	16	32.65	3	14.29	19	27.14
Police advised not to call	1	2.04	1	4.76	2	2.86
No family to contact	5	10.20	2	9.52	7	10
Contacted after a week	7	14.29	2	9.52	9	12.86
Police did not allow any contact	0	0	0	0	0	0
Total	49	100	21	100	70	100

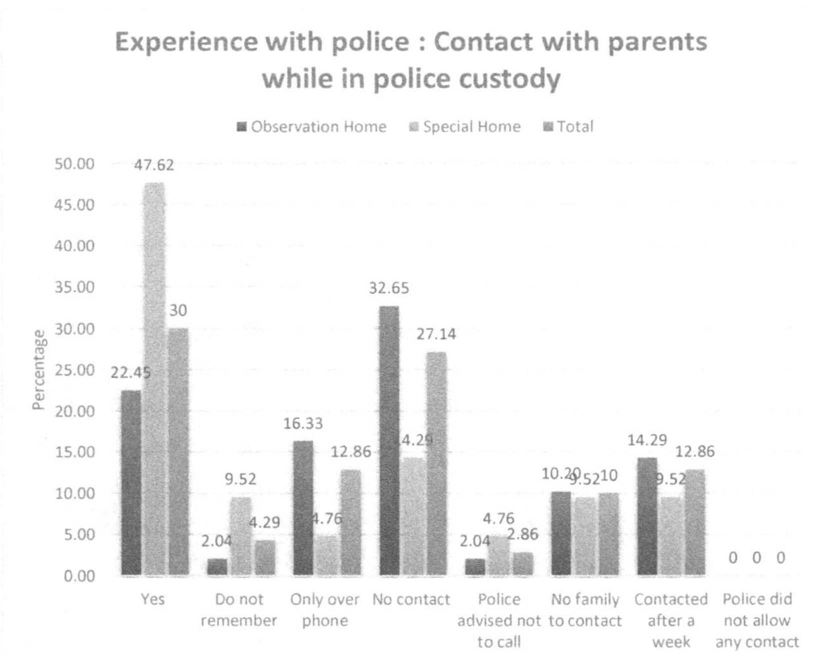

Figure 5.4.1.2 Contact of CICL with parents while in police custody (N =70)

5.4.1.3 Emotional Impact of experience with police

Table 5.4.1.3 revealed that a total of 23% of CICL (33% at the OH) stated that their experience of police was violence. An additional 4% stated that they experienced violence ***and*** a fear of sexual abuse at the hands of the police, while another 4% stated that the violence was to the extent that they felt the fear of death, i.e., they would die from the violence by the police. So, in effect, for a total of 31% of CICL, the experience of police was violence. A total of 20% of CICL (16.33% at the OH and 28.57% at the SH) describe their experience of the police as fear. An additional 12.86% of CICL describe their experience as fear ***and*** helplessness. Hence a total of 32.86% of CICL experience of the police is predominantly fear. 10% of CICL describe their experience of the police as shame and humiliation (Fig. 5.4.1.3).

Table 5.4.1.3 Emotional Impact of experience with police (N =70)

Experience with police : Emotional Impact	**Observation Home**		**Special Home**		**Total**	
	F	%	F	%	F	%
Safe and confident	2	4.08	1	4.76	3	4.29
Fear	8	16.33	6	28.57	14	20.00
Just desserts – got what I deserved	0	0.00	1	4.76	1	1.43
Shame and humiliation	4	8.16	3	14.29	7	10.00
Shock and confusion	2	4	0	0	2	3
Helplessness	0	0	0	0	0	0
Guilt about harm to family	0	0.00	1	4.76	1	1.43
Fear and helplessness	7	14.29	2	9.52	9	12.86
Indifference	0	0.00	2	9.52	2	2.86
Anger	2	4.08	4	19.05	6	8.57
Fear of sexual abuse	2	4.08	1	4.76	3	4.29
Violence and sexual abuse	3	6	0	0	3	4
Violence	16	33	0	0	16	23
Violence to the extent of fear of death	3	6	0	0	3	4
Total	49	100	21	100	70	100

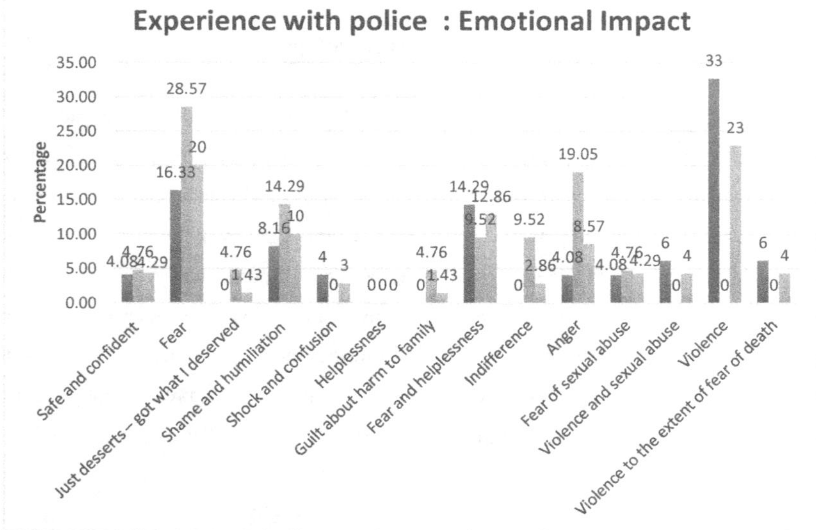

Figure 5.4.1.3 Emotional Impact of experience with police (N =70)

5.4.2 Duration of stay of CICL in OH or Special Home

Table 5.4.2 revealed that 71% of the CICL at the OH have been at the OH for up to one month while 16.33% had been staying at the OH for up to 2 months. 42.86% of the CICL at the SH had been staying at the SH for up to a year, while 19.05% had been staying for up to 3 years, another 19.05% for up to 2 months and 14.29% for up to 24 months. (Fig. 5.4.2) Hence, the average duration of stay of a CICL at the OH was 22 days and that at the SH was 137 days.

Table 5.4.2 Duration of stay of CICL in OH or Special Home (N =70)

Duration of current stay in the institution	Observation Home		Special Home		Total	
	F	%	F	%	F	%
Up to one month	35	71	0	0	35	50
Up to sixty days (2 months)	8	16.33	4	19.05	12	17.14
Up to ninety days (3 months)	2	4.08	1	4.76	3	4.29
Up to 1 year	3	6.12	9	42.86	12	17.14
Up to 18 months	1	2	0	0	1	1
Upto 24 months	0	0.00	3	14.29	3	4.29
Upto 36 months	0	0.00	4	19.05	4	5.71
37 months and above	0	0	0	0	0	0
Total	49	100	21	100	70	100

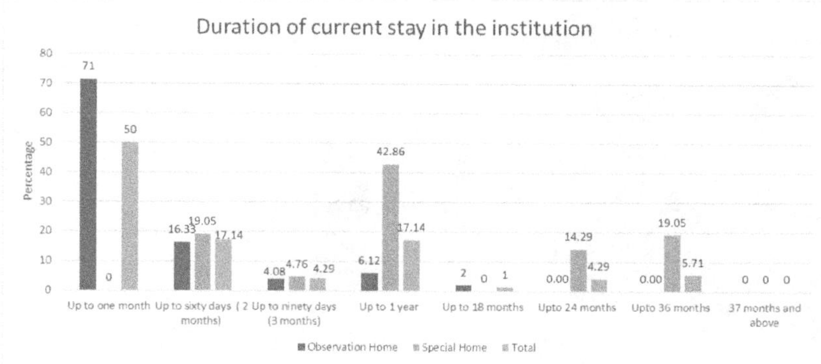

Figure 5.4.2 Duration of stay of CICL in OH or Special Home (N=70)

5.4.3 Type of Offence(s) CICL were charged with

The main categories of offences that CICL had been charged with were petty, serious (non-sexual), heinous (non- sexual) and heinous (sexual). Interestingly, there were no CICLs with serious sexual offences. Table 5.4.3 revealed that a total of 45.71% of CICL (59.17% at the OH and 14.29% at the SH) were found to be charged with heinous non-sexual offences. Further, a total of 28.57% of CICL (20.41% at the OH and 47.62% at the SH) were found to be charged with serious non-sexual offences. A total of 18.57% of CICL (16.33% at the OH and 23.81% at the SH) were found to be charged with heinous sexual offences. Interestingly, 14.29% of the CICL at the SH were found to be charged with petty offences (Fig. 5.4.3).

Table 5.4.3 Type of Offence (s) CICL were charged with (N =70)

Type of Offence Children were charged with	Observation Home		Special Home		Total	
	F	%	F	%	F	%
Petty	2	4.08	3	14.29	5	7.14
Serious (non-sexual)	10	20.41	10	47.62	20	28.57
Serious (sexual)	0	0	0	0	0	0
Heinous (non sexual)	29	59.18	3	14.29	32	45.71
Heinous(sexual)	8	16.33	5	23.81	13	18.57
Total	49	100	21	100	70	100

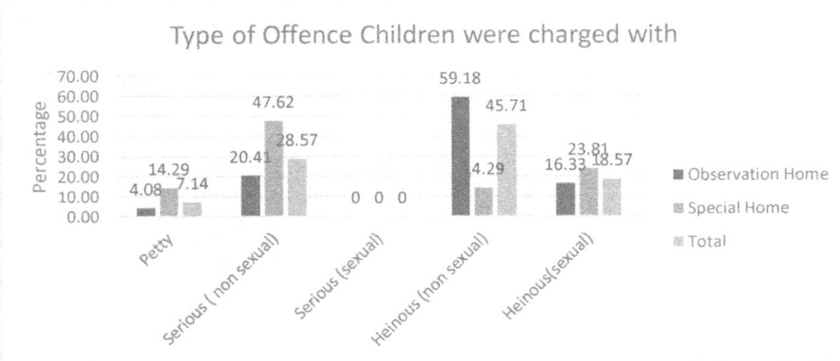

Figure 5.4.3 Type of Offence (s) CICL were charged with **(N =70)**

5.4.4 The Progression trend of offences by children in conflict with law

The Progression trend of offences by children in conflict with law depicted by Table 5.4.4 revealed that a majority of the CICL were first time entrants to the juvenile justice system. Significantly, 95.24% of the CICL at the SH had come into conflict with the law for the first time, thereby indicating that the rate of conviction of even first-time entrants was very high. Further, at the OH, second time offences were found to be almost equal for petty and serious (non-sexual offences) at around 10% each, while at the SH almost all repeat offences were either heinous (non-sexual 9%) or heinous (sexual 3%) (Fig. 5.4.4.).

Table 5.4.4 The Progression trend of offences by CICL (N =70)

Progression Trend of offence (s) by CICL	Observation Home		Special Home		Total	
	F	%	F	%	F	%
Never charged before / first time offender	27	55.10	20	95.24	47	67.14
Petty	5	10.20	1	4.76	6	8.57
Serious (non sexual)	5	10	0	0	5	7
Serious (sexual)	0	0	0	0	0	0
Heinous (non sexual)	9	18	0	0	9	13
Heinous(sexual)	3	6	0	0	3	4
Total	49	100	21	100	70	100

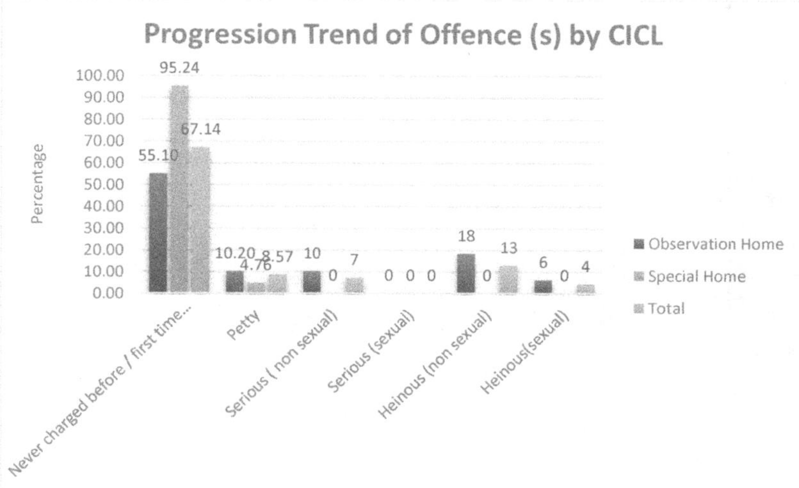

Figure 5.4.4 The Progression trend of offences by CICL (N =70)

5.4.5 Frequency of CICL coming into conflict with the law

Table 5.4.5 revealed that an overwhelming majority of CICL (85.71%), (81.63% at the OH and 95.24% at the SH) had come into conflict with the law for the first time. 8.57% of the CICL (10.20% at the OH and 4.47% at the SH) had come into conflict with the law for the second

Table 5.4.5 Frequency of CICL coming into conflict with the law (N =70)

Frequency of coming into conflict with the law	Observation Home		Special Home		Total	
	F	%	F	%	F	%
First time	40	81.63	20	95.24	60	85.71
Second time	5	10.20	1	4.76	6	8.57
Third time	3	6	0	0	3	4
Fourth time	1	2	0	0	1	1
More than 4 or 5 times	0	0	0	0	0	0
Total	49	100	21	100	70	100

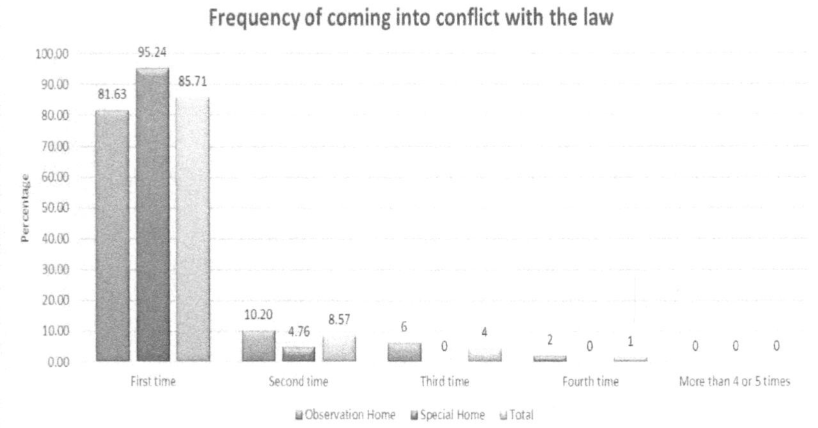

Figure 5.4.5 Frequency of CICL coming into conflict with the law **(N =70)**

5.4.6 Family's contact with justice system

Table 5.4.6 revealed that a total of 64.29% of CICL (63.27% at the OH and 66.67% at the SH) stated that their families had no prior contact with the justice system in any way, with no one in their families ever being arrested, convicted or being in contact with the justice system. However, 12.86% of CICL say they did not know as families did not usually discuss such topics with their children, while 10% of CICL (8.16% at the OH and 14.29% at the SH) admitted that their immediate biological family members were or had been in jail (Fig. 5.4.6).

Table 5.4.6 Family's contact with justice system (N =70)

	Observation Home		**Special Home**		**Total**	
Family contact with justice system	F	%	F	%	F	%
No prior contact	31	63.27	14	66.67	45	64.29
Don't know	8	16.33	1	4.76	9	12.86
Yes	1	2.04	2	9.52	3	4.29
Extended family / blood relatives	5	10.20	1	4.76	6	8.57
Immediate biological family	4	8.16	3	14.29	7	10.00
Total	49	100	21	100	70	100

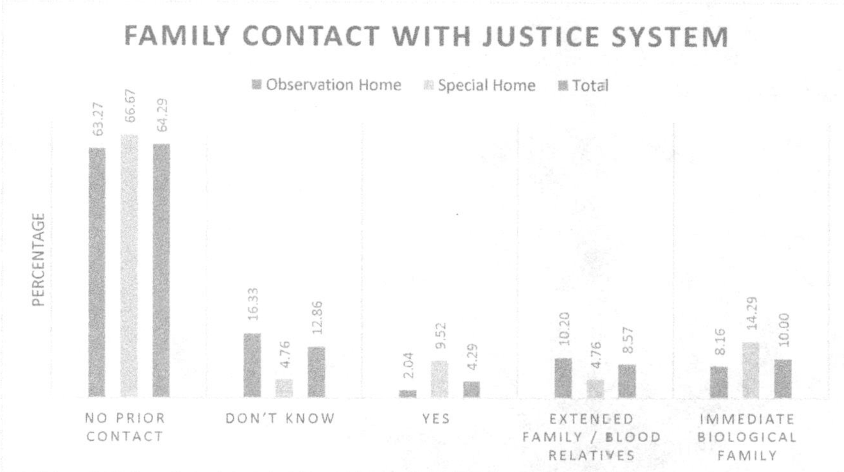

Figure 5.4.6 Family's contact with justice system (N =70)

5.4.7 Adverse Childhood Experiences

5.4.7.1 Number of ACEs of CICL

Table 5.4.7.1 revealed that a total of 54 CICL (77.14%) had 10 or more adverse childhood experiences. The lowest number of ACEs was 4 and highest was 18. Fig. 5.4.7.1 showed that 41.43% of CICL had 10 to 12 ACEs, 21.43% had 13 to 15 ACEs, 20% had 7 to 9 ACEs and 14.28% had 16 to ACEs.

Table 5.4.7.1 Number of ACEs of CICL (N=70)

S.No.	Number of ACEs (out of a max of 20)	Number of children	Percentage of children
1	4 to 6 ACEs	2	2.86
2	7 to 9 ACEs	14	20
3	10 to 12 ACEs	29	41.43
4	13 to 15 ACEs	15	21.43
5	16 to 18 ACEs	10	14.28
	TOTAL	70	100

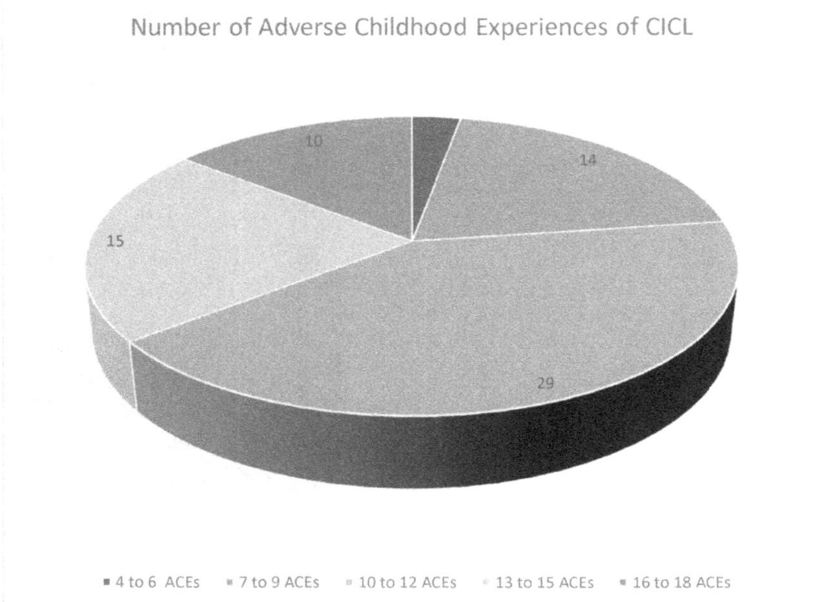

Figure 5.4.7.1 Number of ACEs of CICL (N=70)

5.4.7.2 Magnitude of ACEs of CICL (N=70)

Table 5.4.7.2 revealed that the top three ACEs which were shared by all the CICL (100%) were disruption in education, incarceration and coming into contact with the justice system. The next four ACEs in order of occurrence were poverty (91.42%), experience with police (90%), neglect (78.57%) and lack of parental involvement and poor family relationships (77.14%). The next five ACEs in order of occurrence were child's history of substance abuse (64.28%), child's experience of violence towards himself (60%), child's exposure to violence in the family (58.57%), child's history of prolonged illness or hospitalization (54.28%), family history of substance abuse (54.28%). The last five ACEs in order of occurrence were death of a parent (48.57%), family history of poor health (41.42%), child's history of self harm / attempted suicide (48.57%) family history of mental illness (34.28%)

Table 5.4.7.2 Magnitude of ACEs of CICL (N=70)

S.No.	Type of ACE	Number of children	Percentage of children (%)
1	Contact of child with justice system	70	100
2	Incarceration	70	100
3	Disruption in education	70	100
4	Poverty	64	91.42
5	Experience with police	63	90
6	Neglect	55	78.57
7	Lack of parental involvement and poor family relationships	54	77.14
8	Child's history of substance use	45	64.28
9	Child's experience of violence towards himself	42	60
10	Child's exposure to violence in the family	41	58.57
11	Child's history of prolonged illness, hospitalization due to violence, attempted suicide	38	54.28
12	Family history of substance use	38	54.28
13	Child's history of suicide attempts / self harm	34	48.57
14	Death of a parent	34	48.57
15	Family history of poor health	29	41.42
16	Family history of mental illness	24	34.28
17	Family history of completed suicide / attempts	20	28.57
18	Contact of family with justice system	10	14.28
19	Child charged with sexual offence	14	20
20	Separation or divorce of parents	6	8.57
	TOTAL NUMBER OF ADVERSITIES	821	
	AVERAGE NUMBER OF ADVERSITIES	11.73	

5.5 RESULT V - STATUS OF COUNSELLING IN THE JUVENILE JUSTICE SYSTEM

5.5.1 CICL'S Experience

5.5.1.1 Status of Counselling Services for CICL

For examining the status of counselling services of CICL, the OH Bangalore OH, Mysore OH and Bangalore SH have been studied independently as each of these CCIs have separate institutional counsellors and it was important to compare the services.

5.5.1.1.1 Approachability of Counsellor at CCI

Table 5.5.1.1.1 depicted the approachability of the counsellor at Bangalore OH, Mysore OH and Bangalore SH. It is found that while 40% of the children at the Mysore OH stated that the person that they had approached at the CCI when in distress was the counsellor, not a single CICL at either the OH Bangalore and SH Bangalore did so. Surprisingly, 28.57% of the CICL at the SH mentioned the superintendent as the person that they approach when in distress rather than the counsellor. Further, none of the CICL in either OH or SH ever approached the Probationary Officer, housefather or housemother, guard, cook or any other staff when in distress. A total of 30% of CICL (21% at the OH Bangalore, 33.33% at the OH Mysore and 42.86% at the SH) reported that they talked to their friends within the OH / SH rather than to any adult. Worryingly, a total of 51.43% of the CICL (76.47% at the OH Bangalore, 26.67% at Mysore and 28.67% at the SH) did not talk to anyone at all and just remained silent even in extreme distress. It was noted from the findings that the approachability of the counsellor at the Bangalore OH was very low compared to that of the counsellor at the OH at Mysore and the SH at Bangalore (Fig. 5.5.1.1.1).

Table 5.5.1.1.1 Approachability of Counsellor at CCI (N =70)

S. No	Person at CCI approached by child when in distress	Observation Home (Bangalore)		Observation Home (Mysore)		Special Home (Bangalore)		Total	
		F	%	F	%	F	%	F	%
1	Counsellor	0	0	6	40	0	0	6	8.57
2	Superintendent	0	0	0	0	6	28.57	6	8.57
3	Probationary Officer	0	0	0	0	0	0	0	0
4	Housefather / housemother	0	0	0	0	0	0	0	0
5	Guard	0	0	0	0	0	0	0	0
6	Cook	1	2.94	0	0	0	0	1	1.43
7	Friend within OH /SH	7	20.59	5	33.33	9	42.86	21	30
8	Don't talk to anyone	26	76.47	4	26.67	6	28.57	36	51.43
	TOTAL	34	100	15	100	21	100	70	100

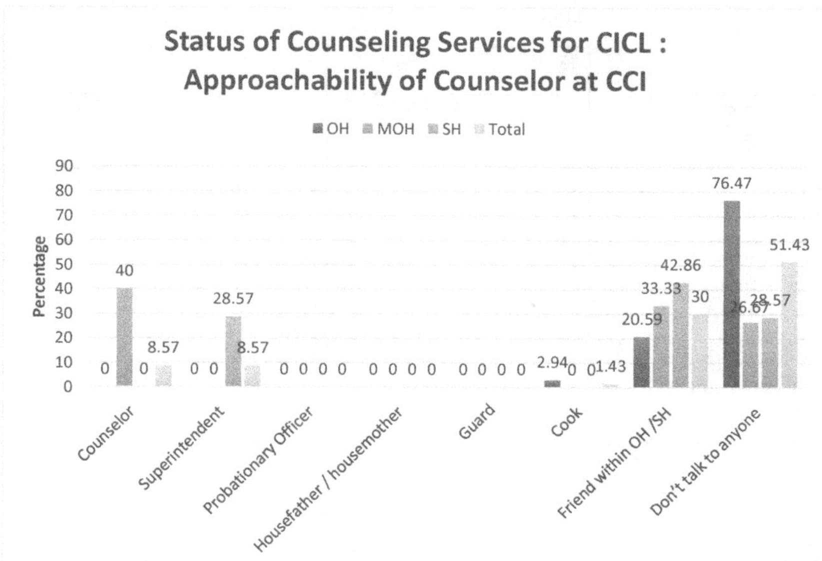

Figure 5.5.1.1.1 Approachability of Counsellor at CCI (N =70)

5.5.1.1.2 Availability of Counsellor at CCI

Table 5.5.1.1.2 described the availability of the counsellor at Bangalore OH, Mysore OH and Bangalore SH. There appears to be a striking difference in the availability of the counsellor at the OH Bangalore, while compared to that at the OH Mysore and at the SH Bangalore. While 100% of the CICL at the SH and 93.33% of the CICL at the OH Mysore stated that they had met the counsellor at their respective CCIs, only 14.71% of the CICL reported that they had met the counsellor at the OH Bangalore. Additionally, 55.88% of the CICL at the OH stated that they had met the counsellor only once when they had first entered the OH Bangalore and had never met the counsellor after that. 17.65% of the CICL at the OH Bangalore did not want to meet the counsellor. It is found that the availability of the counsellor at the Bangalore OH was very low compared to that of the counsellor at the OH at Mysore and the SH at Bangalore (Fig. 5.5.1.1.2).

Table 5.5.1.1.2 Availability of Counsellor at CCI (N=70)

S. No	Availability of Counsellor	Observation Home (Bangalore)		Observation Home (Mysore)		Special Home (Bangalore)		Total	
		F	%	f	%	F	%	F	%
1	Yes met the counsellor	5	14.71	14	93.33	21	100	40	57.14
2	No did not meet the counsellor	1	2.94	0	0	0	0	1	1.43
3	Don't know who / what is counsellor or whom to meet	3	8.82	1	6.67	0	0	4	5.71
4	Yes once when child first came to CCI	19	55.88	0	0	0	0	19	27.14
5	Child does not want to meet counsellor	6	17.65	0	0	0	0	6	8.57
	Total	34	100	15	100	21	100	70	

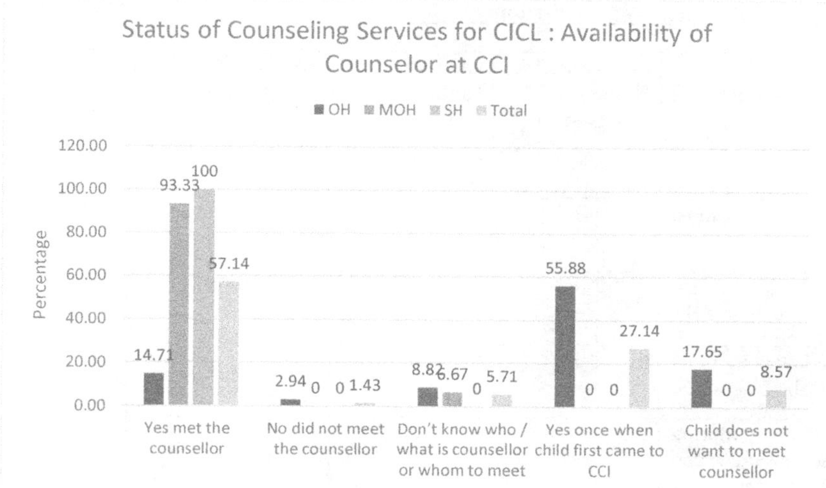

Figure 5.5.1.1.2 Availability of Counsellor at CCI (N=70)

5.5.1.1.3 Frequency of Counselling

Table 5.6.1.1.3 revealed the frequency of counselling at the Bangalore OH, Mysore OH and Bangalore SH. A significant finding is that 40% of the CICL at OH Mysore stated that they had received some form of counselling every day, even if it was not a formal session. Equally significant, 19.05% of the CICL at the SH stated that they had been having formal, regular and scheduled counselling sessions with the counsellor once a week for the last 2-3 years that they had been there and 33.33% of the CICL at the SH stated that they had regular, formal and scheduled counselling sessions once in 2 weeks for the 1 year that they had been at the SH. 33.33% at the OH Mysore and 23.81% at the SH reported that they had weekly once counselling sessions since their admission to the CCI. On the other hand, 26.47% of CICL at the OH Bangalore reported that they had met the counsellor only once during admission and once after that, while 38.24% state that they met the counsellor only once during admission and never after that and 17.65% of the CICL at the OH Bangalore stated that they had never met the counsellor at all. It was found that the frequency of counselling offered by the counsellor at the OH was very low compared to that of the counsellor at the OH at Mysore and the SH at Bangalore (Fig. 5.5.1.1.3).

Table 5.5.1.1.3 Frequency of Counselling (N=70)

S. No	Frequency of Counselling in the institution	Observation Home (Bangalore)		Observation Home (Mysore)		Special Home (Bangalore)		Total	
		F	%	F	%	F	%	F	%
1	Daily or almost daily	0	0	6	40	0	0	6	8.57
2	Once a week for 2-3 years in SH	0	0	0	0	4	19.05	4	5.71
3	Whenever child wishes	0	0	0	0	0	0	0	0
4	Once during admission and once after	9	26.47	0	0	1	4.76	10	14.29
5	Only once during admission	13	38.24	0	0	0	0	13	18.57
6	Whenever instructed to meet	1	2.94	1	6.67	1	4.76	3	4.29
7	Once in 2 weeks for years	0	0	0	0	1	4.76	1	1.43
8	Once in 2 weeks for 1 year	0	0	0	0	7	33.33	7	10
9	Monthly once	0	0	0	0	1	4.76	1	1.43
10	Weekly once since admission	2	5.88	5	33.33	5	23.81	12	17.14
11	Once in 2 weeks since admission	0	0	0	0	1	4.76	1	1.43
12	3-4 times during entire stay	2	5.88	3	20	0	0	5	7.14
13	1-2 times during entire stay	1	2.94	0	0	0	0	1	1.43
14	Never met at all	6	17.65	0	0	0	0	6	8.57
	Total	34	100	15	100	21	100	70	100

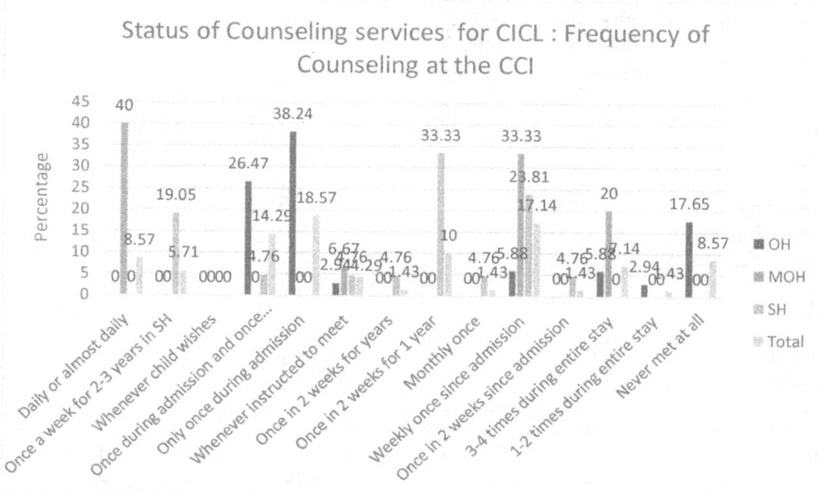

Figure 5.5.1.1.3 Frequency of Counselling (N=70)

5.5.1.1.4 Effect of Counselling

Table 5.6.1.1.4 revealed that there was a significant difference in the findings between the OH, Bangalore as compared to the OH Mysore and SH, Bangalore, with regard to the effects of counselling on the CICL. At the Bangalore OH, CICL reported that counselling did not help them at all (29.41%), found the counsellor to be indifferent and disinterested (20.59%), that counselling did not help and actively harmed them (17.65%), that they did not know what was counselling or who a counsellor was (11.76%). On the other hand, at the Mysore OH, CICL reported that counselling helped them to express their emotions (26.67%), provided momentary relief (20%), gave an opportunity to talk about problems (20%) and helped child to reflect on mistakes and understand right and wrong (20%). At the Bangalore SH, CICL reported that counselling gave momentary relief (14.29%), helped child to reflect on mistakes and understand right and wrong (14.29%), helped the child feel hopeful about self and future (14.29%), helped the child understand his behaviour (14.29%). The findings indicated that the CICL found the counselling offered at the Bangalore OH to be low in effectiveness when compared to that offered at the OH at Mysore and the SH at Bangalore (Fig. 5.5.1.1.4).

Table 5.5.1.1.4 Effect of Counselling (N=70)

S. No	Effect of Counselling	Observation Home (Bangalore)		Observation Home (Mysore)		Special Home		Total	
		F	%	F	%	F	%	F	%
1	Momentary relief	0	0	3	20	3	14.29	6	8.57
2	Emotional expression	1	2.94	4	26.67	2	9.52	7	10
3	Opportunity to talk	1	2.94	3	20	2	9.52	6	8.57
4	Helped solve problem	0	0	0	0	0	0	0	0
5	Helped reflect on mistakes	0	0	3	20	3	14.29	6	8.57
6	Felt safe and hopeful	0	0	1	6.67	0	0	1	1.43
7	Understood behaviour	1	2.94	0	0	3	14.29	4	5.71
8	Helped identify his strengths	0	0	0	0	3	14.29	3	4.29
9	Did not help	10	29.41	1	6.67	0	0	11	15.71
10	Child got irritated	0	0	0	0	1	4.76	1	1.43
11	Too early to tell	2	5.88	0	0	2	9.52	4	5.71
12	Didn't help and actively harmed	6	17.65	0	0	2	9.52	8	11.43
13	Made false promises	2	5.88	0	0	0	0	2	2.86
14	No idea about a counselling	4	11.76	0	0	0	0	4	5.71
15	Counsellor indifferent / disinterested	7	20.59	0	0	0	0	7	10
	Total	34	100	15	100	21	100	70	100

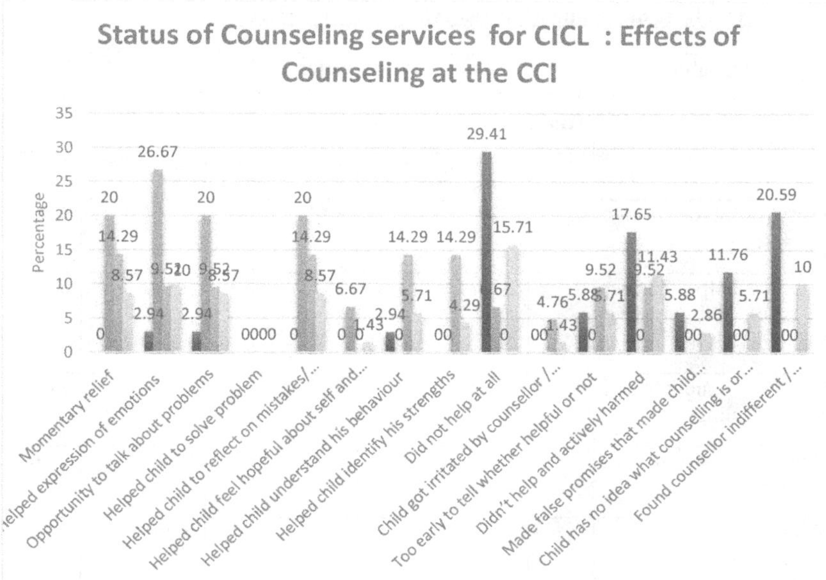

Figure 5.5.1.1.4 Effect of Counselling (N=70)

5.5.1.1.5 Qualities of a Counsellor (as expected by CICL)

Table 5.5.1.1.5 listed the qualities expected in a counsellor by the CICL at Bangalore OH, Mysore OH and Bangalore SH. The most important quality expected out of a counsellor by CICL across all CCIs studied was that the counsellor should be kind (14.71% at Bangalore OH, 20% at Mysore OH and 14.29% at Bangalore SH). Further, while CICL at Bangalore OH (11.76%), and Bangalore SH (14.29%) wanted the counsellor to also understand their feelings, the CICL at Mysore OH wanted the counsellor to help them correct mistakes and negative behaviour (20%) and help them in solving their problems. (13.33%). Additionally, the CICL at Bangalore SH wanted the counsellor to listen (14.29%) and to be able to speak the child's language (14.29%). Interestingly, 11.76% of the CICL at the Bangalore OH stated that they had no idea of who was a counsellor or what was counselling and hence were unable to given any input or opinion in response to this question. Overall, it was found that the top two qualities expected by CICL in a counsellor were being kind and understanding the child's feelings (Fig. 5.5.1.1.5).

Table 5.5.1.1.5 Qualities of a Counsellor (as expected by CICL) (N=70)

S. No	Expected Qualities	Observation Home (Bangalore)		Observation Home (Mysore)		Special Home		Total	
		F	%	F	%	F	%	F	%
1	Trustworthy of stories and secrets	2	5.88	1	6.67	0	0	3	4.29
2	Should help correct mistakes and negative behaviour	1	2.94	3	20	0	0	4	5.71
3	Should understand child's feelings	4	11.76	1	6.67	3	14.29	8	11.43
4	Should be warm and friendly	1	2.94	1	6.67	0	0	2	2.86
5	Should be able to help child in solving problems	2	5.88	2	13.33	1	4.76	5	7.14
6	Should be kind	5	14.71	3	20	3	14.29	11	15.71
7	Should not criticize child for mistakes	1	2.94	1	6.67	1	4.76	3	4.29
8	Should encourage positive behaviour	1	2.94	1	6.67	2	9.52	4	5.71
9	Should be sharp and intelligent	1	2.94	0	0	1	4.76	2	2.86
10	Should be male / female	1	2.94	0	0	1	4.76	2	2.86
11	Should listen	1	2.94	0	0	3	14.29	4	5.71
12	Should treat like a parent	0	0	0	0	2	9.52	2	2.86
13	Should be able to speak my language	0	0	1	6.67	3	14.29	4	5.71
14	Should focus on the future not the past	0	0	0	0	1	4.76	1	1.43
15	Should help in early release from OH	3	8.82	1	6.67	0	0	4	5.71

16	Should not make false promises	1	2.94	0	0	0	0	1	1.43
17	I have no idea of who is counsleor / what is counselling so unable to say anything	4	11.76	0	0	0	0	4	5.71
18	Should meet child regularly	1	2.94	0	0	0	0	1	1.43
19	Should be interested in meeting / talking to the child	3	8.82	0	0	0	0	3	4.29
20	Should encourage to speak the truth	1	2.94	0	0	0	0	1	1.43
21	Should not talk / ask only about offence	1	2.94	0	0	0	0	1	1.43
	Total	34	100	15	100	21	100	70	100

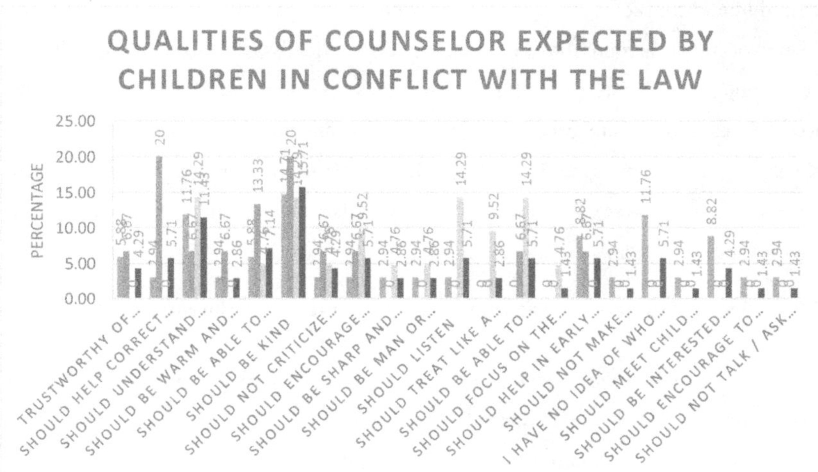

Figure 5.5.1.1.5 Qualities of a Counsellor (as expected by CICL) (N=70)

5.5.2 STATUS OF COUNSELLING SERVICES: COUNSELOR'S EXPERIENCE

5.5.2.1 Profile of Counsellor (at MOH & SH)

5.5.2.1.1 Age and Gender

The counsellors at both the MOH and SH were women. While the MOH counsellor was 30 years old, the SH counsellor was almost 70 years old.

5.5.2.1.2 Educational Profile

The SH counsellor had completed her Pre -University Course and did not have any other formal graduate, post graduate degrees or qualifications. However, she had a Diploma in Theology which is a 2 years course she did as part of her training to be a catholic nun. She also did a 1-year course Personality Human Relations, which was a private training course and not recognized by any Indian university. The MOH counsellor had a post graduate degree with Psychology with additional qualifications in computers, drawing and painting and Hindi.

5.5.2.1.3 Professional profile - Work experience

The SH counsellor was not trained specifically as a counsellor. She had a total work experience of 35-40 years working in an administrative capacity in a school and college convent for girl boarders. This exposure did not involve working directly with children in general or children in conflict with the law in particular, in any capacity. After her retirement, she had been working as a counsellor for 9 years, and specifically as a part time counsellor at the SH for 7 years. The MOH counsellor was a trained psychologist and had a total work experience of 8 years. She had worked as a Program Coordinator and Counselor for children and families with HIV, and specifically trained as a counsellor on areas of sexual and reproductive health for male sex workers for 2 years and then taken on the role as a counsellor at the MOH for the last 6years.

5.5.2.2 Training of counsellors and preparation for the role

Both the counsellors did not have any specific training prior to being posted in their role as counsellor for CICL.The SH counsellor did not have any prior experience of working as a counsellor for boys, or children in custodial settings. However, after she joined as a counsellor at the SH, she had attended several training programs conducted by BOSCO, (an NGO working with children) on different topics like dealing with children, techniques of counselling, case studies, documenting and filming success stories, etc., which helped her to some extent. She also believed that her spiritual training had prepared her well enough for this role. In her words, "I consider counselling not as a job, but as a personal calling and mission. I understand the socio-economic environments that these children come from. I have 'mothered', disciplined and taught the children in my care – right from hygiene to life skills. Of course, those were all girls and now I am working with boys. But these experiences have prepared me to be a counsellor for children in conflict with the law". The MOH counsellor on the other hand, had some exposure to jail as a student, where she had met a young murder convict, who shared his story of how he came to be convicted because he did not have a lawyer, and just because he was a friend of the accused, who was indeed the murderer. Deeply moved by his story, she decided to work with young people in the justice system. She believed that her educational background, gave me exposure to social problems and the lives of disadvantaged people to some extent, though she believed she need more training to understand transfer of children into adult courts better.

5.5.2.3 Counsellor's understanding of psychosocial context of CICL

While the MOH counsellor stated that the psychosocial profile of CICL seemed to vary depending on the nature of offences, while the SH counsellor stated that all CICL were from poor backgrounds and broken families. With respect to the nature of mental health problems in CICL, the MOH counsellor stated that she had encountered drug addiction, neglect by parents, aggression, depression, defiant and rebellious behaviour, suicidal behaviour and sexual abuse, while the SH counsellor stated that she had not encountered any mental illness or mental health problems except some anger issues, emotional problems and behaviour troubles.

5.5.2.4 Referral services by Counsellor

The counsellor at the MOH had referred one child to a psychiatrist while the SH counsellor wanted to refer but did not have any facilities for such referral. With regard to non-psychiatric rehabilitative services, the MOH counsellor was told only the Probationary Officer could make such recommendations, while the SH counsellor stated that she had not referred any child as the support required like facilities, security, escort, and parental support were not there making such referrals difficult to sustain as no support was given for follow-up.

5.5.2.5 Counsellor's Perspective on CICL's capacity for reform and rehabilitation

The MOH counsellor believed that CICL could be reformed and had the potential to change, the SH counsellor believed that CICL were wounded children in need of healing and sinners who needed to be reformed and saved. MOH counsellor believed CICL needed empathy from society and the justice system to reform, while SH counsellor believed CICL needed to repent for reform to happen. MOH counsellor believed that the juvenile justice system needed to understand what was needed for the future of CICL and based on that rehabilitation was to be planned, while the SH counsellor believed that unless the root cause for the child coming into conflict with the law was understood, rehabilitation was not possible and that follow – up of these children after they leave SH was a must for real rehabilitation.

5.5.2.6 Support required by child for reform and rehabilitation

The support required by child for reform and rehabilitation from the counsellor, family and the government were listed by the counsellors. While the MOH counsellor stated that counsellor's support to the child was through reassurance to the child that there was someone to help him and make sense of his actions, the SH counsellor stated that support to the child was by confronting them with their actions to teach them right and wrong and that the child first needed to repent for reform to happen. The MOH counsellor listed acceptance from family, financial support to study and not compelling the child to work as support required for the child from the family, while the SH counsellor listed independent living skills and telling his story once he leaves the institution as areas where the child needs support from family. The child needed the support of the government through less harsh punishment and for children to be treated as children and not as adults, according to the MOH counsellor, while the SH counsellor stated that government support was through schemes that would keep children engaged productively in different ways, vocational and income generating activities.

5.5.2.7 Counselling Competence of counsellor at OH and SH

Both the counsellors at the MOH and SH were not aware of their role or that of mental health professionals in conducting preliminary assessment of children charged with heinous offences. Both counsellors were also not aware of reporting procedures to be followed in the event of any child disclosing sexual abuse to them. While the MOH counsellor stated that she had the experience of some children sharing experiences of their sexual abuse with her and that she had listened and appreciated them for their courage in sharing, the SH counsellor stated that no child had ever shared any experience of sexual abuse with her. Further the SH counsellor stated that she felt anger if any child shared about their sexual crime and believed that it was their criminal mentality that made them commit such acts.

In terms of counselling practices used, the MOH counsellor stated that she included the child's statement whenever any child claimed that he was innocent as she believed that it may help him in some way in the legal process and was also the ethically right thing to do. However, on the other hand, if a child admitted to having committed the offence he had been charged with, she did not include it in the report as she felt that it would be self-incriminating for the child. The SH counsellor on the other hand, stated that she used practices like painting of Ganesha idols with lots of colours and 'mirror therapy' to sharpen their skills of observation and self- awareness. Personal strengths of the MOH counsellor were that she encouraged and motivated the children by teach them new skills (like typing, computers and drawing), while SH counsellor stated that her strength was that she helped the children to form their conscience through singing prayer songs that helped them feel and express emotions.

5.5.2.8 Role Performance of the counsellor

The MOH counsellor used to engage with the mothers and families, had not prepared or contributed to SIR, ICP or Home Visit and had been recently trained on how to prepare an ICP. She had conducted group sessions on education opportunities, health, conflict resolution, job options, alcoholism, and relationship with parents, motivation stories, etc. The SH counsellor stated that she had not never engaged with any families, never submitted any documents including SIR, ICP, nor involved in Home visit or any other legal procedure. She had, however, conducted group activities for children by making them act 'the prodigal son' as a role play as well as enacting stories from the Bible, which she believed were methods to bring them out of their evil ways.

5.5.2.9 Factors influencing role performance of the counsellor

The factors influencing role performance of the counsellor, namely, gender, emotional intensity of work, stress and burn out and challenges in performing the role were inquired into. While the MOH counsellor stated that gender did not impact her relationship as children shared quite freely with her, the SH counsellor stated that her age (nearly 70 years) as well as her gender was an advantage as it encouraged boys to cry freely in her presence. Both the counsellors admitted that the emotional intensity of their work sometimes overwhelmed them. Both counsellors also admitted that they felt stressed and burnt out by the demanding nature of their work, and the MOH counsellor stated that she had felt additionally stressed when she learnt that a staff member had sexually abused a boy. Even though that staff person had left, she had continued feeling stressed about that matter. The SH counsellor stated that she felt frustrated about the lack of lack of qualified staff to teach the children even though many of them were very eager to learn. While the MOH counsellor listed the lack of autonomy for the counsellor, restrictions placed by the superintendent and reporting on police atrocities as the main challenges of the role, the SH counsellor stated that her inability to speak Hindi and not understanding the different cultures that many children came from, were the challenges she faced.

5.5.2.10 Coping strategies of counsellor

The MOH counsellor washed her face, drank water and listened to music to calm her down as a strategy to deal with the stress at work, while the SH counsellor turned to prayer, meditation and her religion to deal with the stress at work. The MOH counsellor believed that it was very important for every counsellor to go for personal counsellor in order to be emotionally stable to do this work, while the SH counsellor felt that self-awareness was more important than personal counselling for the counsellor. The MOH counsellor stated that she had sought professional help for her personal as well as family problems while the SH counsellor said that she did not have any facility to report feeling stressed and hence had never sought help even if she felt depressed.

5.5.2.11 Support received and required by counsellor

The support received and required by counsellor for effective counselling, professional supervision and nature of supervision, support for personal growth and wellbeing, and personal safety were enquired into. The MOH counsellor stated that she required support from staff and Department of Women and Child development while the SH counsellor expected support in understanding the language of some of the children from other States as her inability to speak the language affected her ability to connect or build rapport with the child. While the MOH counsellor believed that she should not be supervised only by the administrative head or reviewed by the JJB as was the current practice, but that a psychologist or mental health professional must also supervise and guide the counsellor on technical aspects of her job to monitor what kind of counselling process / models she was using. However, the SH counsellor believed that she had been sent and empowered by god, and hence did not feel the need for any professional supervision. The MOH counsellor stated that there was a need for staff to also be counselled, to create a more cordial work atmosphere which would enable personal growth of the counsellor, while the SH counsellor stated that her faith and religious beliefs gave her the strength to do her work as a counsellor. The counsellors at both the MOH and the SH stated that safety of counsellors was an issue and that they had felt scared many times, and while the MOH counsellor stated that she had been lucky that no untoward incident had taken place till now, the SH counsellor stated that she had been threatened with violence and a child had once even brought a big needle to the session and told her that he intended using it on her.

5.5.2.12 Impact of counselling services

The counsellors at both the MOH and SH believed that the counsellor could make a difference and impact on the life of a CICL. The MOH counsellor believed that children could be moulded and taught good values, while the SH counsellor stated that the counsellor could help to identify their strengths, make them feel wanted and instil self-belief and confidence. According to the MOU counsellor, the factors that worked for some of the children who had been successfully reformed were being sent to the Special Home, the gap and distance from peer circle and break in addiction habits, (some children could give up drugs only after going Special Home), and going back to parents and family. While motivation and support from parents, and the young age and sense of hope amongst these young boys were the factors that worked in the reform and rehabilitation, according to the SH counsellor.

5.6. RESULT VI : REFORM, REHABILITATION AND RESTORATION

5.6.1 REFORM – Resilience, Accountability & Goal Orientation

5.6.1.1 Potential for Reform: Self-Description & Resilience - I AM

Table 5.6.1.1 depicts the self-description of CICL in terms of how many positive qualities they are able to identify and describe about themselves, when asked to complete the sentence, “I am …” A total of 42.86% of CICL (61.90% at the SH and 34.69% at the OH) stated that they could only recognize one positive trait within themselves. Interestingly, 19.05% of ICCL at the SH recognized four positive qualities within themselves, while the CICL at the OH, 28.57% recognized two positive traits, 18.37% recognized three positive qualities and 12.24% could not recognize any positive trait within themselves (Fig. 5.6.1.1).

Table 5.6.1.1 Potential for Reform : Self-Description & Resilience - I am (N=70)

Perception of Self in terms of resilience : I AM	Observation Home		Special Home		Total	
	F	%	F	%	F	%
Recognized 4 positive qualities within himself	3	6.12	4	19.05	7	10
Recognized 3 positive qualities within himself	9	18.37	0	0	9	12.86
Recognized 2 positive qualities within himself	14	28.57	2	9.52	16	22.86
Recognized only one positive trait within himself	17	34.69	13	61.90	30	42.86
Unable to recognize any positive trait in himself	6	12.24	2	9.52	8	11.43
Total	49	100	21	100	70	100

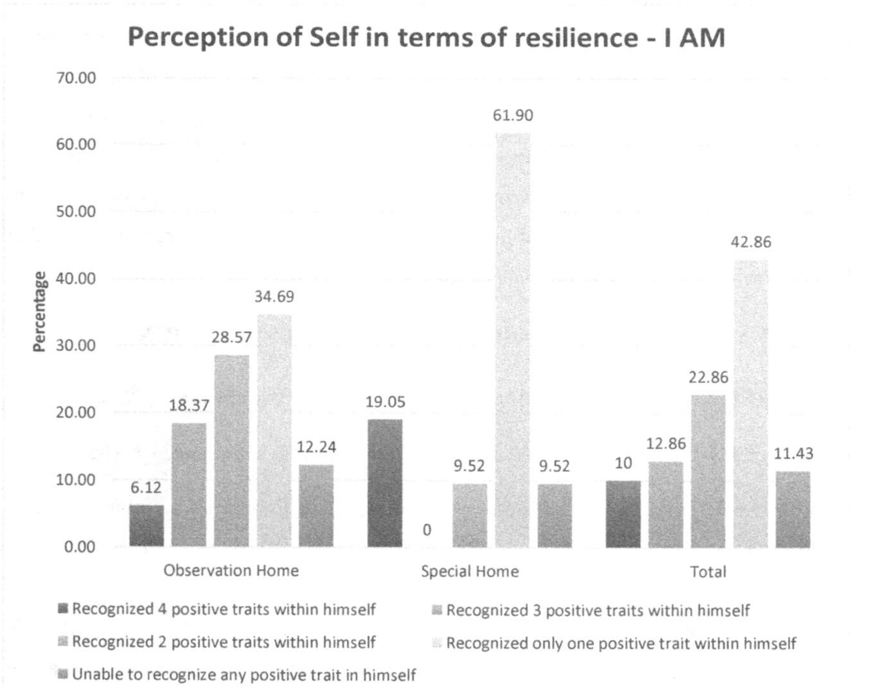

Figure 5.6.1.1 Potential for Reform : Self-Description & Resilience - I am (N=70)

5.6.1.2 Potential for Reform : Self Description & Resilience - I can

Table 5.6.1.2 depicts the self-description of CICL in terms of how many positive qualities they are able to identify and describe about themselves, when asked to complete the sentence, "I can …" A total of 41.43% of CICL (42.86% at the OH and 38.10% at the SH) stated that they could only recognize one positive trait within themselves. Interestingly, 14.29% of ICCL at the SH recognized four positive qualities within themselves, 28.57% recognized three positive qualities within themselves and 19.05% recognized two positive qualities within themselves. On the other hand, 36.73% of the CICL at the OH recognized two positive qualities within themselves. (Fig. 5.6.1.2).

Table 5.6.1.2 Potential for Reform : Self Description & Resilience - I can (N=70)

Perception of Self in terms of resilience - I CAN	Observation Home		Special Home		Total	
	F	%	F	%	F	%
Recognized 4 positive qualities within himself	2	4.08	3	14.29	5	7.14
Recognized 3 positive qualities within himself	4	8.16	6	28.57	10	14.29
Recognized 2 positive qualities within himself	18	36.73	4	19.05	22	31.43
Recognized only one positive trait within himself	21	42.86	8	38.10	29	41.43
Unable to recognize any positive trait in himself	4	8.16	0	0	4	5.71
Total	49	100	21	100	70	100

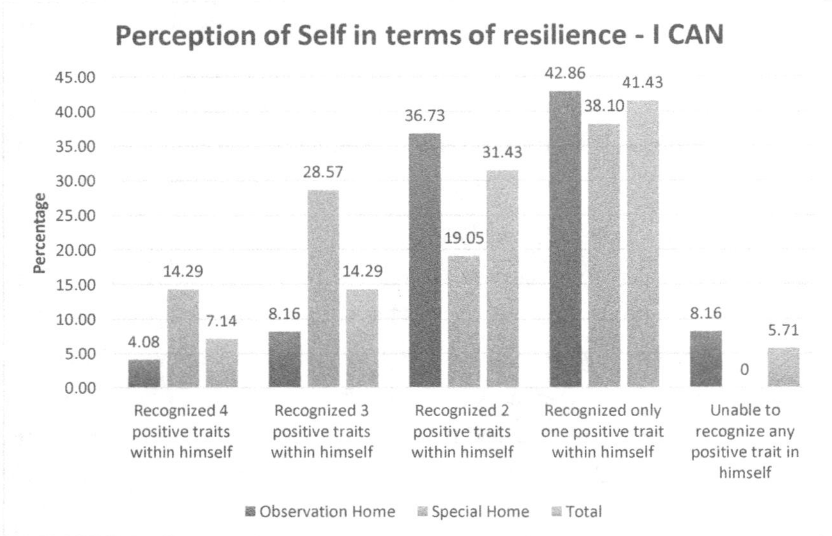

Figure 5.6.1.2 Potential for Reform : Self-Description & Resilience - I can (N=70)

5.6.1.3 Potential for Reform: Self-Description & Resilience: I have

Table 5.6.1.3 depicts the self-description of CICL in terms of how many positive qualities they are able to identify and describe about themselves, when asked to complete the sentence, "I have …" A total of 52.86% of CICL (48.98% at the OH and 61.90% at the SH) stated that they could only recognize one positive trait within themselves. Further, total of 20% of CICL (20.41% at the OH and 19.05% at the SH) stated that they could recognize two positive qualities within themselves. Disturbingly, 18.57% of the CICL (22.45% at the OH and 9.52% at the SH) were unable to recognize any positive trait within themselves (Fig. 5.6.1.3).

Table 5.6.1.3 Potential for Reform : Self Description & Resilience - I have (N=70)

Perception of Self in terms of resilience: I HAVE	Observation Home		Special Home		Total	
	F	%	F	%	F	%
Recognized 4 positive qualities within himself	1	2.04	2	9.52	3	4.29
Recognized 3 positive qualities within himself	3	6.12	0	0	3	4.29
Recognized 2 positive qualities within himself	10	20.41	4	19.05	14	20

Recognized only one positive trait within himself	24	48.98	13	61.90	37	52.86
Unable to recognize any positive trait in himself	11	22.45	2	9.52	13	18.57
Total	49	100	21	100	70	100

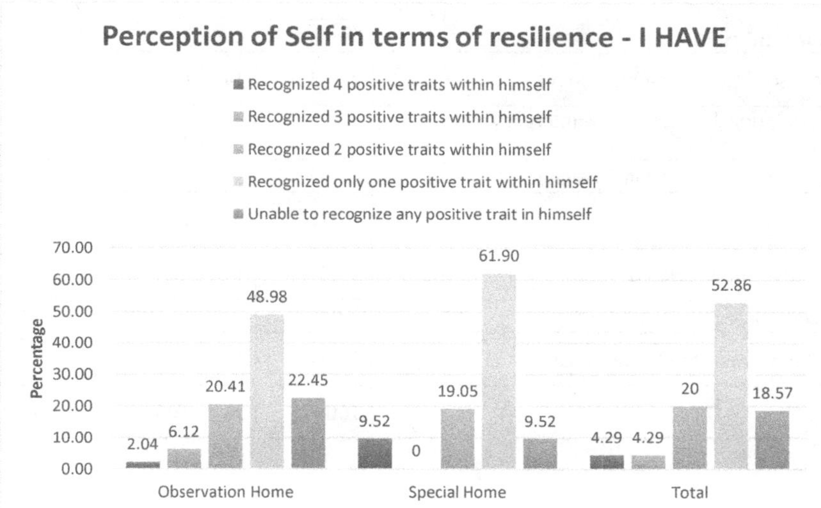

Figure 5.6.1.3 Potential for Reform : Self Description & Resilience - I have (N=70)

5.6.2 Potential for Reform : Willingness to take Accountability for behaviour - what can he change by himself

Table 5.6.2 described the willingness of the CICL to take responsibility for what aspects of his behaviour he can change by himself. A total of 35.71% of CICL (22.45% at the OH and 66.67% at the SH) stated that they can change many aspects of intrapersonal behaviour like his own beliefs, thinking patterns, emotional expression, responding and coping styles, etc. It was interesting to note the difference between the CICL at the OH and the SH with regard to willingness to take accountability. While 19.05% of the CICL at the SH stated that they could change aspects of their behaviour related to their family and other social behaviour, CICL at the OH stated they could change aspects of education related behaviour (20.41%) , job and employment related behaviour (14.29%) and social and community related behaviour

(12.24%). Interestingly, 20.41% of the CICL stated that they did not know or could not think of what aspect of their behaviour they could think of changing by themselves (Fig. 5.6.2).

Table 5.6.2 Potential for Reform : Willingness to take Accountability for behaviour - what can he change by himself (N=70)

Accountability	Observation Home		Special Home		Total	
	F	%	F	%	F	%
Self focused – intrapersonal behavior	11	22.45	14	66.67	25	35.71
Family/relationship related – interpersonal behavior	4	8.16	4	19.05	8	11.43
Society / community related behavior	6	12.24	1	4.76	7	10
Education related	10	20.41	0	0	10	14.29
Job / Employment related	7	14.29	1	4.76	8	11.43
Financial related	1	2.04	0	0	1	1.43
Don't know/can't think / can't say	10	20.41	1	4.76	11	15.71
Total	49	100	21	100	70	100

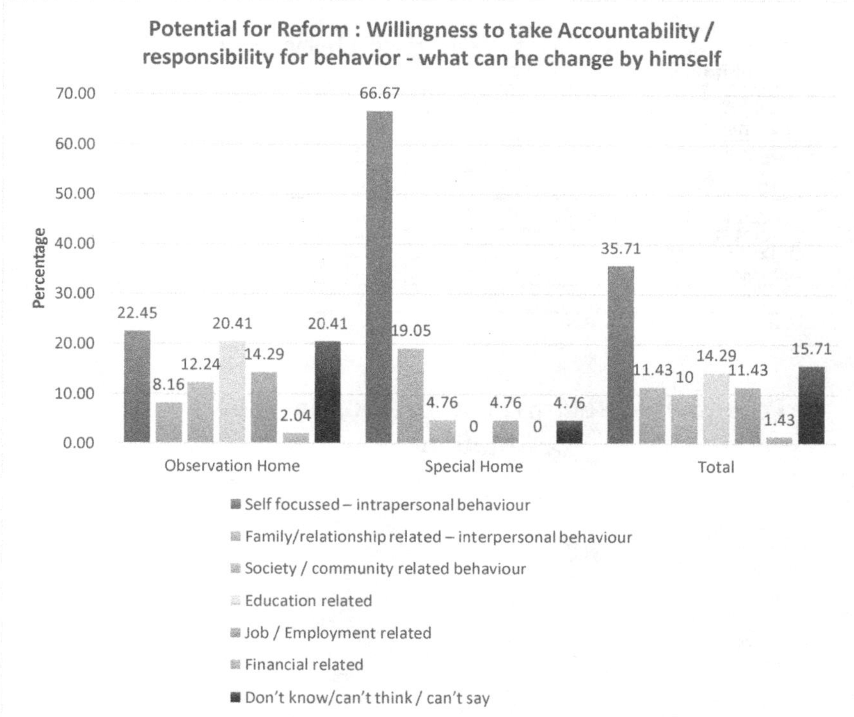

Figure 5.6.2 Potential for Reform: Willingness to take Accountability for behaviour - what can he change by himself (N=70)

5.6.3 Potential for Reform: Future Plans and Goal Orientation

Table 5.6.3 depicted the plans and goals CICL had set for themselves once they got out of the institutions. A total of 28.57% of CICL (22.45% at the OH and 42.86% at the SH) stated that their plans were all job and employment related, while another 27.14% of CICL (32.65% at the OH and 14.29% at the SH) stated that their goals were all education and studies related. Significantly, 14.29% of the CICL (16.33% at the OH and 9.52% at the SH) were afraid of the future, while 11.43% of the CICL (12.24 % at the OH and 9.52% at the SH) were unable to think or decide about their future. Interestingly, 19.05% of the CICL at the SH wanted to care for their parents and give back to society in some way (Fig. 5.6.3).

Table 5.6.3 Potential for Reform : Future Plans and Goal Orientation (N=70)

Plans of the children	Observation Home		Special Home		Total	
	F	%	F	%	F	%
Education Related	16	32.65	3	14.29	19	27.14
Job / Employment related	11	22.45	9	42.86	20	28.57
want to care for parents / society	3	6.12	4	19.05	7	10
Not to get in conflict with law	4	8.16	0	0	4	5.71
Only focused on getting out of OH / SH	1	2.04	1	4.76	2	2.86
Unable to think / decide	6	12.24	2	9.52	8	11.43
Fear of the future	8	16.33	2	9.52	10	14.29
Total	49	100	21	100	70	100

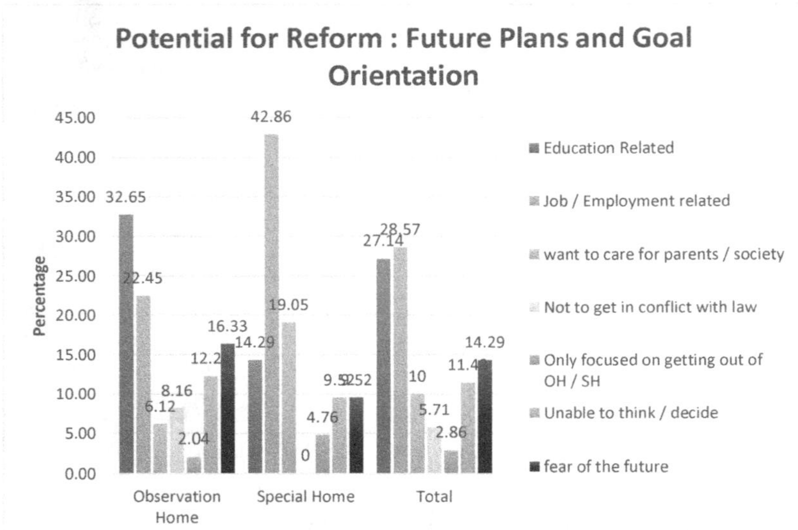

Figure 5.6.3 Potential for Reform : Future Plans and Goal Orientation (N=70)

5.6.4 REHAB – Support to meet goals & Positive impact of JJ system

5.6.4.1 Support required to meet his goals

Table 5.6.4.1 depicted the type of support required by the CICL to meet his personal and professional goals. A total of 24.29% of CICL (14.29% at the OH and 47.62% at the SH) stated that the main support that they required for achieving their goals was from parents and family. Followed by 18.57 of CICL (20.41% at the OH and 14.29% at the SH) who stated that they required financial support to achieve their goals. Interestingly, 26.53% of the CICL at the OH stated that they did not know what kind of support they required. Revealingly, 23.81% of the CICL at the SH stated that they need social support in the form of community acceptance, jobs and moral support in order to achieve their goals. Other types of support cited also include support to stay away from crime, protection from police harassment, protection from the victim's family and mental health support like counselling, de-addition services etc. (Fig. 5.6.4.1). Very uniquely, one CICL at the CICL stated that the support he needed was forgiveness and unless society and the victim could forgive him, he would not be able to achieve any goal for himself.

Table 5.6.4.1 Support required to meet his goals (N=70)

Type of support	Observation Home		Special Home		Total	
	F	%	F	%	F	%
Financial Support	10	20.41	3	14.29	13	18.57
Social Support (acceptance, job, moral support)	4	8.16	5	23.81	9	12.86
Parental / Family Support	7	14.29	10	47.62	17	24.29
Legal Support	4	8.16	0	0	4	5.71
Support to stay away from crime	3	6.12	1	4.76	4	5.71
Protection from police harassment	4	8.16	1	4.76	5	7.14
Protection from victim's family	1	2.04	0	0	1	1.43
Forgiveness	0	0	1	4.76	1	1.43
Mental Health support – counselling, de-addiction, etc.	3	6.12	0	0	3	4.29
Don't know	13	26.53	0	0	13	18.57
Total	49	100	21	100	70	100

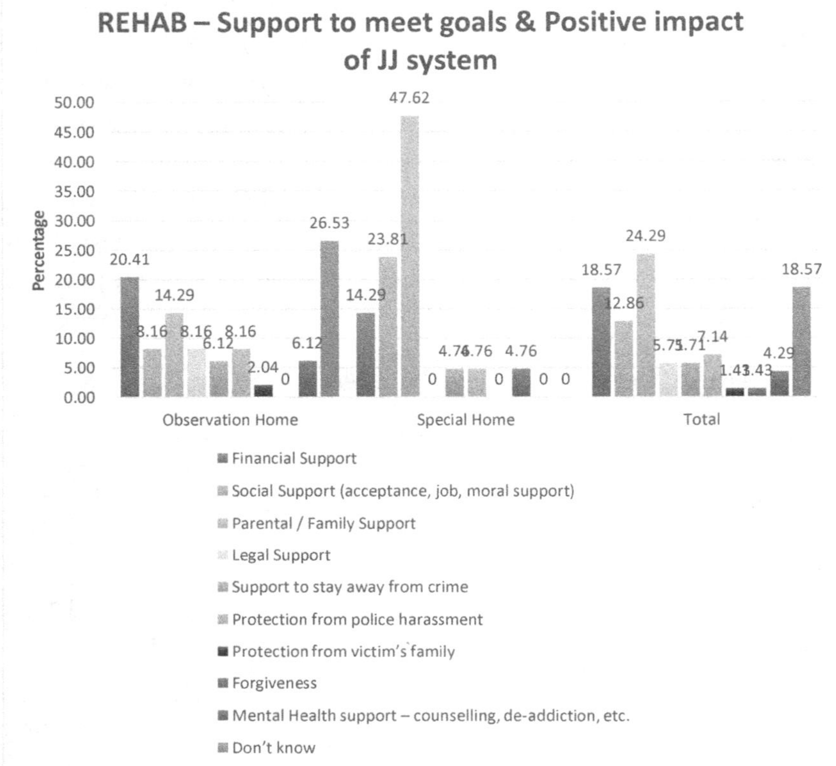

Figure 5.6.4.1 Support required to meet his goals (N=70)

5.6.4.2 Supporting person in meeting his goals

Table 5.6.4.2 depicted the person(s) who, in the CICL's view can support him in meeting his personal and professional goals for his future. 24.29% of the CICL (32.65% at the OH and 4.76% at the SH) stated that they did not know who could help them achieve their goals. However, a total of 22.86% of the CICL (22.45 % at the OH and 23.81% at the SH) stated their parents and / or family would help them in achieving their goals. Specifically, 10% of CICL, (14.29% at the SH) stated that their mother was the one person whose support would help them achieve their goals. Interestingly, 10.20% of CICL at the OH stated that their teachers or educational institution could help them achieve their goals if they provided them support. Very interestingly, 42.86% of the CICL at the SH stated that the Superintendent at the SH was that one person whose support could make their goals become reality (Fig. 5.6.4.2).

Table 5.6.4.2 Supporting person in meeting his goals (N=70)

Person /agency	Observation Home		Special Home		Total	
	F	%	F	%	F	%
Parents / Family	11	22.45	5	23.81	16	22.86
Mother	4	8.16	3	14.29	7	10
Siblings	1	2.04	1	4.76	2	2.86
NGO	3	6.12	0	0	3	4.29
Teachers / Educational Institution	5	10.20	0	0	5	7.14
Friends	4	8.16	0	0	4	5.71
Relatives/ neighbors / community	3	6.12	1	4.76	4	5.71
JJB	1	2.04	0	0	1	1.43
Don't know	16	32.65	1	4.76	17	24.29
Superintendent of SH	0	0	9	42.86	9	12.86
No one to support	1	2.04	1	4.76	2	2.86
Total	49	100	21	100	70	100

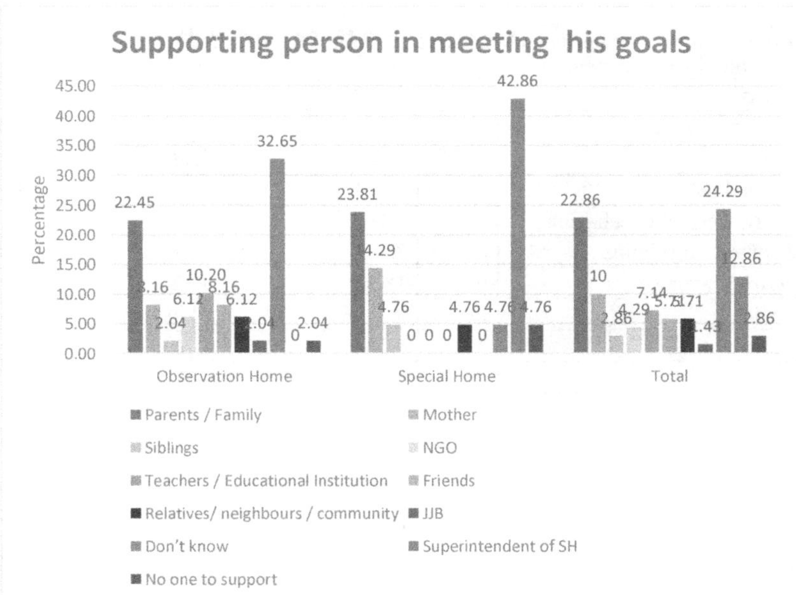

Figure 5.6.4.2 Supporting person in meeting his goals (N=70)

5.6.4.3 Positive impact of JJ system

Table 5.6.2.3 depicted the positive impact of the juvenile justice system on children in conflict with the law. A total of 22.86% of CICL (28.57% at the OH and 9.52% at the SH) stated that they had increased self-awareness after coming into the juvenile justice system. 15.71% of CICL (18.37% at OH and 9.52% at the SH) stated that they had learnt to differentiate right from wrong after coming into the juvenile justice system. In another positive feedback, 14.29% of CICL (10.20% at the OH and 23.81% at the SH) stated that they had learnt a new skill after coming into the juvenile justice system, while 11.43% of CICL (12.24% at OH) stated that they had learnt a new good habit after coming into conflict with the law. Interestingly, 14.29% of CICL at the SH specifically mentioned that they had learnt empathy after coming into the SH (Fig. 5.6.2.3).

Table 5.6.4.3 Positive impact of JJ system (N=70)

Positive things learnt / experienced from the juvenile justice system	**Observation Home**		**Special Home**		**Total**	
	F	%	F	%	F	%
Self-awareness	14	28.57	2	9.52	16	22.86
Gave up drugs /smoking	4	8.16	2	9.52	6	8.57
Learnt new skill	5	10.20	5	23.81	10	14.29
Learnt new good habit	6	12.24	2	9.52	8	11.43
Learnt socially acceptable behavior	4	8.16	2	9.52	6	8.57
Emotional control / discipline	4	8.16	2	9.52	6	8.57
Learnt right from wrong	9	18.37	2	9.52	11	15.71
Learnt empathy	0	0	3	14.29	3	4.29
Can't say / don't know	3	6.12	1	4.76	4	5.71
TOTAL	49	100	21	100	70	100

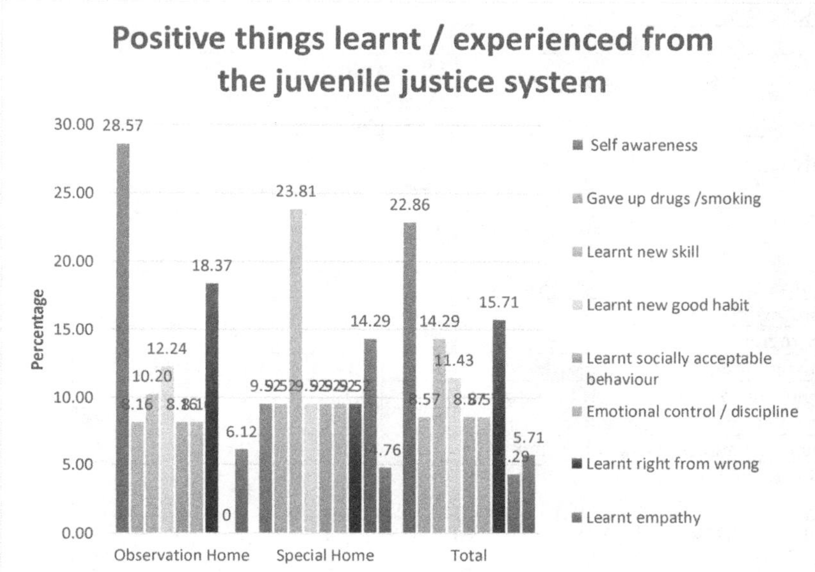

Figure 5.6.4.3 Positive impact of JJ system (N=70)

5.6.5 RESTORATION – Remorse, Harm, Empathy & Making Amends

5.6.5.1 Remorse about harm caused

Table 5.6.5.1 depicted the remorse of the CICL about the harm caused by them. A total of 44.29% of CICL (30.61% at the OH and 76.19% at the SH) stated that they strongly regretted their actions that caused harm and brought them in conflict with the law. Further, 11.43% of CICL (10.20% at the OH and 14.29% at the SH) stated that they regretted the harm caused by them and another 10% of CICL stated that they wished they acted differently (14.29% at the OH). Therefore, a total of 67.15% of CICL expressed remorse about the harm caused by them. Interestingly, some CICL (21.42%) stated that they were innocent and hence felt different emotions, innocent and hence no remorse (5.71%), innocent and angry and being framed (5.71%), innocent but felt terrible about the victim (4.29%), innocent and didn't know who was the victim (5.71%). 10.20% of CICL at the OH did not know whether they were innocent or not (Fig. 5.6.5.1).

Table 5.6.5.1 Remorse about harm caused (N=70)

Remorse	Observation Home		Special Home		Total	
	F	%	F	%	F	%
Strongly regret what I did	15	30.61	16	76.19	31	44.29
Yes I regret	5	10.20	3	14.29	8	11.43
I often regret what I did	1	2.04	0	0	1	1.43
Sometimes I wish I had acted differently	7	14.29	0	0	7	10
I seldom regret what I did	0	0	0	0	0	0
I rarely regret what I did	0	0	0	0	0	0
I don't want to think about it all (denial)	2	4.08	1	4.76	3	4.29
I am innocent so I have no regret or remorse	3	6.12	1	4.76	4	5.71
I don't know whether I am innocent or not	5	10.20	0	0	5	7.14
I am innocent and angry at being framed	4	8.16	0	0	4	5.71
I am innocent but feel terrible about the victim	3	6.12	0	0	3	4.29
I am innocent and don't know who is the victim	4	8.16	0	0	4	5.71
Total	49	100	21	100	70	100

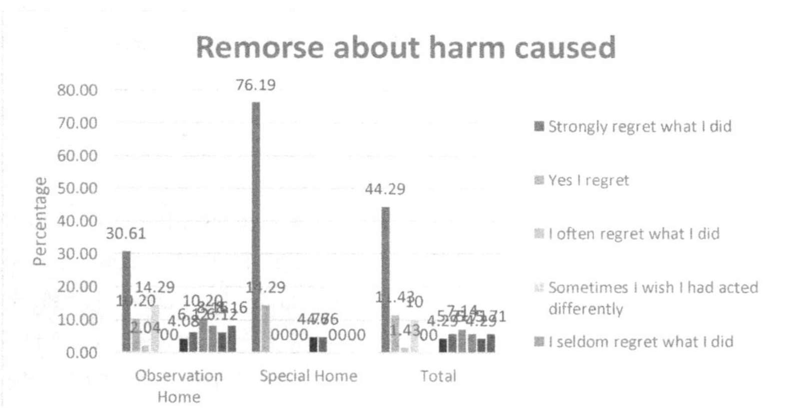

Figure 5.6.5.1 Remorse about harm caused (N=70)

5.6.5.2 (Perceived) Harm caused: Who was harmed ?

Table 5.6.5.2 depicted the persons whom the CICL perceives as having caused harm to. Interestingly, while a total of 14.29% (10.20% at OH and 23.81% at the SH) stated that they had caused harm to their family, including parents and siblings, an equal 14.29% of CICL stated that they had caused harm to their own family, as well as the victim and victims' family. A total of 12.86% of CICL (16.33% at the OH) stated that they had caused harm to their own parents. Interesting, among the CICL at the SH, 14.29% stated that they had caused harm to themselves while another 14.29% stated that they had harmed the victim and victim's family (Fig. 5.6.5.2).

Table 5.6.5.2 (Perceived) Harm caused: Who was harmed ?(N=70)

	Observation Home		Special Home		Total	
Who was harmed	F	%	F	%	F	%
Self	3	6.12	3	14.29	6	8.57
Own Parents	8	16.33	1	4.76	9	12.86
Family (parents and siblings)	5	10.20	5	23.81	10	14.29
Extended family (relatives)	2	4.08	0	0	2	2.86
Own family and extended family	1	2.04	2	9.52	3	4.29
Victim	4	8.16	1	4.76	5	7.14
Victim and victim's family	3	6.12	3	14.29	6	8.57
Own family, victim and victim's family	7	14.29	3	14.29	10	14.29
Own family and extended family, victim and victim's family	1	2.04	0	0	1	1.43
Self, own family and extended family, victim and victim 's family	4	8.16	2	9.52	6	8.57
I don't want to think / talk about it	3	6.12	1	4.76	4	5.71
I don't think I have harmed anyone	4	8.16	0	0	4	5.71
I don't know	4	8.16	0	0	4	5.71
TOTAL	49	100	21	100	70	100

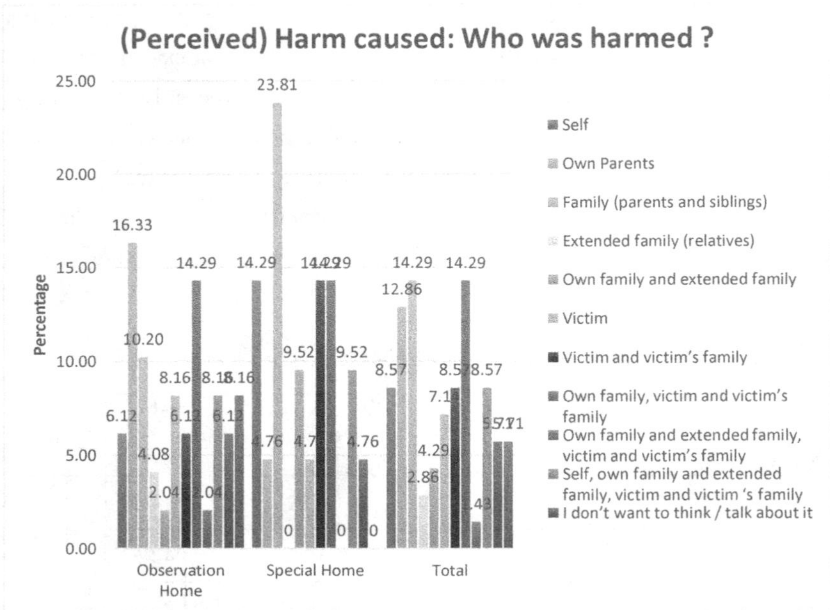

Figure 5.6.5.2 (Perceived) Harm caused: Who was harmed ?(N=70)

5.6.5.3 Kind of harm caused

Table 5.7.5.3 described the kind of harm caused by the CICL by coming into conflict with the law. A total of 15.71% of CICL (18.37% at the OH and 9.52% at the SH) stated that the kind of harm caused by them was the loss of life of the victim. 12.86% of CICL (especially 23.81% at the SH and 8.16% at the OH) stated that the kind of harm caused by them was the shame brought on their family on account of their actions. Significantly, 11.43% of CICL (14.29% at the OH) stated that the kind of harm caused by them was that relationships with their own family as well as the victim's family were broken. Interestingly, CICL at the SH stated that their actions had caused financial loss for the victim and victim's family (19.05%) and relationships with their own families to be broken (19.05%) (Fig. 5.7.5.3).

Table 5.6.5.3 Kind of harm caused (N=70)

Kind of harm caused	Observation Home		Special Home		Total	
	F	%	F	%	F	%
Shame to self	2	4.08	1	4.76	3	4.29
Shame to own parents	4	8.16	0	0	4	5.71
Shame to family	4	8.16	5	23.81	9	12.86
Loss of wage and employment for family	0	0	0	0	0	0
Loss of education for self	3	6.12	1	4.76	4	5.71
Physical harm to victim	3	6.12	0	0	3	4.29
Physical and sexual harm to victim	1	2.04	0	0	1	1.43
Financial loss for self and family	1	2.04	0	0	1	1.43
Financial loss for victim and victim's family	1	2.04	4	19.05	5	7.14
Relationships with family broken	3	6.12	4	19.05	7	10
Relationship with family and victim's family broken	7	14.29	1	4.76	8	11.43
I don't think I have harmed anyone	0	0	0	0	0	0
I don't want to think / talk about it	1	2.04	1	4.76	2	2.86
Harassment of self and family by police	5	10.20	1	4.76	6	8.57
Death of mother	0	0	1	4.76	1	1.43
Loss of life of victim	9	18.37	2	9.52	11	15.71
I don't know	5	10.20	0	0	5	7.14
Total	49	100	21	100	70	100

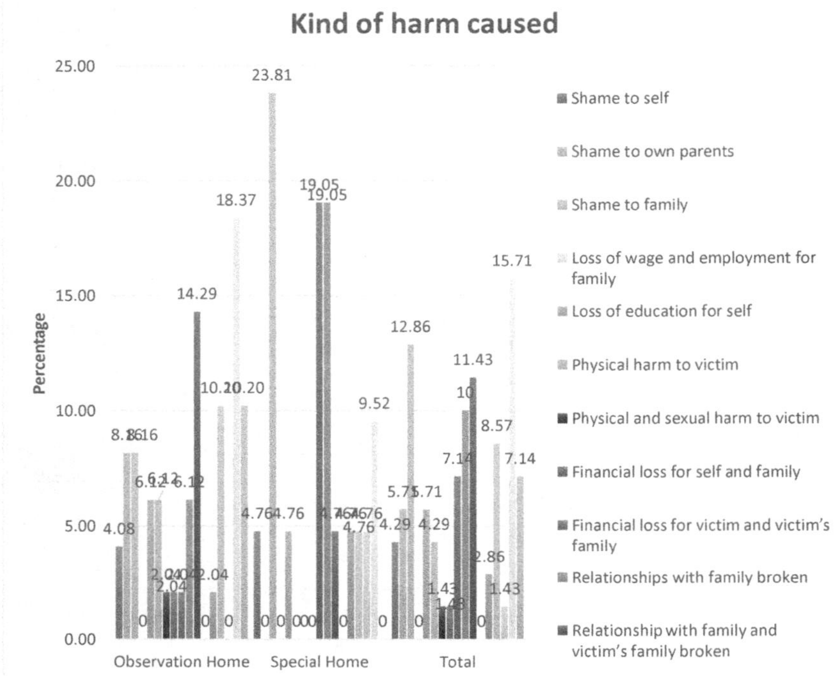

Figure 5.6.5.3 Kind of harm caused (N=70)

5.6.5.4 Empathy for victim

Table 5.6.5.4 revealed that a total of 45.71% of the CICL (36.73% at the OH and 66.67% at the SH) stated that they always felt empathy for the victim and / or their families. Further, a total of 12.86% of CICL (10.20% at the OH and 19.05% at the SH) stated that they felt often empathy for the victim and/or their families. 11.43% of CICL (16.33% at the OH) stated they did not know and felt confused. Interestingly, 18.57% of CICL (26.53% at the OH) stated that they and their families were the victims themselves. Very significantly, not a single CICL stated that they did not feel any empathy at all (Fig. 5.6.5.4).

Table 5.6.5.4 Empathy for victim (N=70)

Empathy for Victim	Observation Home		Special Home		Total	
	F	%	F	%	F	%
Yes always	18	36.73	14	66.67	32	45.71
Yes Often	5	10.20	4	19.05	9	12.86
Yes Sometimes	3	6.12	1	4.76	4	5.71
Rarely	1	2.04	0	0	1	1.43
Not at all	0	0	0	0	0	0
Don't want to think / talk about it	1	2.04	1	4.76	2	2.86
Don't know	8	16.33	0	0	8	11.43
I and my family are the victims	13	26.53	0	0	13	18.57
Have not harmed anyone	0	0	1	4.76	1	1.43
Total	49	100	21	100	70	100

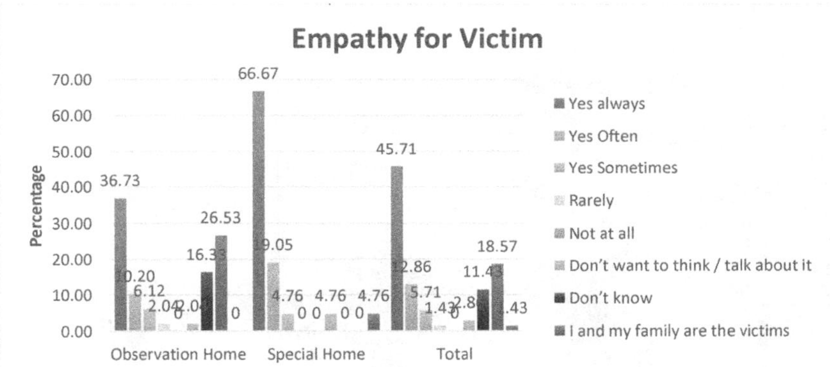

Figure 5.6.5.4 Empathy for victim (N=70)

5.6.5.5 Making amends

Table 5.6.5.5 revealed that a total of 40% of CICL (40.82% at the OH and 38.10% at the SH) expressed the desire to apologize and beg for forgiveness from the victim and / or victim's family. Another 14.29% of CICL (12.24% at the OH and 19.05% at the SH) wanted to make amends and beg forgiveness but did not know how to go about doing it. 11.43% of CICL (14.29% at the OH) even wanted to meet the victim's family and make amends, while 14.29% of the CICL at the SH stated that the best way to make amends was not cause any harm to anyone in the future. However, 12.86% of CICL (18.37%) stated that they themselves were victims needing help and had been falsely implicated (Fig. 5.6.5.5).

Table 5.6.5.5 Making amends (N=70)

Ways in which to make amends	Observation Home		Special Home		Total	
	F	%	F	%	F	%
Meet Victim's family	7	14.29	1	4.76	8	11.43
Apologize / beg forgiveness	20	40.82	8	38.10	28	40
Financial Support	0	0	3	14.29	3	4.29
Change in behavior	1	2.04	1	4.76	2	2.86
No future harm	1	2.04	3	14.29	4	5.71
Want to but don't know how	6	12.24	4	19.05	10	14.29
Don't want to think / talk about victim	1	2.04	1	4.76	2	2.86
Himself a victim needing help	9	18.37	0	0	9	12.86
Don't know victim	4	8.16	0	0	4	5.71
Total	49	100	21	100	70	100

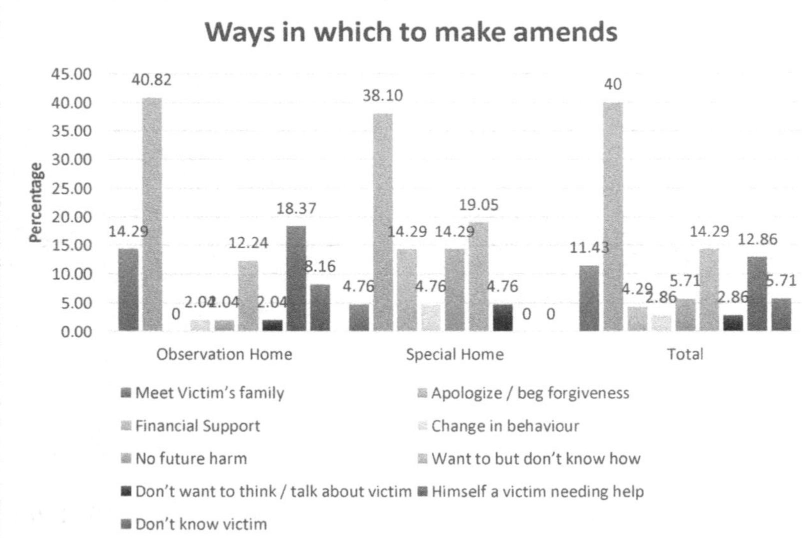

Figure 5.6.5.5 Making amends (N=70)

5.7 RESULT VII - RIGHTS

5.7.1 RIGHT TO LEGAL REPRESENTATION

5.7.1.1 Right to Legal Representation

Table 5.7.1.1 revealed that a total of 82.86 % of the CICL (77.55 % at the OH and 95.24% at the SH) stated that they had a lawyer who represented them, thus indicating that the right to legal representation was upheld. However, 18.37% of CICL at the OH and 4.76% of CICL at the SH stated that they did not have a lawyer. Worryingly, 4% of the CICL at the OH stated that they did not know they were supposed to have a lawyer or about any other legal procedure or entitlement (Fig. 5.7.1.1).

Table 5.7.1.1 Right to Legal Representation (N=70)

Right to Legal Representation: Access to Lawyer	Observation Home		Special Home		Total	
	F	%	f	%	F	%
No	9	18.37	1	4.76	10	14.29
Yes	38	77.55	20	95.24	58	82.86
Does not know	2	4	0	0	2	2.86
Total	49	100	21	100	70	100

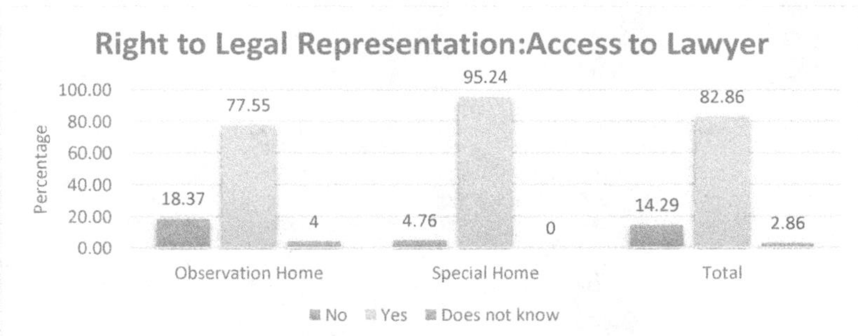

Figure 5.7.1.1 Right to Legal Representation (N=70)

5.7.1.2 Reasons for lack of access to Legal Representation

Reasons for lack of access to a lawyer included poverty, lack of legal awareness lack of faith in the justice system and not having any family to appoint a lawyer. Table 5.8.1.2 depicted that among those who could not access legal representation, a total of 81.43% of the CICL (75.51% at the OH and 95.24% at the SH) stated that poverty and lack of financial resources were the main reason why they could not get legal representation. 14.29% of the CICL at the OH stated parents and family related reasons for not having a lawyer. Disturbingly, 4.76% at the SH stated that they did not have any faith in the justice system and hence had not appointed any lawyer (Fig. 5.8.1.2).

Table 5.7.1.2 Reasons for lack of access to Legal Representation (N=70)

Reasons for lack of access to Legal Representation	Observation Home		Special Home		Total	
	F	%	F	%	F	%
Financial constraints	37	75.51	20	95.24	57	81.43
Parents and family related reasons	7	14.29	0	0	7	10
No family to appoint lawyer	2	4.08	0	0	2	2.86
Lack of legal awareness	3	6.12	0	0	3	4.29
Lack of faith in justice system	0	0	1	4.76	1	1.43
Total	49	100	21	100	70	100

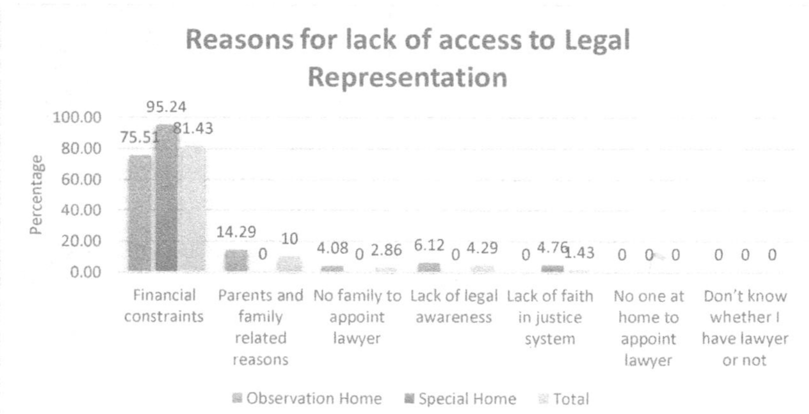

Figure 5.7.1.2 Reasons for lack of access to Legal Representation (N=70)

5.7.2 RIGHT TO CONTACT WITH FAMILY

It was found that 33.33% of the CICL at the SH stated that were allowed to meet or talk to their parents any time they expressed such a wish, while another 23.81% of the CICL at the SH stated that there were no specific restrictions placed on them for contact with their family. Table 5.8.2 showed that a total of 24.29% of the CICL (35% at the OH) stated that they were allowed to speak or meet their parents once a week. This was done through a system of weekly "Parents Day" at the OH, wherein parents were allowed to visit their children on Mondays between 10.00 am to 6.00 p.m. A disturbing 22% of the CICL at the OH stated that their family members were afraid the police would harass them if they maintained contact with their children and hence avoided coming to visit them at the OH or even to speak on the phone with them. This, however did not extend to the CICLs at the SH. Equally saddening, however, was that 14.29% of the children at the SH did not have any visit from family but had some occasional telephonic contact and another 14.29% at the SH did not have anyone to call family who could visit them (Fig. 5.7.2).

Table 5.7.2 Right to contact with family while in custody (N=70)

Right to contact with family while in custody	**Observation Home**		**Special Home**		**Total**	
	F	%	F	%	F	%
No restrictions at all	1	2	5	23.81	6	8.57
Whenever child expresses wish	1	2.04	7	33.33	8	11.43
Once a week	17	35	0	0	17	24.29
Twice or thrice a month	2	4	0	0	2	2.86
Once a month	0	0	0	0	0	0
Only when family visits	0	0	0	0	0	0
Never (not allowed to meet / call)	0	0	0	0	0	0
Child does not want to meet	0	0	0	0	0	0
No one in family who can visit	3	6.12	3	14.29	6	8.57
Family disowned child & does not want to visit.	3	6	2	9.52	5	7.14
No visit from family but telephonic contact sometimes	4	8	3	14.29	7	10
Family in jail and unable to visit	0	0	1	4.76	1	1.43
Once a week by phone	4	8	0	0	4	5.71
Family is afraid of police so don't come to meet	11	22	0	0	11	15.71
Family does not know and hence no visit	3	6.12	0	0	3	4.29
Total	49	100	21	100	70	100

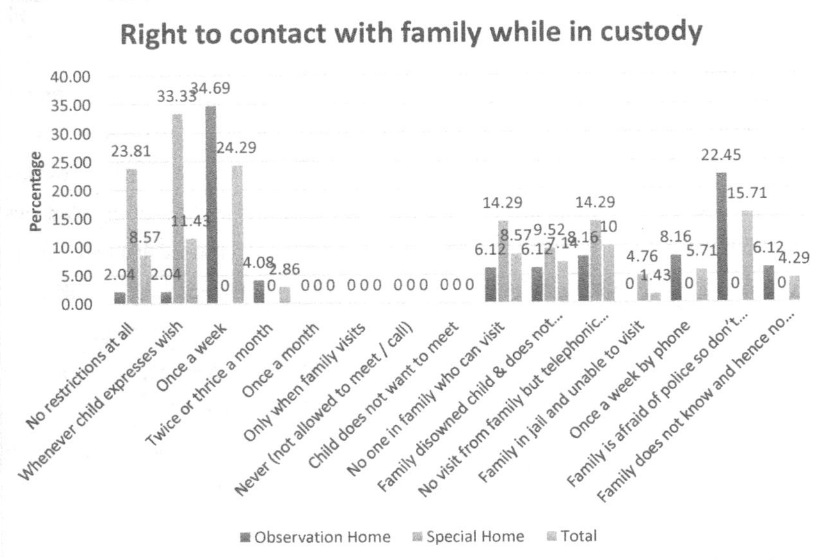

Figure 5.7.2 Right to contact with family while in custody (N=70)

5.7.3 RIGHT TO ETHICAL RESEARCH PARTICIPATION

5.7.3.1 Consent and willingness to talk about family

Table 5.7.3.1 depicted that 100% of the CICL in the study, both at the OHs and the SH, had given their consent to talk about their family. Many of the children specifically stated that they were happy to talk about themselves, their families and their lives. (Fig. 5.7.3.1).

Table 5.7.3.1 Consent and willingness to talk about family (N=70)

S. No	Consent and willingness	Observation Home (Bangalore)		Observation Home (Mysore)		Special Home (Bangalore)		Total	
		F	%	F	%	F	%	F	%
1	Consent given	34	100	15	100	21	100	70	100
2	Consent not given	0	0	0	0	0	0	0	0

	Total	34	100	15	100	21	100	70	100

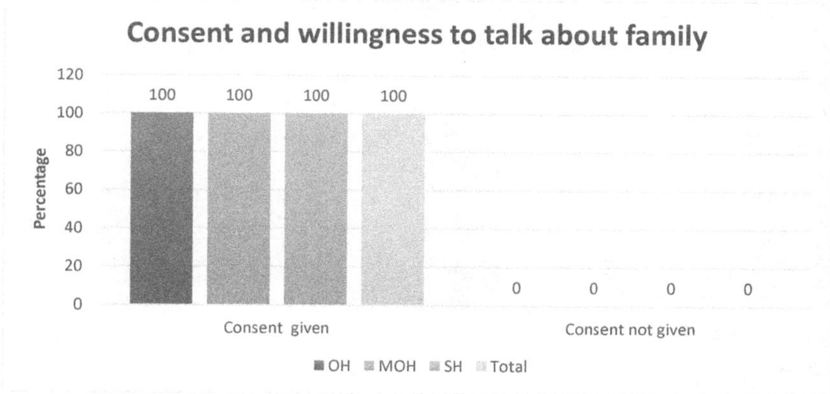

Figure 5.7.3.1 Consent and willingness to talk about family (N=70)

5.7.3.2 Experience of participation in research

Table 5.7.3.2 showed that 100% of the CICL at the OHs as well as the SH reported their experience of participation in the report as happy (Fig. 5.7.3.2).

Table 5.7.3.2 Experience of participation in research (N=70)

S. No	Experience of participation in research	Observation Home (Bangalore)		Observation Home (Mysore)		Special Home (Bangalore)		Total	
		F	%	F	%	F	%	F	%
1	Happy	34	100	21	100	15	100	70	100
2	Can't say	0	0	0	0	0	0	0	0

3	Not happy	0	0	0	0	0	0	0	0
	Total	34	100	21	100	15	100	70	100

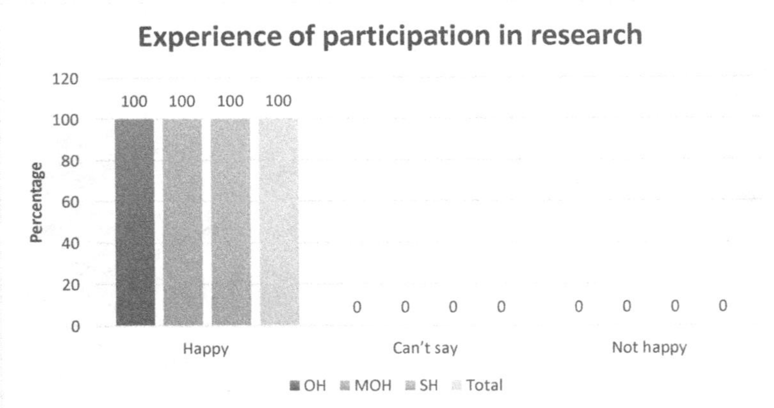

Figure 5.7.3.2 Experience of participation in research (N=70)

5.7.3.3 Experience of participation in research : Distress due to research

Table 5.7.3.3 showed that 100% of the children at the OHs and SH stated that they did not experience any distress on account of participation in the research study (Fig. 5.7.3.3).

Table 5.7.3.3 Experience of participation in research : Distress due to research (N=70)

S. No	Distress due to research	Observation Home (Bangalore)		Observation Home (Mysore)		Special Home (Bangalore)		Total	
		F	%	F	%	F	%	F	%
1	No distress	34	100	15	100	21	100	70	100
2	Unable to decide	0	0	0	0	0	0	0	0

3	Yes I was distressed	0	0	0	0	0	0	0	0
	Total	34	100	15	100	21	100	70	100

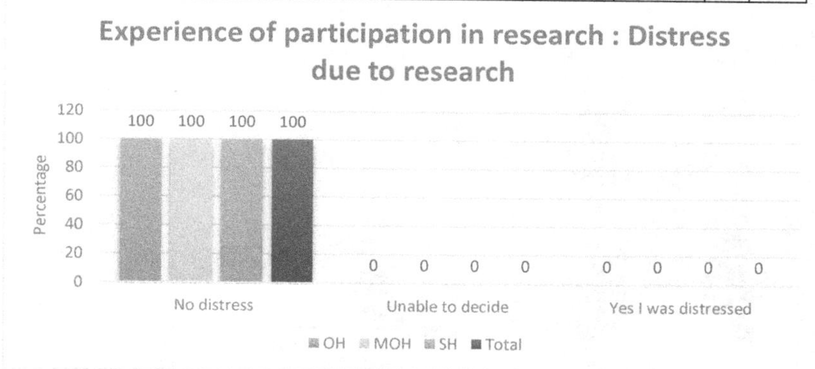

Figure 5.7.3.3 Experience of participation in research : Distress due to research (N=70)

5.7.3.4 Experience of participation in research : Usefulness of research to child

Table 5.7.3.4. showed that a total of 94.29% of CICL (97.96% at the OH and 85.71% at the SH) stated that their participation in the research study was useful to them to a great extent, while 14.29% of the CICL stated that their participation was useful to some extent (Fig. 5.7.3.4).

Table 5.7.3.4 Experience of participation in research : Usefulness of research to child (N=70)

Experience of participation in research : Usefulness of research to child	**Observation Home**		**Special Home**		**Total**	
	F	%	F	%	F	%
Yes, useful to a great extent	48	97.96	18	85.71	66	94.29
Useful to some extent	1	2.04	3	14.29	4	5.71
Not useful at all	0	0	0	0	0	0
Total	49	100	21	100	70	100

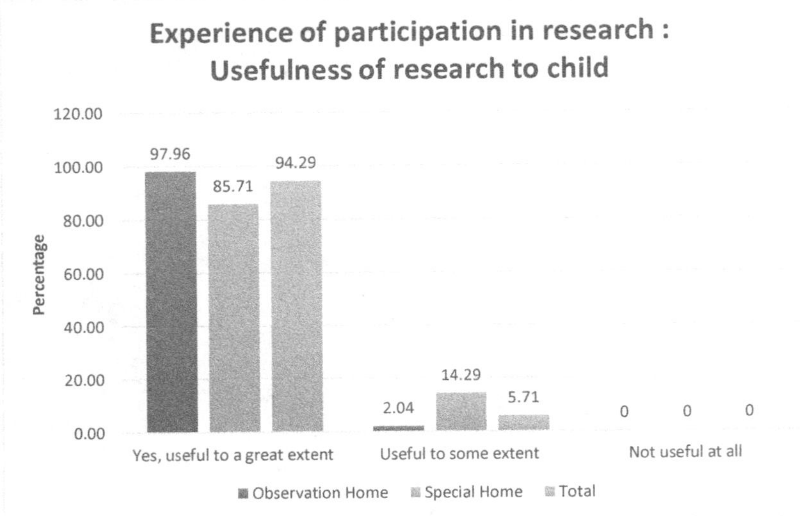

Figure 5.7.3.4 Experience of participation in research : Usefulness of research to child (N=70)

5.7.3.5 Experience of participation in research : Willingness to participate in the future

Table 5.7.3.5 showed that a total of 98.57% of CICLs (100% at OHs and 95.24% at the SH) stated that they would be willing to participate in a similar study in the future (Fig. 5.7.3.5).

Table 5.7.3.5 Experience of participation in research : Willingness to participate in the future (N=70)

Experience of participation in research : Willingness to participate in the future	**Observation Home**		**Special Home**		**Total**	
	F	%	F	%	F	%
Yes	49	100	20	95.24	69	98.57
Maybe	0	0	1	4.76	1	1.43
No	0	0	0	0	0	0
Total	49	100	21	100	70	100

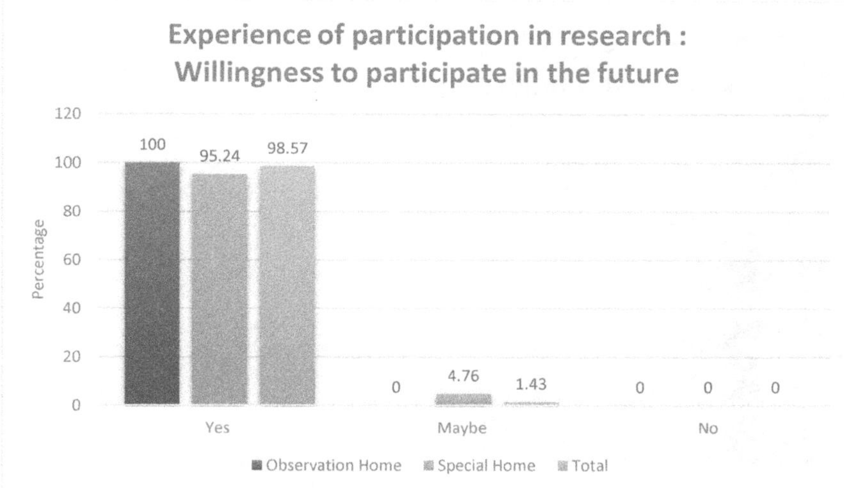

Figure 5.7.3.5 Experience of participation in research : Willingness to participate in the future (N=70)

5.7.3.6 Experience of participation in research : Current feelings check as closure

Table 5.7.3.6 showed that a total of 87.14% of the CICL (97.96% at the OH and 61.90 % at the SH) reported feeling happy at the end of the interview with the researcher while a total of 12.86% of the CICL, with 38.10% at the SH reported feeling relieved and lighter at the end of the interview with the researcher (Fig. 5.7.3.6).

Table 5.7.3.6 Experience of participation in research : Current feelings check as closure (N=70)

Experience of participation in research : Current feelings check as closure	**Observation Home**		**Special Home**		**Total**	
	F	%	F	%	F	%
Happy	48	97.96	13	61.90	61	87.14
Relieved / lighter	1	2.04	8	38.10	9	12.86
Can't say	0	0	0	0	0	0
Not happy	0	0	0	0	0	0
Total	49	100	21	100	70	100

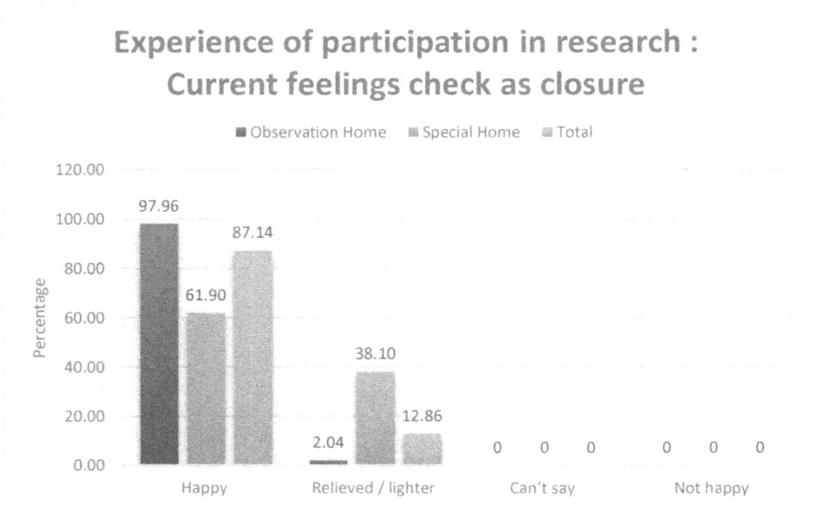

Figure 5.7.3.6 Experience of participation in research: Current feelings check as closure (N=70)

5.8 RESULT VIII: CASE STUDIES

5.8.1 Introduction

It has often been speculated that children in conflict with the law in India suffer from several serious mental health risks but there have been very few evidence-based researches to confirm this assumption, either in the fields of psychiatry, psychology, sociology, law or any other related disciplines. Parallelly, it has also long been conjectured that the provision of counselling services in the juvenile justice system are not adequate to address the mental health needs of children in conflict with the law.

The present study was therefore undertaken to provide quantitative and qualitative evidence on the mental health status and counselling of children in conflict with the law in India.

5.8.2 Methodology for case study

Of the total of 70 children interviewed for the research study, a total of 10 interviews have been presented as case studies for a qualitative understanding of the combination of factors that may have contributed to the mental health status of the child in question. These 10 interviews were chosen on the basis of the number of adverse childhood experiences they had faced and the themes of adversities that the study aimed to be highlighted through the case studies. The theoretical framework used to understand the case studies was the Adverse Childhood Experiences (ACE) Study which examined the relationship between chronic stress caused by adversities in the childhood (the first 18 years of life) and later-life health. Names of all the children, their families and other identifying details in the case studies have been changed to protect their identity and maintain confidentiality.

The 10 ACEs studied in the original ACE study (Felitti, Vincent J; Anda, Robert F; et al. 1998) were:

1. Childhood abuse -Emotional -Physical -Sexual
2. Neglect -Emotional -Physical
3. Growing up in a seriously dysfunctional household as evidenced by:
    a. Witnessing domestic violence
    b. Alcohol or other substance abuse in the home
    c. Mentally ill or suicidal household members
    d. Parental marital discord (as evidenced by separation or divorce)
    e. Crime in the home (as evidenced by having a household member imprisoned)

The present study listed each of these experiences as individual adverse childhood experiences and added a few more ACEs for the purposes of this study. The additional adverse childhood experiences chosen for inclusion in this study were based on prior research that has shown such childhood experiences to have significant adverse health implications. Child sexual abuse was excluded even though it is known to be a significant ACE that affects mental health, due to reasons of legal reporting mandated by Indian law.

The present study checked for the presence of the 20 following ACEs in the research sample. The 20 ACEs listed were:

1. Poverty: Non–fulfilment of basic needs, education, inability to pay / hire a lawyer as the child's narration of his experience of poverty
2. Disruption in education
3. Death of a parent

4. Divorce/ separation of parents
5. Neglect: Non- fulfilment of basic needs, emotional neglect
6. Lack of parental involvement and poor relationship with and among family members
7. Family history of poor health
8. Child's history poor health: hospitalization, illness, accident, violence, attempted suicide, etc.
9. Family history of substance use
10. Child's history of substance use
11. Family history of mental illness
12. Family history of suicide / attempts at suicide
13. Child's history of suicide / attempts at suicide / self harm
14. Exposure of child to violence in the family
15. Exposure of child to violence towards himself
16. Contact of family with justice system
17. Contact of child with justice system
18. Incarceration
19. Experience with police
20. Charged with sexual offence (sexual encounter of any kind before the age of 18 years is considered" child sexual abuse" and irrespective of consent or victim or offender status as per law, the CICL would be considered as having undergone CSA and hence an adverse childhood experience.

Each case study described the number and magnitude of ACEs undergone by the CICL. Based on the nature of each individual cases, some key themes were highlighted and the main areas of the focus for psychological counselling were identified for each case.

An effective counselling process for children in conflict with the law must focus on two main goals:

1. To create self-awareness in the CICL about his strengths and limitations as well as that of his life situation.
2. The counseling process must connect the CICL to resources and support systems in the family, State and civil society that would enable his rehabilitation and social reintegration.

The counsellor for children in conflict with the law, unlike counsellors in other settings for children, is required to play a multi-dimensional role. She/ he is expected to not only focus on counselling of the child, but to also contribute to reports like the Social Investigation Report, the Individual Care Plan, etc. which are submitted to the JJB and form important inputs in deciding the legal as well as the rehabilitative outcomes of the case of the child. The counsellor is also expected to refer children to multiple services including medical, psychiatric, vocational, educational, rehabilitative, community services, etc. which would help them in their rehabilitation and social reintegration. The counsellor is also expected to interact with the family of the CICL and understand his family background and social milieu in order to make appropriate recommendations in the Counselling Report, which is submitted to the JJB.

5.8.3 CASE 1 - PRAVEEN

"Dropping out from school changed my life"

Basic demographic profile

Praveen was 16 years old when he came to the Special Home where he has spent the last one year. He was 17 years old when interviewed. Praveen belonged to a poor family with a family income of approximately Rs. 5,000 per month.

Praveen loved to study and enjoyed reading and writing, but failed his 6th standard exam by 3 marks and his school asked him not to come back. According to Praveen, **this changed the entire direction of his life**. He still nurtured the dream to study and believed that if given the opportunity and supported by his mother, he could study and pass the 10th standard exam.

Education, however, remains a distant dream for many children in conflict with the law like Praveen, who are forced to drop out of school due to a variety of reasons. The reasons include financial reasons like poverty, an inability to pay the fees and compulsion to go to work to support the family, academic reasons like not being good at studies, failing in the exams or parental pressure to study subjects they are not interested in, family related reasons like death or separation of parents, illness of self or others in the family or a problematic school environment (discrimination due to caste / religion, ill-treatment by teachers, distance from school, etc.)

For Praveen, it was a combination of ill-treatment by his school authorities, the death of his father and his mother's poor health that **forced him to give up his education** and try to look for some work that would earn him some money. However, once he was out of school, he also came into contact with older boys and young adults from the neighbourhood who were involved in illegal activities – mainly petty theft. Praveen also took to roaming the streets, hitting people and throwing stones when asked to by the gang.

Legal profile

Praveen was charged and found guilty under Section 380 of the Indian Penal Code for Theft in a dwelling house. This is a serious, cognizable and non-bail able offence under the law. Cognizable offences are those in which the police can arrest without any warrant. These are more serious in nature. Non-cognizable offences on the other hand are those for which a police officer has no authority to arrest, unless with a warrant. Praveen was in the Special Home since one year and was waiting for completion of his term. He did not have any previous history of crime and this was the first time he was coming into conflict with the law.

Social profile

Praveen belonged to a very poor family, his father Late Muniswamy was a daily wage earner who died due to excessive drinking when Praveen was around 12-13 years old. Praveen's mother, Raji, also worked as a daily wage earner and barely managed to make ends meet. Praveen has a younger brother who is 10 years old. Praveen's father **could not provide basic necessities** of food, clothes or education for his children and was either sick or intoxicated most of the time. This forced his mother to go out and try to earn some money for the family but it made Praveen feel that she too had **abandoned** her children as she was **not available** to show any affection and did not know much about his day –to-day activities. He wished that his father did not drink, that his mother took care of him and that he went to school – all of which, he felt, were not possible as his parents had failed him and his brother as parents. Yet, as the oldest son, he also felt responsible and said he understood how difficult life was for his mother as a single, sick, female and poor parent.

Health profile

Praveen met with a bike accident as a young child and fractured his leg, for which he was hospitalized for a month. Praveen's family has a poor health history. His **father died of liver failure** due to excessive drinking. His mother suffered from tuberculosis and memory loss and often fell unconscious. However, his father's alcoholism appeared to have had a strong impact on Praveen, who said he hated alcohol as it took his father's life. He also never took alcohol or drugs in his life, though he experimented with cigarettes once and gave up. Though there was no violence from his parents, Praveen's **uncle hit him** often. **Praveen did not retaliate** though he felt very angry and sad at the violence shown towards him.

Current Mental Health Status

Praveen appeared to be struggling to cope with the **challenges of custodial settings** and being separated from his mother and brother. He had disturbed sleep and recurrent thoughts about ending his life, though he tried to keep himself **motivated by thinking about his responsibilities** towards his mother and younger brother. He also admitted that he had attempted suicide a few years earlier after his uncle had beaten him up severely for going out with his friends. In a fit of despair, Praveen drank poison and was taken to a hospital. However, it turned out that the poison was a 'duplicate' poison (fake, adulterated) and hence not fatal. Praveen took this incident as a sign from life that he was meant to live. This incident also showed him the distress his mother and brother went through believing him to be dead and **he resolved that he would never do such a thing** again. His survival after his suicidal attempt was a lesson for him which made him realize the importance of his family and value of his own life. However, his maternal aunt, who also used to live with his family, had attempted suicide multiple times and Praveen would feel very disturbed every time it happened.

Coming into conflict with the law

Praveen and his friends had broken into a house and stolen some household articles and jewellery. Along with jewellery, they also took away the thaali – mangalsutra of the girl who was getting married, without understanding the **socio-cultural consequences** of it. In Indian custom, the 'thaali' is a jewelry worn to symbolize the marital status of a woman. For this, Praveen was booked under section 380 of IPC for housebreaking and theft. He was found guilty of the charge after inquiry and ordered to be placed at the Special Home. At the time of interview, he spent had spent 1 year at the SH.

Experience with police

After committing the offence, Praveen left his house and went into hiding with his gang a little distance away from his home. Upon receiving the complaint of housebreaking and theft, and information about the possible involvement of Praveen in the offence, the police visited Prakash's house and caught Praveen's 9-year-old younger brother and took him to the police station. The police then hit his brother to find out about Praveen's whereabouts and told his mother to inform Praveen wherever he was that they would not release his younger brother unless he surrendered himself. After 4 days of the offence, when Praveen contacted his mother to inform her about his whereabouts, he was shocked to find out that his younger brother was being beaten up by the police in the lock-up and that the beatings would be continued if he did not surrender. Praveen immediately rushed to the police station and surrendered himself to the police within the next two hours and gave detailed information about the offence and the other accused.

Praveen was very angry at the police at that time. However, at the time of the interview a year later, he felt that it was his actions that had brought these consequences for his brother.

Experience of Counsellor and counselling

Praveen felt that having an older adult person who could help young adolescents like himself was very necessary and helpful. He expected the older adult person to help the young adolescent understand his / her socio—cultural milieu and personal problems. He felt that through this counselling process, children like himself, must be enabled to understand their responsibility towards family and society. According to him, a counsellor should listen calmly and patiently. He felt that the counsellor at the Special Home was more focused on 'reforming and correcting' him than in understanding him and helping him heal.

Remorse and empathy for victim

Praveen expressed deep remorse and helplessness that he could not repay the money stolen nor make the wedding happen and that made him feel totally disturbed about his actions. According to Praveen, the jewellery they stole included the 'thaali – mangalsutra' of the daughter of the house, whose wedding was stopped because of this robbery. The victim was told that she was not 'auspicious' as her thaali itself was stolen before the marriage and hence the wedding was called off.

When Praveen was out on bail, he tried to approach the victim's family and express his remorse. He apologized to the victim's family but they did not accept it. He fell at the feet of the victim, her father and mother – but they said that they could not forgive him for having ruined her life, as the wedding had been called off. He now **realized what a blunder** he had made.

During his stay at the Special Home, Praveen learnt a few positive things like learning how to behave in a group and that he should not be violent.

Adverse Childhood Experiences

Praveen scored a total of **17 out of 20** adverse childhood experiences. The list of adverse childhood experiences undergone by Praveen include :

Poverty, disruption in education, death of a parent, neglect, lack of parental involvement and poor family relationship, family history of poor health, child's history of prolonged illness/hospitalization, family history of alcoholism, family history of suicide, family history of mental illness, child's history of attempted suicide, exposure to violence in the family, violence towards child, violence by police, involvement of family with justice system (family member convicted or in jail) , incarceration of child, contact of child with justice system.

Scope for Reform, Rehabilitation and Restoration

Praveen was keen to study and pass his 10th class exams. He also had a strong desire to take care of his mother and brother. He was especially worried about being a negative role model for his younger brother and did not want his brother to become like him or get into 'conflict with the law'. He had a dream of sending his brother to a good school with hostel facilities, where his brother would be would be away from the influence of negative peer group and a disadvantaged socio-cultural milieu. He felt that if brother could access quality education, at least he would not end up like Praveen. Praveen believed that his coming into 'conflict with the law' was the result of the adverse impact of school environment, treatment given by teachers to him at school due to his **caste and poverty status.**

Praveen had come to realize that he could not continue his education and he wanted to become a car driver and **earn sufficient money to support his mother and brother**. In a casual interaction a few days after the formal interview, Praveen, expressed that he was a very good cook and if placed in a training institution to formally learn cooking, he was confident he would turn out to be a good chef. For this purpose, he could be helped through ECHO's Hotel Management Program which has the provision of integrated learning programs leading to Diploma / Degrees in Hotel Management.

Positive impact of JJ system :

Praveen felt that he had benefitted from his stay at the Special Home. He believed he was disciplined, had learned to read and write again after a gap of some years and also learnt two new languages, English and Hindi, which he did not know before. He believed that this learning would be very helpful for him once he left the Special Home.

Focal Points for Counseling Praveen :

The themes sought to be highlighted in Praveen's case study are disruption of education, caste and poverty, underlying psychosocial problems which created a pathway for Praveen to come into conflict with the law.

For Praveen, the main psychological points to be focused on by the counsellor are :

1. **Appreciation and positive affirmation** for Praveen's restraint at not being violent, not consuming alcohol or substances or smoking, deciding not to commit suicide and admitting to his offence and taking accountability for his actions and making the attempt to apologize to his victim and family. These are hugely positive and prosocial behaviours that must be acknowledged and appreciated and thereby reinforced in Praveen, through the process of counselling.
2. **Grief Counselling** – Counselling on coping mechanism with grief to work through his feelings of loss and allowing him to grieve for the absence of his father and mother, loss of his childhood, education, lack of love and affection from his parents. The counsellor could co-create a safe space for Praveen where he is able to be vulnerable and process his feelings of loss and grief.
3. **Reflection and motivation** - Encouraging Praveen to reflect on the reasons and situations leading to the disruption of his education, including the role played by caste and poverty, and then motivating him to pursue his dream of completing his basic education.
4. **Rehabilitation and vocational training** – Motivating Praveen to enrol for vocational training programs offered at the Special Home for Hotel Management so that he fulfils his ambition of becoming a chef, educating his brother, looking after his mother and becomes financially independent as well.

5.8.4 CASE 2 - SANDESH

"My mother never gave up on me. And then she died."

Basic demographic profile

Sandesh was 17 years old when he came to the Special Home where he has spent the last one year. He was 18 years when interviewed. Sandesh belonged to a poor family, where his father was unemployed and in jail and mother was dead, leaving the family with almost no family income. Some months they managed to scrape by with a family income of approximately Rs. 5,000/- a month.

Sandesh had studied till the 6th standard and then dropped out of school. He was struggling with his studies in his school, when his friends, many of whom were older adults, encouraged him to try different kinds of substances, including cigarettes and alcohol and he stopped going to school and preferred spending time with them.

Legal profile

Sandesh was charged and found guilty under Section 380 of the Indian Penal Code for Theft in a dwelling house. This is a serious, cognizable and non-bailable offence under the law. Cognizable offences are those in which the police can arrest without any warrant. These are more serious in nature. Non-cognizable offences on the other hand are those for which a police officer has no authority to arrest, unless with a warrant. Sandesh did not have any previous history of crime and this was the first time he had come into conflict with the law. Sandesh's father and brother were in jail for other offences.

Social profile

Sandesh father, Gowrappa, was in jail and mother Sharada was dead. Both used to work as coolies for a meagre daily wage. Sandesh father, Gowrappa, used to be mostly unemployed and only occasionally go to work before he got incarcerated. His mother, Sharada, died a few months after Sandesh was placed in custodial care. It was his mother who worked odd jobs and earned some money. Sandesh has an older brother and a younger brother. **Sandesh's father and older brother were in jail** at the time of the interview.

Sandesh described his father as an alcoholic, who would get into regular and violent fights with his mother and beat Sandesh and his siblings. Sandesh's father would not go to work and forced his mother to work and earn money to run the household. Sandesh's father also got into violent fights with neighbours and people in the community. According to Sandesh, one of their neighbours even committed suicide because of problems with his father.

Sandesh's **mother died after he came into conflict with the law** and Sandesh grieved for her intensely. Sandesh's mother came to the police station where he was detained and also visited the Observation Home at least 30 times just to assure him that she was trying her best to get him out on bail. He had fond memories of his mother and said she treated all her three children equally and died out of stress and worry about him and his brother who was also in jail.

Sandesh talked about the extreme poverty faced by his family due to his **father's unemployment, alcoholism and quarrelsome behavior.** He also felt that this caused the ill health of all the family members, as result of which, the family went hungry for many days and did not have many of their basic needs met. His mother was the only source of hope and affection for Sandesh and his brothers.

Health profile

Sandesh had fallen down from a tree when he was around 12-13 years old and had a spinal dislocation for which he was hospitalized for around a month and was on total bed rest. Incidentally, this was also the time that he was not attending school regularly and he used this as an excuse to stop going to school altogether.

Sandesh's **father used to hit his wife and children** with sticks, belt, mudde kol (stick used to mix ragi)**. Sandesh also used to hit others**, especially the boys in his area, when they used to talk badly about him and his family. Sandesh also used to slap and kick his dad when he used to hit his mother.

Sandesh had a **history of smoking** (cigarettes, beedi), alcohol (local arrack, beer, rum, vodka) **and substance addiction** (ganja and solution.) He was introduced to all these habits by his friends, many of whom were many years older to him and friends of his older brother. He also felt grown up spending time with these older boys. He felt as if his mind was free, relaxed and in a fantasy world when he was high and intoxicated.

Current Mental Health Status

Sandesh tried to commit suicide once after a violent outburst from his father, but his mother saved him. He again, **often thought of committing suicide** while in police custody but his mother kept coming to see him every single day and giving him hope. Sandesh and both his brothers suffer from what he described as 'devva fits' (dissociative episodes ?) frequently - every few months. During these 'fits', Sandesh and his brothers used to talk in strange voices, feel as if their bodies were floating in a fantasy world with no connection to their bodies and behave strangely and act like a different person altogether.

Experience with police

Sandesh was kept in police custody for 3 days and beaten on his back, hands, legs and face, even though he admitted right from the beginning that he had committed the offence. His mother tried to plead with them to let him go but the police refused to relent. Sandesh believed that if his mother had been able to pay some money to the police, perhaps he may have been released. After 3 days, he was taken to the OH, where his mother would come to visit him regularly. He described his experience with the police as one filled with fear.

Experience of Counsellor and counselling

Sandesh was thankful to the counsellor at the Special Home who encouraged him to read and write. However, he also felt that she was too focused on discussing only his past and not helping him move forward or plan his future. His expectation of a counsellor was that she should treat him like a parent – that is with love and not with threats. He was annoyed when he was told, "If you tell this, I'll include good things about you in my report to JJB". He felt he should be allowed to be truthful and not forced to confess. He also felt that the counsellor's **excessive focus on his offence** kept reminding him of his painful past which he wanted to forget.

Remorse and empathy for victim

Sandesh prided himself on being a very self-aware person. He felt that he must take the responsibility for his own reformation by first acknowledging all the crimes that he had committed – including the ones for which he had not been caught or punished by the law. He owned up that he had indulged in small thefts in the past for which he had not been caught. He also admitted that not being caught by the police did not mean that he had not done it. Sandesh insisted that he had to change his life on his own, and that he did not have anyone who could help or support him in his reformation and rehabilitation.

Sandesh felt a deep sense of guilt over his brother being in jail and his mother's death. He felt that he was the reason for his brother going to jail and that his mother died worrying about her sons and their future. He felt a sense of deep loss that he had lost all his friends due to coming in to conflict with the law as no one wanted to associate with him anymore.

Sandesh was willing **and eager to ask forgiveness** as well as **make material amends to the victim** by paying back twice the value of what he robbed from the victim. He was willing to continue apologizing and seeking forgiveness from the victim for the rest of his life as he felt that they may not be ready to forgive him in the first attempt.

Adverse Childhood Experiences

Sandesh scored a total of **18 out of 20** adverse childhood experiences. The list of adverse childhood experiences undergone by Sandesh include :

Poverty, disruption in education, death of parent (mother), neglect, lack of parental involvement and poor family relationship, family history of poor health, child's history of prolonged illness/hospitalization, family history of alcoholism, child's history of substance abuse, family history of attempted suicide, family history of mental illness, child's history of attempted suicide, exposure to violence in the family, violence towards child, violence by police, involvement of family with justice system (family member convicted or in jail) , incarceration of child, contact of child with justice system.

Scope for Reform, Rehabilitation and Restoration

Sandesh can dance, do mimicry and believed he is skilled enough to join a circus. He also felt he was humble and could work hard. He believed that his mother never gave up on him and cared for him right till the end of her life. Her faith in him gave him the strength to keep trying to reform himself and be a better person. Sandesh wanted to join a dance academy, but he did not have the financial support he needed in order to learn dance.

Positive impact of JJ system :

Sandesh shared that he never used to listen to anybody, but after coming into the JJ system, he had now learnt to listen, to respect others and to understand other people's pain because of what he had himself gone through.

Focus Points for Counseling Sandesh:

The themes sought to be highlighted in Sandesh case study are loss of the mother – who was the sole and central figure of support, family's involvement with the justice system, violence at home, poor family health which created the environment which most likely brought Sandesh into conflict with the law.

For Sandesh, the main psychological points to be focused on by the counsellor are:

1. **Grief Counselling** – Sandesh was in deep grief over the death of his mother as well as his brother being in jail. He felt guilty that he was responsible for both these tragic life events. Counselling must focus on helping him process both his grief and his guilt.
2. **Referral for psychiatric evaluation –** The counsellor must consider referring Sandesh for psychiatric evaluation as two significant factors – history of substance addiction and

suspected dissociative episodes which may be indicative of underlying mental illness, must be further investigated.

3. **Restorative approaches** - The counselling process must leverage Sandesh's self-awareness and willingness to reform as indicated in his readiness to admit all the other earlier offences and misdoings for which he had not been caught. Sandesh was also eager to make amends for his behavior towards his victims and restorative practices which encourage seeking an apology from the victim or offering to take corrective action to make amends for the harm caused, must be explored as part of the counselling process.
4. **Strengths – based counselling** focusing on his physical skills (dance), desire to be a responsible citizen and live up to his mother's expectations must be further reinforced through the counselling process.

5.8.5 CASE 3 - SAIF KHAN

"It doesn't cost money to give love to your children - even if it costs money to give them food."

Basic demographic profile

Saif Khan was 17 years when he came to the Special Home a year ago and 18 years when interviewed. Saif belongs to an extremely poor family struggling to make ends meet. Saif has no education. Although he was very excited about going to school, just a few weeks into school, he got into a fight with some children at school. As a punishment, his parents sent him to work as a child labourer in an almirah factory. He was only 5 years old at that time. He then went on to work in different places for small sums of money. When he was a little older, he was sent to work in a meat shop. So instead of learning to read and write and feeling proud of it, Saif grew up learning to butcher animals and saying proudly that he could butcher a cow all by himself. Saif often wondered if that was something to be proud of – knowing to kill someone or something ? As he put it, "I wanted to go to school but ended up learning how to butcher a cow" Saif's father was an auto driver and mother was a domestic help. Saif's father did not contribute to the family income. Saif's family income was less than Rs. 5,000/- per month.

Legal profile

Saif was charged and found guilty under Section 302 of the Indian Penal Code for murder. This is a heinous, cognizable and non-bailable offence under the law. Cognizable offences are those in which the police can arrest without any warrant. These are more serious in nature. Non-cognizable offences on the other hand are those for which a police officer has no authority to arrest, unless with a warrant. Saif did not have any previous history of crime and this is the first time he has come into conflict with the law.

Social profile

Saif's father, Allah Baksh, was an auto driver who remarried and abandoned his family. He did not contribute anything financially or socially to the family. Saif believed that his **father and their poverty were the main causes** for all the problems in his family. Saif longed for the affection of his father which he never got. As he put it, "It doesn't cost money to give love to your children - even if it costs money to give them food. Fathers should know this and not use poverty as an excuse to abandon the family."

Saif was one of five children. He had an older brother, a young sister, and two younger brothers. Saif's mother, Dilsha, worked as a domestic help and struggled to raise her many children. She and Saif's older brother were in jail (at the time of interviewing) in connection with the same offence, one younger brother was in a Madrassa (an Islamic religious school) and another younger brother lived in a neighbour's house. His younger sister was disabled (suffered from polio) and at the time of interviewing, she was missing with her whereabouts not known since **almost all his family members were incarcerated.**

Saif was angry about his father abandoning his family and believed that he should not have had so many children if he could not take care of them. Saif also felts helpless that there was no one to help him or his mother. He was able to see the **struggles she went through as a single parent** with so many children. He broke down several times during the interview while talking about his mother and sister. He worried about his sister and that someone may be abusing her, given her disability and the unsafe neighbourhood in which they lived. He was **angry, sad and afraid at the same time** about how vulnerable his mother and sister were – both physically and sexually, from predatory men in the neighbourhood.

Saif had faced **severe parental neglect** from his father with most basic needs also being often not fulfilled. He felt that his father was indifferent towards them and used his poverty as an excuse to not care for them. His mother, on the other hand, was experienced by him as loving despite their poverty and her poor health. She struggled to take care of all of her children despite her husband abandoning them. Despite receiving little affection or parenting, Saif stated that he was very emotionally attached to his family.

Health profile

Saif was admitted to NIMHANS for 3 days, when he was around 6-7 years old, after he was hit by a hammer on his head during a fight in his home. Saif's father used to hit his mother and all his children with belt as well as other household objects. Saif had also experienced violence from neighbours and adults on several occasions. Saif also punched and broke the teeth of his neighbour who used to sexually trouble his mother. "Yes I violently attacked the man who sexually troubled my mother," admitted Saif. Unable to bear the constant stress and conflicts, his **mother had tried to commit suicide many times**.

Saif had a **history of substance addiction**. He smoked cigarettes daily and took marijuana twice or thrice a week. Saif recollected feeling high and then tired and again to have some energy, he would use marijuana again. He felt he needed that kind of energy to be able to do his job as a butcher, which he described as physically as well as emotionally hard and exhausting.

Current Mental Health Status

Saif's mother had tried to commit suicide many times. He also **planned to commit suicide many times** but could not succeed. Saif even ran away from the Observation Home for 3 months and decided to kill himself. Then he thought about his sister and went and surrendered himself. He was conflicted between ending his life and staying alive to take care of his mother and sister.

Coming into conflict with the law

Saif was asked by one of his friends (an adult) to accompany him to a neighbourhood area where they had a fight planned with another gang. Saif went along as this friend had helped him many times in the past with small amounts of money. The members of the other gang were also known to Saif and during the fight one of the men whom they attacked got severely injured and later died in hospital. The person who died was also a friend of Saif's.

Experience with police

Saif and his family members had been harassed so many times by the police over the years that Saif said he did not really care anymore. He was convinced that there was no use saying anything as he would not be believed. From the time he was young child, he had seen the police take his family members and people from his neighbourhood, all Muslims, to the station and being tortured with all kinds of cases foisted on them. Though he admitted that he was very scared when he was taken to the police station after the incident, he did not think it would end up as a murder case. He assumed that they would get beaten up soundly by the police and sent home. He described his experience with the police as a combination of fear and helplessness.

Experience of Counsellor and counselling

Saif's lawyer had told him not to confess, but sister (a nun who is a counsellor at the SH) told him to speak the truth and assured him that she would stand by him if he spoke the truth. Saif did not receive any counselling while at the OH and stated that he did not even know that there was a counsellor at the OH. It was only when he came to the SH that he learned that there was a counsellor whom he could speak to. Saif believed that a counsellor should smile, talk kindly and encourage the children in custodial settings. Saif was also grateful to the superintendent of the Special Home who played the role that the counsellor should have played. The superintendent persuaded and arranged for Saif's uncle (father's brother) to meet him at the SH and this united him with his family again. He had been feeling very despondent thinking about how his family members were all scattered, some in jail, one in a madarassa, one at the mercy of neighbours, one whose whereabouts were unknown and he, himself also in custody. However, this meeting with his uncle gave Saif a lot of hope and he wanted to live again for the sake of his mother and sister.

Remorse and empathy for victim

Saif felt a great sense of guilt about the harm his actions had caused to the victim's family. The victim's sister's marriage was fixed and due in 3 months. Saif wanted to give some money for her wedding but he was certain that she (victim) would not accept anything from a person who had killed her brother. Saif said he cried inside all the time thinking about the murder and kept asking himself, 'how could I kill my own friend?' He repeatedly kept thinking about how he had not thought that a person's life could be lost in a fight.

Saif stated that his strengths are that he knows to cook biryani and butcher a cow all by himself. Saif said he was keen to change and give up his bad habits but wanted support and encouragement and believed that the Superintendent of the SH and his mother could help him become a better person.

Adverse Childhood Experiences

Saif scored a total of **18 out of 20** adverse childhood experiences. The list of adverse childhood experiences undergone by Saif include:

Poverty, disruption in education, separation of parents (abandonment of mother and family by father), neglect, lack of parental involvement and poor family relationship, family history of poor health, child's history of prolonged illness/hospitalization, family history of alcoholism, child's history of substance abuse, family history of attempted suicide, family history of mental illness, child's history of attempted suicide, exposure to violence in the family, violence towards child, violence by police, involvement of family with justice system (family member convicted or in jail) , incarceration of child, contact of child with justice system.

Scope for Reform, Rehabilitation and Restoration

Saif wanted to join the traffic police. But first, he wanted to search his sister and bring his family together again. He wanted help to access his mother and brother in jail and wanted to bring them out of jail on bail first. He wanted to find his sister and ensure that she was safe and taken care of. Saif's goal was to see his family together, safe and happy.

Positive Impact of JJ System

Saif believed that he had changed a lot over the last one year. He had given up drugs and learnt to control his anger. He struggled with both for a long time. He had learnt to talk with respect and help others.

Focus Points for Counselling Saif :

The themes sought to be highlighted in Saif's case study are the all-pervasive nature of violence at home and his neighbourhood, substance abuse, high risk of suicide, parental neglect and conflicts which created the environment which most likely brought Saif into conflict with the law.

For Saif, the main psychological points to be focused on by the counsellor are:

1. **Crisis Intervention for suicide and referral for psychiatric evaluation** - Given the combination of volatile risk factors in Saif's history - substance abuse, attempted suicide of self and mother, distress about separation from family and anxiety about their safety, whereabouts and wellbeing, Saif would be at high risk for suicide, depression and self-harm and hence , crisis intervention for the same would be the first and immediate counselling intervention for Saif. The counsellor could facilitate a visit to his mother in jail

which could also contribute to alleviating his anxiety to some extent. A referral for psychiatric evaluation might also be helpful for Saif given his history of addiction and self-harming behaviours.

2. **Reflection and reassessment of his life situation** - Saif believed that his father and poverty were the main reasons for all his problems. The counselling process must enable him to become aware that while he cannot have control over either his father's behaviour or his family's poverty, he could learn to gain control over his own behaviours.
3. **Identifying and understanding emotions and learning emotional regulation** - Saif suffered a lot of guilt about killing his friend. Enabling his to process his feelings of guilt, loss and shame over the death of his friend would need to be a key focus of the counselling process.
4. **Learning non-violent coping mechanisms** - Saif had exposure to severe violence at home and neighbourhood at a very young age. Encouraging him to access life skills relating to how to use non-violent communication, conflict resolution and coping mechanisms would form part of the counselling focus.

5.8.6 CASE 4 - BABU

"Someone has to pay the price for crimes by kinfolk – I am that someone"

Basic demographic profile

Babu was 17 years old when came to the SH. He had been at the SH for 6 months and was 18 years at the time of being interviewed. Babu was studying in 10th standard when he was forced to leave school. He belongs to a poor family and his family's income is approximately around 10,000/- per month (which he used to earn by working as a construction labourer. Babu is the sole earning member in his family, as his father is dead, mother is mentally ill and his two sisters do not go to work.) He was forced to give up his studies and go for work due to his **father's death, mother's illness** and lack of employment opportunities in his home state of Bihar.

Legal profile

Babu was charged and found guilty under Section 380 of the Indian Penal Code for Theft in a dwelling house. This is a serious, cognizable and non-bail able offence under the law. Cognizable offences are those in which the police can arrest without any warrant. These are more serious in nature. Non-cognizable offences on the other hand are those for which a police officer has no authority to arrest, unless with a warrant. Babu does not have any previous history of crime and this is the first time he has come into conflict with the law.

Social profile

Babu's father, (Late) Babulal Sharma was a coolie and his mother, also used to occasionally work as a coolie till some years ago. But ever since she fell ill, she is unable to work. Babu's **father was an alcoholic** who picked up fights at home and did not help in solving any of the family's problems. His **mother is alcoholic as well as mentally ill** and hence unable to work regularly or consistently. Babu's mother would often scold him and his siblings very harshly. Both his parents were alcoholic and Babu grew up being used to beatings, hunger and fights at his home. Babu has 2 sisters and he felt that their mother was not available to look after them, while their father did not care. Babu felt that he was forced to grow up much before his age and take on the responsibilities of his family. He was good at his studies and school was a place he could escape to from the problems of his home. But he learnt to adjust with the situation at his work place, living with adult men and their families and focusing on the work given to him. Though, he often sat alone and cried thinking about his broken family.

Health profile

Babu was hospitalized for a week as a young child for a fracture which was his first experience of hospitalization. His mother, who is alcoholic as well as mentally ill was **hospitalized for depression**. But the family could not sustain her treatment financially and she returned home. Babu would smoke occasionally (maybe weekly once) when he felt stressed. It made him feel grown up and accepted by the adult men who worked with him on the construction site. Babu's father used to hit his mother and all his children with firewood, sticks etc. and Babu also learnt to hit and kick other boys in his area during fights. When asked about his father's health habits, Babu's question was, " Do only poor people become violent after drinking? Do rich people still behave decently even if they are drunk? This question has always troubled me so I want to know."

Current Mental Health Status

Babu **tried to commit suicide many times** over the years, but according him, there was always some problem or the other going on in his house and he would get distracted and give up. Once his mother had a heart attack, then she had a kidney failure, another time she was hospitalized for trying to commit suicide, etc. and Babu got busy trying to cope with the problems and forgot about committing suicide.

Coming into conflict with the law

Babu appears to be confused about whether he is guilty or not with regard to the incident that brought him into conflict with the law. Babu had been staying with a group of adult men and their families in a shack and they would go for any construction work as and when they found work. These men and families are all from his village or nearby places in Bihar and most of them have learnt to speak Kannada though not too well. According to Shiv, there was some argument over payment by some local construction contractor for the work done by this group of laborers. Repeated requests by the laborers had not been heeded to, so they went to the office of the contractor to ask for their pending dues. But soon things got heated and the argument turned into a fight and some things in the contractor's office were damaged. Later in the evening, the contractor and a group of men came to the shack where Babu lived and beat up everyone, threw out their things and threatened that they would have them sent back to Bihar. They also said that they had filed a case with the local police that these laborers had stolen and damaged things from the contractor's office / construction site. Over the next two days, many of the adults from Babu's shack told Babu that he had to take the blame of the theft / damages and that he would have to go to jail otherwise they would all lose their jobs and be sent back to Bihar to die out of starvation and poverty. They also assured him that it would be only for a short duration as he was below 18 years while they were all adults and could end up for years in jail. Initially Babu was very afraid and refused but after 2 days he felt he had no other option. He knew there was no one either in Karnataka or in Bihar who would or could help him. He requested that his mother and sisters should be sent some money till he returned from jail. His elders then took him to the station and surrendered him admitting that he had broken into the office and stolen the office items.

Experience with police

Babu was handed over to the police by some of the adult men from his village with whom he had been staying. They told him that he must 'confess' that he had broken and stolen some things in the contractor's office, which Babu did. Babu says that the police kept him the in the station for 3 days during which time some negotiations were going on between the police, the contractor and his co-workers. He is not sure whether there was any money exchanged but after 3 days, he was remanded to custody at the OH. He describes his experience with the police as one of shame and humiliation.

Experience of counsellor and counselling

Language was a huge barrier for Babu as he does not speak or understand Kannada. He felt emotionally isolated from everyone around him as he could not understand what others were saying not could he make himself understood. He felt that it is was really important to have at least few staff members at child care institutions who could speak multiple languages. When asked why he did not confide in anyone about what had really happened, he replied that , "No one asked and no one would have believed me, so I just kept quiet".

Counselling sessions were not happy times for Babu as he felt that the counsellor was discriminating against him. She could not speak in Hindi and so would not include him in any group activities. Even though Babu can understand and speak a little bit of English which the counsellor also knew, she showed very little interest in sessions with him. He felt angry and frustrated as the counsellor pointed out his faults in every session and this made him shut down further. Babu feels that a counsellor should help to cheer the child up and focus on the future not only on the past and on his mistakes.

Remorse and empathy for the victim

Babu felt a sense of great guilt and repeatedly says that he has brought shame and humiliation to his family. He often wonders whether he did the right thing by admitting to the offence. At the same time, he also feels that there was no other way to 'save' or protect his community people from the wrath of the locals. Babu has not revealed any of these details to anyone and feels it is best that he quietly completes his term and goes back to work. He also is very confused about what to do next.

Adverse Childhood Experiences

Babu scored a total of **17 out of 20** adverse childhood experiences. The list of adverse childhood experiences undergone by Babu include :

Poverty, disruption in education, death of a parent (father), neglect, lack of parental involvement and poor family relationship, family history of poor health, child's history of prolonged illness/hospitalization, family history of alcoholism, child's history of substance abuse, family history of attempted suicide, family history of mental illness, child's history of attempted suicide, exposure to violence in the family, violence towards child, violence by police, incarceration of child, contact of child with justice system.

Scope for Reform, Rehabilitation and Restoration

Babu repeatedly said he would not repeat his mistakes again but still seems unsure of what exactly is the mistake he has committed. Babu describes himself as a reflective person who thinks a lot about his life, choices, and his feelings but felt unable to think about his future as his mind is fully occupied worrying about the fate of his mother and sisters. Babu can also sing, read and write well and was good at his studies. He just wants to get back to work, earn money so that he can support his mother and sisters. His immediate goal is to get his mother treated and he believes that the Superintendent of the SH could help him with that.

Positive impact of JJ System :

Babu believes that his stay away from home as well as at the Special Home has taught him about the different types of difficulties faced by children from many different backgrounds and even helped him to handle difficult situations to some extent.

Focus Points for Counseling Babu:

The themes sought to be highlighted in Babu's case study are broken family, poor family health, violence, suicide, coercion on children to accept crimes they have not committed which created the environment which most likely brought Babu into conflict with the law.

For Babu, the main psychological points to be focused on by the counsellor are:

1. **Mental Health Assessment** : The counsellor must refer Babu for a detailed mental health assessment to assess depression and other mental health problems, given his mother's history of depression as well as multiple attempts to commit suicide.
2. **Referral of Babu's family for counselling, medical and other rehabilitative services.** His mother needs medical treatment as well as mental health assessment. The counsellor is empowered to make recommendations to refer families of children in conflict with the law for such services, which could be made as part of orders by the JJB.
3. **Focus on individual goals and self-discovery** - As the sole earning member of his large family shouldering all the financial responsibilities, Babu appears to be weighed down under the burden of several adult responsibilities. The counselling process must encourage and enable him to explore his own ambitions as well and help his resume his studies as he was academically good.

4. **Life skills – especially assertiveness and communication**. The counselor must enable Babu to communicate his feelings and his expectations clearly and assertively. His experiences of being bullied into submission, coerced into complying with decisions made by others run the risk of becoming a pattern of behavior, which must be dismantled through the counseling process.
5. **Restorative approaches** – There is a need for the adults involved in this case to apologize to Babu and offer some restitution. The counseling process must explore restorative approaches which could make this possible.

5.8.7 CASE 5 - MADHAV

"I don't know what I have confessed to"

Basic demographic profile

Madhav was 15 years old and had been staying at the Observation Home for 3 months, when he was interviewed. Madhav had studied up to the 2nd standard. He loved going to school. Both his parents were unemployed and he was forced to drop out of school and look for work from the age of 6 years. He did not have a family or family income. **Both his parents were dead**. He worked for a tent-house owner, who rented tents and furniture for small events. He was given the food served at these events / functions and paid around Rs. 50/- or Rs. 100 / - for each event. According to Madhav, his employer was a kind person who gave him food from time to time.

Legal profile

Madhav was charged under Section 457 and 380 of the Indian Penal Code for Theft in a dwelling house. This is a serious, cognizable and non-bail able offence under the law. Cognizable offences are those in which the police can arrest without any warrant. These are more serious in nature. Non-cognizable offences on the other hand are those for which a police officer has no authority to arrest, unless with a warrant. Madhav did not have any previous history of crime and this was the first time he had come into conflict with the law. There was **no one in Madhav's family to engage a lawyer** for him.

Social profile

Madhav's parents were both dead. His father, Boppana and mother Devika were both unemployed even whilst alive and not earning anything and hence the family lived in abject poverty. Madhav's **mother died by committing suicide** when he was 3 years old and his sister who was a small baby at that time was given away to an orphanage by his relatives. His **father remarried shortly and abandoned** the family. Madhav was then forced to drop out of school (from class 2) and start looking for work in order to survive. Madhav did not have food or clothes most of the time and did not have anyone to look after him even when he fell sick. He did not remember any affection from his parents. Madhav's father used to hit him and his mother. After he remarried, his step-mother also used to drink and frequently quarrel over lack of money. Madhav's father fought with his employer, who was a mason and killed him with a stone - for which he went to jail. Madhav lived his with maternal grandmother who suffered from diabetes and was immobile as she had severe gangrene –related wounds on her legs and feet. Madhav gave her whatever money he earned.

Health profile

Madhav had never seen a doctor in his life though he had fallen ill many times. No one had ever taken him to a doctor or hospital and he would just recover on his own. His father died when he was 13 years old and his mother died when he was 3 years old. His father remarried and his step mother also used to drink. His **father spent a few years in jail** for a murder and when he returned his health was really bad. He was diagnosed with blood cancer at St. John's hospital and died to lack of treatment. Madhav's mother committed suicide when he was 3 years old by pouring kerosene on her body and setting herself on fire in front of his eyes. Madhav did not smoke, consume alcohol or any other substances.

Current Mental Health Status

Madhav **tried to hang himself** when his father died. He used to have terrible **nightmares**. He could not forget his mother's burning body which keeps flashing before his eyes. His father used to hit his step mother and sent her also away, otherwise Madhav often felt that perhaps she might have at least been there for him in his times of distress. Madhav used to get more hours of the sleep at the OH but could not fall asleep. All the old nightmares kept flashing before his eyes and he just could not fall asleep. Madhav recalled that his father vomited blood and died and that his mother burnt herself and died and often **kept questioning himself as to why he was still alive.**

Coming into conflict with the law

Madhav was quite confused about why he had been placed at the OH. He had collected his wages (Approx Rs. 200/-) from his employer and was walking back home when the police apprehended him and asked him to accompany them to the station. They asked him where he got the money from and did not believe him when he said it was his wages for the work done for putting up a pandal (temporary tent) for a funeral.

Experience with police

Madhav's experience with the police was very traumatic. The police also beat him continuously for 4 days. They put chilly powder in his eyes and gave him electric shocks in his private parts. Madhav stated that the only thought in his head was , ' How much are they going to hit me? And "Will they ever stop hitting me?" They hit him so much that he kept fainting. Finally he just said yes. He didn't know what he had confessed to.

Madhav also asked the researcher if she could tell him why the police had arrested and brought him to the OH. He felt scared to ask anyone. The police told him that if he confessed he would get out soon, so he said yes. He thought he had said yes to stealing, but he was afraid that he may have confessed to murder. The police also told him that they would prove that he was a murderer just like his father and that everyone would believe it. Madhav broke down and wept and said that he had not killed anybody and that he hoped that at least the researcher believed that he was innocent.

Experience of counselor and counseling

Madhav had no idea of who or what is a counselor and stated that he had never met one in his life. He was completely unaware about any information related to the counselor at the OH and said he had no idea of what should be the qualities of a counselor as he had not met any such person in his life and hence was unable to even imagine why any adult would want to sit and talk or listen to him about his life.

Remorse and empathy for victim

Madhav had no idea about who are the victims. He was unaware of what charges have been filed against him and believed it is murder or some other 'dodda crime' (big offence).

Adverse Childhood Experiences

Madhav scored a total of **17 out of 20** adverse childhood experiences. The list of adverse childhood experiences undergone by Madhav include :

Poverty, disruption in education, separation of parents (abandonment of mother and family by father), neglect, lack of parental involvement and poor family relationship, family history of poor health, child's history of prolonged illness/hospitalization, family history of alcoholism, family history of attempted suicide, family history of mental illness, child's history of attempted suicide, exposure to violence in the family, violence towards child, violence by police, involvement of family with justice system (family member convicted or in jail), incarceration of child, contact of child with justice system.

Scope for reform, rehabilitation and restoration

Madhav is confused about what to do next. He wants to try to get a job or go back to him his employer Anwar who was a tent house owner and ask for a job. But he was not sure whether he would be taken back now that he had been to the police station and 'jail'. He did not know who could or would help him. Madhav believed that he was hardworking and that his two greatest skills were that he could fix a puncture and put up a pandal anywhere. Madhav did not have anyone who cared for him. The only kind adult in his life was his employer who fed him occasionally but Madhav hinted that he feared he would be asked for sexual favors in return. Madhav wanted to take care of his sister and make her study well. She was studying 9th standard and staying at a hostel in Marathalli. Madhav believed that if he worked hard, he could take care of his sister and his dream was to get her married.

Positive impact of JJ System

Madhav was unable to think of anything positive he had learnt through his contact with the juvenile justice system. He ended the interview with the question, 'Will someone help me and my sister?

Focus Points for Counselling Madhav :

The themes sought to be highlighted in Madhav's case study were no parents, neglect, suicide of mother, violence and false charges by police, which created the environment which most likely brought Madhav into conflict with the law.

For Madhav, the main psychological points to be focused on by the counselor are:

1. **Suicide intervention counselling and referral for psychiatric evaluation** : Madhav appeared to suffering from flashbacks, sleep disturbances, nightmares, suicidal thoughts, etc. post the traumatic events that he had undergone, both the violence at the hands of the police and the suicide of his mother that he had witnessed as a young child. The counsellor could refer Madhav for a detailed psychiatric evaluation.
2. **Legal Representation :** Madhav was unaware about the exact nature of the charges against him. The counsellor would need to alert the JJB about this fact through her report so that his lawyer is able to take it up before the JJB as well.
3. **Referral to Child Welfare Committee (CWC) as a "Child in Need of care and protection"** : Madhav clearly was a child in need of care and protection – as his parents were both dead, he did not have anyone to look after him and was working as a child labourer. The counsellor could make a recommendation to the JJB to declare Madhav a child in need of care and protection and refer him to the Child Welfare Committee under provisions of the JJ Act, so that he could access the rehabilitative services entitled to a child in need of care and protection under the law.
4. **Rehabilitative measures** : The Counselor must take care to prepare an Individual Care Plan highlighting the facts that Madhav was in an exploitative child labour employment, was facing physical and emotional neglect as he did not have parents, was vulnerable to abuse and violence on account of his position as a child labourer and hence could be considered for rehabilitative measures like placement with a fit person or fit facility, foster care or sponsorship for his grandmother to be able to look after him in a better manner.

5.8.8 CASE 6 - PRAMOD

" I know the pain of losing a loved one"

Background demographic profile

Pramod was 17 years old when he came to the Observation Home where he had spent the last one month and 10 days. Pramod belonged to a poor family with a family income of less than Rs. 5,000 per month. Pramod had studied till 7th standard, failed in his exams as his mother died and gave up his studies.

Legal profile

Pramod was charged and found guilty under Section 302 of the Indian Penal Code for murder. This is a heinous, cognizable and non-bailable offence under the law. Cognizable offences are those in which the police can arrest without any warrant. These are more serious in nature. Non-cognizable offences on the other hand are those for which a police officer has no authority to arrest, unless with a warrant. Pramod did not have any previous history of crime and this is the first time he is coming into conflict with the law.

Social profile

Pramod's father, Raghu was a house painter. His mother, (Late Reshma) died when he was 12 years old. She poured kerosene on herself, set herself on fire and died. His father used to drink and fight with his mother all the time and was never happy with his family. His father moved out the house when his mother died and abandoned his children, and does not support them either financially or emotionally. He wished that his father did not drink or fight with his mother and lived happily with his family. Pramod and his sister struggled to have even their basic needs met. Pramod believed that a mother should love her children a lot, should be at home and not have to work outside. He sometimes believed that maybe if his mother had loved him or his sister a little more, she may not have killed herself. After the death of his mother, his chinamma (mother's sister) took care of Pramod and his sister.

Health profile

Pramod was hospitalized when he was younger for some heart problem but he does not know the details. His **father is an alcoholic** and had both kidney and liver failure due to drinking. **Mother committed suicide** by pouring kerosene on herself and setting herself on fire. Pramod smokes daily and says it gives him relief from tension. His father was a very violent man who used to hit, beat and punch Pramod and his sister regularly. Pramod used to **watch violence** in his family frequently - stabbing with knife, hitting with grinding stone, etc. and it used to make him very afraid. Pramod continued to be scared of violence and would run away whenever there was violence. He has not hit anyone in his life and does not want to hit anyone either. He believed it was a terrible thing to hit others and stated that he had never initiated violence even though he had faced much violence in his life. He found it **ironic that a person like him who was so afraid of violence, had been charged with murder.**

Current Mental Health Status

Pramod **had cut himself many times** with a knife and blade while feeling totally frustrated. He had seen his mother and his cousin (sister) set themselves on fire and burn to death. He was haunted by the fact that his 16-year-old sister lives alone at home. She lives with another 15-year-old orphan girl and both work in a matchbox making shop. He keeps getting nightmares about her and is worried that she might be raped or killed someday.

Coming into conflict with the law

Pramod was **not sure for what he was arrested** or why he was charged with this particular crime. He was named as an accomplice by two other adults who were arrested in another case for theft. These two adults were known to Pramod, lived in his neighbourhood and Pramod admitted that he knew that they were involved in some illegal activities. However, he was quite angry with them when he found out that they had named him as a gang member.

Experience with police

The police kept Pramod in the station for 6 days. He called his chinnamma but she didn't come. The police tied his hands and hit him badly on both feet, back and forced him to confess. There were 2 more persons who were arrested for the same case. The police took 1 lakh each from them and released them. They didn't allow Pramod to sleep till he confessed. He was not sure what he said yes to, he just wanted the beating to stop. He thought he was being beaten up for being friends with anti-social elements. It was only after coming to the OH that he realized that he had been charged with murder. Pramod was terrified and felt that he needed to hide from the police as they would come after him the moment he was released on bail.

Experience of counsellor and counselling

Pramod felt that the counsellor should encourage children to speak the truth and not automatically assume that every child who comes to the OH is a criminal or is guilty. The counsellor at the OH never really talked or listened to Pramod . She directly asked Pramod , 'Yenney madditthu?" (meaning - what crime have you committed?). "I didn't do anything, so I didn't know what to say and I never spoke to her again" says Pramod . "She could have at least asked me Yennu aithu? (meaning - what happened). If only she had asked me I would have told her that the police kept me in the station for 6 days and told her the truth about my life."

Remorse and empathy for victim

Pramod had feels a deep sense of sorrow that the victim (who was also the son of someone) died, but he kept wondering why the police chose him to put the blame of the murder. He was not able to understand it. He stated that he would like to be a son to the victim's parents. He wanted to tell the victim's family that he had not done anything and that he was not involved in their son's death in any way. He said that he knew the pain of losing a loved one - and wished he could do something to help them understand.

Adverse Childhood Experiences

Pramod scored a total of **17 out of 20** adverse childhood experiences. The list of adverse childhood experiences undergone by Pramod include :

Poverty, disruption in education, death of a parent (mother), neglect, lack of parental involvement and poor family relationship, family history of poor health, child's history of prolonged illness/hospitalization, family history of alcoholism, child's history of substance abuse, family history of attempted suicide, family history of mental illness, child's history of attempted suicide, exposure to violence in the family, violence towards child, violence by police, involvement of family with justice system (family member convicted or in jail) , incarceration of child, contact of child with justice system.

Scope for Reform, Rehabilitation and Restoration

Pramod was unable to think of anything good or positive about him or his life at present. Pramod believed that his strengths were his chinnamma and his sister. He did not swear or use bad language and did not initiate violence even though he had faced much violence in his life. Pramod wanted to get a job and go back to work. He used to work in a painting shop and believed that a former colleague might help him find a job again. He wanted to make sure his sister was safe.

Positive Impact of the JJ system

Pramod 's stay at the OH had taught him to be careful about friendships, to focus on his work and to respect elders. He had never spoken about his mother's death to anyone as it made him feel scared and ashamed as she had committed suicide. Being able to talk about his mother and her death to the researcher was stated as a huge relief by Pramod who said he was 12 years old when his mother died.

Focus Points for Counseling Pramod :

The themes sought to be highlighted in Pramod 's case study were witnessing suicide of mother, physical and emotional neglect, violence and false charges by police, suicidal thoughts and self-harm, violence at home which created the environment which most likely brought Pramod into conflict with the law.

For Pramod , the main psychological points to be focused on by the counselor are:

1. **Referral for psychiatric evaluation**: Pramod's witnessing of the suicide of his mother and not having talked about her death to anyone for more than 3 years was a serious concern that needed to be addressed immediately, also given that he appeared to be suffering from flashbacks, sleep disturbances, nightmares, suicidal thoughts, etc. post the traumatic events that he had undergone, both the violence at the hands of the police and the suicide of his mother that he had witnessed as a young child. The counsellor could refer for a detailed psychiatric evaluation.
2. **Legal Representation:** Pramod was unaware about the exact nature of the charges against him. The counsellor would need to alert the JJB about this fact through her report so that his lawyer is able to take it up before the JJB as well.
3. **Referral for educational services :** The counsellor must put forth in her counsellor's report to the JJB that both Pramod and his 16 year old sister are "children in need of care and protection" – as their mother was dead, father had abandoned them, they were homeless and at risk of further abuse and violence. The counsellor could make a recommendation to the JJB to declare Pramod and his sister as "children in need of care and protection" and refer him to the Child Welfare Committee under provisions of the JJ Act, so that they could access the rehabilitative services entitled to children in need of care and protection under the law, like exploring education for both the children in a residential educational institution.
4. **Intensive Counselling to address suicide and self-harm :** Pramod 's risk of suicide was considerably higher as there are two completed suicide in his family (mother and cousin) and the chronic stress he appeared to be suffering from on account of the violence he had seen and undergone. The counsellor also would need to support Pramod understand and cope with his feelings of victimhood.

5. **Life skills training –** The counsellor would need to recommend Pramod for life skills training especially in areas of how to cope with violent situations, assertiveness and communicate his feelings. Identifying safe, positive adults who could support him in coping with his distress over the violence in his life would be an important task that the counsellor could support Pramod with.

5.8.9 CASE 7 – PRAKASH

"I thought it was like collecting firewood for our household"

Basic demographic profile

Prakash was 17 years old and had been at the OH only for 24 days at the time of interviewing. He was studying in 1st PUC and his education had been disrupted as he had come into conflict with the law. Prakash was also working in a brick kiln and earning around 12,000/- per month. He was the sole earning member in his family.

Legal profile

Prakash was charged under Section 390 and 392 of the Indian Penal Code for robbery. This is a heinous, cognizable and non-bail able offence under the law. Cognizable offences are those in which the police can arrest without any warrant. These are more serious in nature. Non-cognizable offences on the other hand, are those for which a police officer has no authority to arrest, unless with a warrant. He did not have any previous history of crime and this was the first time he was coming into conflict with the law. Sandalwood smuggling is considered a serious offence under the Indian law.

Social profile

Prakash did not know much about his parents as he and his brother were abandoned by their parents at a young age. The occupation of both his father, Mani and mother Muniamma were not known to him. Prakash also **did not know whether both his parents were alive or dead**. Prakash's father was an alcoholic who had abandoned him when he was around 4-5 years old. Prakash often wished that his father would not drink, would be affectionate towards and him and have a job. His mother married someone else after his father left them and she too abandoned Prakash and his younger brother. Prakash often wished that at least she had not abandoned her children. Prakash and his younger brother were looked after by his grandmother who was very harsh with them and often starved and beat them. She sent Prakash to work at a nearby brick kiln in their village when he was around 10 years old and he had got used to working and studying side by side. Prakash was not able to attend classes regularly due to his work and household chores but he wrote all his exams without fail and had managed to pass all these years. Prakash was keen on studying even though he was not very good academically. He had been paying for his own education and that of his brother, who was a few years younger than him.

Health profile

Prakash stated that he had fallen sick many times but had never been taken to a doctor. Once he even fell down from a tree and was seriously sick and almost died, but he was still not taken to a doctor. Both his parents had tuberculosis and his father was severely alcoholic. Prakash was told about this by his grandmother who used to talk about his parents sometimes. Prakash did not smoke or drink. Prakash did not know whether his parents were violent with each other. But his grandmother used to beat both Prakash and his brother very violently with a stick. She used to curse them and their parents while beating them and often wished them dead.

Current Mental Health Status and Risks / hazards

Prakash felt like killing himself the first few days when he came to the OH. His grandparents were not aware or informed that he was at the OH and only a distant uncle knew about his coming into conflict with the law. But still Prakash repeatedly wondered why his grandparents did not even bother to find out what had happened to him as he had not gone home for so many days. It made him think that would no one even miss him even if he just disappeared or died someday. He recalled trying to kill himself once before when his grandmother had beaten him very badly. His grandmother's sister's son who used to live with them committed suicide in front of Prakash and that used to keep flashing before his eyes too. But he also thought that, "If I die, my younger brother will have no one and will become an orphan. I am all that he has, so I have to live for his sake and take care of him."

Coming into conflict with the law

Prakash had gone with a few men from his village to collect firewood from a nearby 'thota' (garden / orchard). This was a regular activity that he had been used to since childhood. On the day of the incident, he went with a few men who asked him to wait outside the compound wall and keep a lookout in case anyone came to chase them away, and proceeded to go inside the thota. Prakash collected some dried wood from nearby and was waiting for them to return when he heard loud noises and realized that some fight had broken out. Prakash suspected that the watchman of the thota had become alert and was trying to stop them from taking the wood. Fearing trouble, Prakash ran away from there and headed home. Later, he came to know that the watchman had been injured in the fight and that the men he had gone with had also been arrested.

Experience with police

Prakash was caught by the police from a nearby shop in the village. The police beat him in the night when he was arrested. They tied his hands and beat him on his hands and back with a lathi. Next day again they slapped him a lot and threatened him that if he opened his mouth before the magistrate, they would come to his home and trouble him.

Experience of counsellor and counselling

Prakash met the counsellor at the OH once during admission. She said 'all you people from 'halli' (village) are trouble makers'. Prakash got scared hearing this and just kept quiet after that. He felt that the counsellor should talk positive things to the children and should not have discouraged them, especially since they have gone through so much suffering already before coming into conflict with the law.

Remorse and empathy for victim

Prakash was very confused about who the victim was or what wrong he had done. He thought the victim might have been the watchman of the 'thota' but he could not say for sure. Prakash was told by the police that he was caught for sandalwood smuggling and that it was a very big crime. Prakash was confused about this because he thought it was like collecting firewood for his household, which he had done many times for his grandmother. He had gone many times with some people in his village who used to take him with them and give him food and some money. So, he was not able to exactly understand why and how he had come into conflict with the law now.

Adverse Childhood Experiences

Prakash scored a total of **17 out of 20** adverse childhood experiences. The list of adverse childhood experiences undergone by Prakash include :

Poverty, disruption in education, abandonment by parents and separation of parents, neglect, lack of parental involvement and poor family relationship, family history of poor health, child's history of prolonged illness, family history of alcoholism, family history of suicide, family history of mental illness, child's history of attempted suicide, exposure to violence in the family, violence towards child, violence by police, incarceration of child, contact of child with justice system.

Scope for Reform, Rehabilitation and Restoration

Prakash was initially very homesick at the OH but slowly he started feeling that at least some people at the OH seemed to care about him. The superintendent madam would often ask him whether he was alright and that cheered him up a lot. He also mentioned that the researcher was talking to him and asking about his life, which was something that nobody had ever done for him in his entire life. In his words, "My grandmother used to often say I wish you died. But here you (researcher) are asking me about my future plans. So I feel that perhaps I should know more good people who can help me understand myself better and try to correct myself." Prakash believed that his strengths were that he had never hurt anyone and was a hardworking person who was always willing to do any work that was given to him.

Positive impact of JJ System

Prakash did not know what his goals or future was or what it should be. He also did now know who could help or support him to achieve his goals. But he felt that after coming to the OH he had started thinking that maybe he should have a goal in life for himself.

Focus Points for Counselling Prakash :

The themes sought to be highlighted in Prakash's case study were death of family and abject neglect, violence in family, family history of mental illness and suicide and his lack of awareness about the seriousness of the offence, which created the environment which most likely brought Prakash into conflict with the law.

For Prakash, the main psychological points to be focused on by the counsellor are:

1. **Referral for National Child Labour Project (NCLP) Scheme** – The counsellor could refer Prakash for enrolment to the NCLP Scheme as he was studying in Ist PUC and working as a child labourer. This would give access to Prakash to education as well as help him become aware of socially and legally appropriate behaviour and their consequences.
2. **Family Counseling** for his grandmother, uncle and any other relatives (close or distant) who might be able to provide support for Prakash. The counsellor could play an active role in informing the JJB about Prakash's family circumstances. Family members, especially grandparents could be facilitated to apply for financial assistance through sponsorship and encouraged for counselling to be able to provide better parental support for Prakash and his brother.
3. **Counselling to build self-esteem and strengths based counselling :** The counsellor must focus on building Prakash's self esteem by highlighting his many positive qualities so that is feelings of rejection and abandonment are mitigated.
4. **Legal Awareness :** The counsellor must help Prakash to become legally aware of the consequences of his actions.

5.8.10 CASE 8 - SUBASH

" If having sex is wrong, then why is she still outside?"

Background demographic profile

Subash was 17 years old when he came to the OH at Mysore where he had been staying for the last 135 days, at the time of being interviewed. Subash parents were both dead and he was being raised by his aunt (mother's sister). He belonged to a very poor family which had a monthly family income of less than Rs. 10,000/- per month. He had studied upto 5th standard. His teachers in school hit him very badly and he decided that he would not go to school anymore.

Legal profile

This is the **fourth time that Subash** is coming into conflict with the law. The first time he was charged under IPC Section 380 for housebreaking and theft, which is a heinous, cognizable and non-bailable offence. While he was out on bail two more cases of IPC 380 were filed against him. Again, when he was out on bail the third time, he was charged under the Protection of Children from Sexual offences Act (POCSO) and remanded to custody at the

Mysore OH. The **first three cases are heinous**, cognizable, non-bailable offences, while the **fourth cases is a heinous, cognizable, non-bailable, sexual offence**. Cognizable offences are those in which the police can arrest without any warrant. These are more serious in nature. Non-cognizable offences on the other hand are those for which a police officer has no authority to arrest, unless with a warrant.

Social profile

Subash's had never seen his father, Prakash, who abandoned him when he was barely a few weeks old. His mother, Shrikala, died when he was a week old. Subash was then taken care of by his mother's sister who did not get married for his sake and was the ideal mother in Subash's eyes. He had heard that his father used to hit his mother and troubled everyone in the family. His father committed suicide a month after his mother's death.

Health profile

Both of Subash's parents died within a short span of time and when Subash was barely a few weeks old. His mother had a stroke a week after giving birth to him and died. His **father committed suicide a** month after his mother's death. His father used to hit his mother. In school, the teachers also used to hit Subash so badly that he decided he would not go to school anymore after he completed his 5th standard. Subash was hospitalized for over a month when a truck ran over him once as a child. His chikkamma, whom he considers his mother lovingly nursed him back to health. Subash's uncle (mother's brother) used to hit his chikkamma after getting drunk using any household object. He also used to hit Subash with firewood. Subash grew up hating him and waiting to grow a little stronger when he could hit him back. Once he grew up a little, he showed his uncle a knife when he tried to hit him – though he hit him back with his hand. After that his uncle did not dare to hit him again. Subash did not know about his family's history of substance use and himself also did not take to smoking, drinking or any substance use of any kind. He was taken for a medical examination by the police after being charged under POCSO.

Current Mental Health Status

Subash used to get very bad **nightmares** and felt like crying a lot. The counsellor, Ms. Visalakshi at the OH and Dr. Krishna (a psychiatrist from an NGO who treated Subash on the insistence of the counsellor) helped him a lot. He often cried a lot and felt **intense rage** that he felt he could not express. Subash also felt very angry that he had not done anything wrong and had still been wrongfully detailed since the last 135 days. He often expressed this anger in his question to the counsellor that, "If having sex is wrong, then why is she still outside? **I didn't force her, she too said yes, didn't she?"**

Coming into conflict with the law

This is the fourth time that Subash was coming into conflict with the law. Subash admitted that the first time he did some 'thappu kelasa' (wrong job) was with his friends. He went along with them for housebreaking and it seemed like a great adventure and they picked up some small household things. It was only after the police caught them that Subash realized what a big crime it was. He confessed to the police and decided that henceforth he would keep his distance from such friends and such activities. However, to his misfortune, after that first incident, every time there was any theft in his area, the police would apprehend him, ask his mother for money and bring him to the OH. Then a few months ago, the police filed a POCSO case against Subash. He had gone out with his girlfriend. Subash and his girlfriend had known each other for around a year and had had sex several times and she was also willing and happy. But a few months before Subash's apprehension, when his girlfriend's parents found out that he had no money, no family and no job, they stopped her from seeing him and filed a POCSO case against him.

Experience with police

The police kept Subash in the station for a week and did not allow him to talk to his girlfriend. They tried to get money from his aunt but she could not pay the amount they asked. Subash was confident that his girlfriend would not testify against him.

Experience of counsellor and counselling

Subash found a lot of comfort in the counsellor. According to him, she would speak to all the children on a daily basis and spent a lot of time with them. Even though the formal counselling sessions were scheduled only once a week or so, she would ensure that there was some interaction or the other with the children, which Subash felt had been very important in keeping him positive. He felt that a counsellor should teach the children in her care good habits and help them to correct their mistakes.

Remorse and empathy for victim

Subash was filled with guilt and remorse over having hurt his aunt for what he now believed was his selfish pleasure. The shame that he saw in her eyes at the police station haunted him every day. He felt that because of him, she had to put her head down in shame in front of her friends. He felt he would need a lifetime to undo that harm to her. Subash believed that the biggest victim of all his criminal behaviour was his mother –aunt and that he needed to apologize to her. Subash felt that both he and his girlfriend were equally **victims of a law and society that did not understand that it was normal and natural for teenagers in love to express their love through sex.**

Adverse Childhood Experiences

Subash scored a total of **16 out of 20** adverse childhood experiences. The list of adverse childhood experiences undergone by Subash include : Poverty, disruption in education, death of a parent (both parents), neglect, lack of parental involvement and poor family relationship, family history of poor health, child's history of prolonged illness, family history of attempted suicide, family history of mental illness, child's history of attempted suicide, exposure to violence in the family, violence towards child, violence by police, incarceration of child, contact of child with justice system.

Scope for Reform, Rehabilitation and Restoration

Subash was unable to think of his future course of actions clearly. He admitted that all he could think about was going home to his mother. He felt that he had some inherent strengths like being helpful and self-reliant. He was confident that he could rebuild his life as he had good relationships to support him. He wanted to learn driving and become a driver. Sometimes Subash also thought that he should try for a government job but was not sure how to go about it or who could help or guide him for it. He felt that it had been a very long time since he had left home and wanted to go back home soon.

Positive Impact of the JJ system

Subash had realized the worth of his mother-aunt only after coming into the juvenile justice system. He realized how much she had sacrificed her life for his sake and being in custody, made him understand the value of home.

Focus Points for Counselling Subash :

The themes sought to be highlighted in Subash's case were recidivism, consensual sex amongst adolescents resulting in legal conflicts, family violence, severe violence in school leading him to drop out which created the environment which most likely brought Subash into conflict with the law.

For Subash, the main psychological points to be focused on by the counsellor are:

1. **Personal Counselling to create awareness on sexuality, personal safety and boundaries** – The Counsellor would need to enable Subash to understand biological, psychological, emotional and relational aspects of his own sexuality and that of others. The counsellor would also need to enable Subash to understand the legal and social consequences of his sexual behaviour as an adolescent.
2. **Life skills education** – The counselor could enable Subash to develop life skills in the area of interpersonal communication, relationship boundaries, problem solving and future planning skills, decision making in terms of behaviour and consequences, and so on.
3. **Reform and restorative based approaches** – The counsellor could capitalize on Subash's high potential for reform as evinced by his prosocial behaviours like intense desire and motivation to make amends for his behaviour with his mother -aunt, his self-confidence about his own strengths, wanting to take up a government job, etc. and encourage his reform process.
4. **Prevention of recidivism** – Counselling must focus on reinforcing prosocial behaviours, encouraging Subash to dissociate himself from negative peers and gang affiliations so that he does not get in get into conflict with the law again and reoffend. The counsellor could help him build his coping strategies to resist temptations from gangs and antisocial peers.

5.8.11 CASE 9 - MOHIT

"One life lost but so many other lives destroyed too - all because of me and my friends"

Basic demographic profile

Mohit A was 17 years old and had been at the OH Mysore for 39 days at the time of being interviewed. It was interesting to note how many children counted their stay in custodial care in number of days, highlighting how every single day is a very long time for them. Mohit belonged to a poor family, his father was a construction labourer and mother was a housewife and their monthly family income was less than Rs. 10,000/- per month. Mohit had studied up to high school 9th standard and then dropped out as his family told him that they could not afford to send him to school anymore and that he should start working. He was looking for a job at the time of the incident.

Legal profile

Mohit was charged under Section 304 of the Indian Penal Code for culpable homicide not amounting to murder. This is a heinous, cognizable and non-bail able offence under the law. Cognizable offences are those in which the police can arrest without any warrant. These are more serious in nature. Non-cognizable offences on the other hand are those for which a police officer has no authority to arrest, unless with a warrant. Mohit had been at the OH Mysore for 39 days and was awaiting bail. He did not have any previous history of crime and this was the first time he was coming into conflict with the law.

Social profile

Mohit's father, Anjaneya, used to do some odd jobs at at construction sites. His mother, Ammu was a housewife. His father was not always employed and that created a lot of friction in his family. He wished that his father would correct him gently and not hit him to discipline him. Mohit was emotionally attached to him mother even though she did not always take care of him.

Health profile

Mohit had never been hospitalized in his life though he had suffered from many childhood illnesses from time to time. His father was an alcoholic who used to drink heavily and suffered from poor health. His mother also suffered from anaemia and malnutrition as there was often no food to eat in the house on many occasions. The entire family used to go hungry for many days when his father could not find work. Mohit had a younger brother who had also stopped going to school as his family could not afford sending them both to school. Mohit admitted that he drank beer once or twice during festivals, but otherwise, he did not smoke or take drugs. Mohit 's father would slap his mother often and hit her with a stick also in front of his children. Both of Mohit 's parents used to hit him and his brother with sticks. Mohit used to feel very angry but he did not hit back and had never showed violence to anyone else.

Current Mental Health Status and Risks / hazards

Mohit was very sad when he was arrested by the police and taken to the OH, Mysore and he often thought of committing suicide in his initial days there. Then he thought that he must die after achieving something. His **grandmother had committed suicide**, he didn't want to be like that and wanted to achieve something and then die.

Coming into conflict with the law

Mohit and 3 of his friends from his neighbourhood had gone for an outing on the outskirts of Mysore. One of his friends worked in a welding workshop where Mohit also planned to join, another friend worked with his brother in a garage, while Mohit and the fourth friend (the deceased victim) were looking for a job. All the four of them went to play in a small water-body and started playing in the water even though none of them knew how to swim. The victim went deeper into the water and though Mohit and his friends tried to pull him out, they could not and themselves started almost drowning. One of Mohit's friends then managed to get out of the water and shouted for help and some people came and rescued them. However, by that time, the victim had drowned and he could not be revived. Mohit and his two other friends (who were also rescued from the water) were apprehended by the police and charged with the murder of their friend who had drowned. Both his friends were also with him at the Mysore, OH.

Experience with police

The police apprehended Mohit and his two friends and took them to the station within a few hours of the incident. Mohit and his friends fell sick and developed high fever and were in shock over the death of their friend. The police threatened to beat them if they did not confess to the murder of their friend. All the three of them started crying and begged to be allowed to go home as they were really scared of getting into trouble with their parents. But the police refused and said they would release them only if they confessed to the murder of their friend. Mohit and his friends were really afraid of the beatings and kept pleading that it was an accident but the police insisted that they confess that they had murdered their friend.

Experience of counsellor and counselling

Mohit met the counsellor at the OH Mysore daily and felt that she had helped him to face his fears of staying in a custodial institution. He stated that the affectionate and cheerful nature of the counsellor was very comforting to him during this difficult time of his life.

Remorse and empathy for victim

Mohit felt deeply saddened and guilty about the death of his friend and often used to wish that he could just undo all that happened on that fateful day. He had never imagined that things would turn out the way they did and one of his friends would end up dead and that the rest of them would end up in jail. His uncle's son had gone to jail years ago and Mohit did not want to become like his cousin and end up in jail too. Mohit was acutely aware that a life had been lost and he wanted to apologize to the victim's family but felt helpless that his apology would not bring his friend back to life. He wanted to just fall at the feet of the victim's parents and beg for forgiveness but felt that may never happen. As he put it, " One life lost but so many other lives destroyed too - all because of me and my friends."

Adverse Childhood Experiences

Mohit scored a total of **16 out of 20** adverse childhood experiences. The list of adverse childhood experiences undergone by Mohit include :

Poverty, disruption in education, neglect, lack of parental involvement and poor family relationship, family history of poor health, family history of alcoholism, family history of suicide, family history of mental illness, child's history of attempted suicide, exposure to violence in the family, violence towards child, violence by police, incarceration of child, contact of child with justice system.

Scope for reform, rehabilitation and restoration

Mohit was aware of the abject poverty in his home and his responsibilities towards his family and wanted to start working somewhere at the earliest. He recognized that his family could not afford to send him or his brother to school anymore and wanted to take up a welding job that he knew of. He believed that his uncle would help him in this. Additionally, he believed that he is helpful, does his work neatly, is friendly, can sing, draw, make people laugh and has a kind heart – all of which would help him in the future.

Positive impact of the JJ system

Mohit stated that he had learnt drawing, prayer and yoga at the OH, Mysore.

Focus Points for Counselling Mohit :

The themes sought to be highlighted in Mohit's case were peer pressure, family violence, severe violence in school leading him to drop out which created the environment which most likely brought Subash into conflict with the law.

For Mohit, the main psychological points to be focused on by the counsellor are:

1. **Trauma informed counselling** – The fact that Mohit had seen a close friend die under tragic circumstances, that he had also been involved and almost lost his life himself and that he was apprehended for the 'murder' of this friend are all life -events that most likely had a strong impact on Mohit and the counsellor would need to offer counselling to address these issues.
2. **Personal Counselling to create self awareness and encourage introspection** – The counsellor could enable Mohit to reflect on some of his life choices and decisions with regard to his relationships, friendships and behaviour while with friends.
3. **Life skills education on resisting peer pressure**
4. **Legal awareness** on how to contact his family and legal representation to fight his case before the JJB.

5.8.12 CASE 10 - SATYA

"I wish someone had told me that"

Basic demographic profile

Satya was 14 years old and had been at the OH Mysore for 65 days at the time of being interviewed. He had studied till primary school and then dropped out as both his had parents died. Satya did not have any family and no steady source of income either. He used to do odd jobs and people used to give him some food or money in return.

Legal profile

Satya was charged under Section 376 of the Indian Penal Code and under the Protection of Children from Sexual Offences Act, for rape and sexual assault against a minor. This is a heinous, cognizable and non-bailable offence under the law. Cognizable offences are those in which the police can arrest without any warrant. These are more serious in nature. Non-cognizable offences on the other hand are those for which a police officer has no authority to arrest, unless with a warrant. Satya did not have any previous history of crime and this was the first time he had come into conflict with the law.

Social profile

Satya's father, Basavarja was unemployed, while his mother, Sarasu did cleaning work. His **father committed suicide after murdering his mother**. It was his aunt who told him that his father had murdered his mother and gone to jail for it. Satya often felt very sad about this and wished that his father was not a criminal. He did not remember his mother very clearly but did remember that she was very loving towards him and wished she had not died. His grand–aunt (grandmother's sister) took care of him for some time but after she died, he had no one and had been living on his own. He would sleep wherever he got work. On account of growing up as an orphan, Satya experienced **deep poverty, starvation, violence and emotional neglect** from a very young age. He had practically no adult affection, supervision, guidance or monitoring.

Health profile

Satya had got injured many times while working in the fields and while laying roads. He learnt to just carry on with his work otherwise he would get scolded, beaten or thrown out of the job. Satya had been beaten by many people - mostly strangers and employers. When he used to ask for food or money, he used to get beaten. He had been slapped, kicked, punched, hit with stick, etc. Many people used to swear at him calling him bastard, orphan, thief, beggar etc. When he was younger, Satya used to feel bad about these insults and cry. But as he grew older, he learnt to just keep quiet and do his work. He did not smoke, drink or consume drugs.

Current Mental Health Status

After being apprehended by the police, Satya felt that his life was over and that perhaps he too might someday commit suicide in jail like his father. He believed that no one would miss him even if he committed suicide. He thought about taking his life many times but never had the courage to go ahead and do it.

Coming into conflict with the law

The victim was Satya's grand - aunt's daughter and biologically related to him. She was older than him by a few years. She and Satya had grown up together for some time in the same house when her mother used to take care of him when his parents died. She was a kind person and sometimes used to give Satya food to eat. She went to live with some other people in the village after the death of her mother. She used to take Satya to the pump house in the fields and have sex with him. They had had sex many times, but once they were caught, she told everyone that Satya had raped her and so he was apprehended and taken to the police station.

Experience with police

The police beat Satya very badly and gave electric shock to his private parts. He was terrified and thought he would die from the pain but just kept quiet. After a week, he was taken to the OH. He was terrified worrying about whether the police would kill him first or the villagers.

Experience of counsellor and counselling

Satya experienced the counsellor at OH Mysore as a kind person who believed him when he told her what had actually happened. He felt happy that at least someone in the world believed him when he spoke the truth. This was the first time in his life that he had met somebody like her.

Remorse and empathy for the victim

Satya realized only after coming to the OH that it was wrong for him to have had sex with the victim, whom he regarded as his cousin. He wished someone had told him that it was wrong to have sex with a girl who is biologically related. He also felt that he didn't even realize that what he was doing with her was wrong as **no one had ever told or taught him right and wrong.** He wanted to apologize to his cousin. Someone told him that no one would marry her now because he had raped her. That bothered Satya and he hoped that she got married and had a happy family.

Adverse Childhood Experiences

Satya scored a total of **17 out of 20** adverse childhood experiences. The list of adverse childhood experiences undergone by Satya include :

Poverty, disruption in education, death of parents (murder and suicide), neglect, lack of parental involvement and poor family relationship, family history of poor health, child's history of prolonged illness, family history of attempted suicide, family history of mental illness, child's history of attempted suicide, exposure to violence in the family, violence towards child, violence by police, involvement of family with justice system (family member convicted or in jail) , incarceration of child, contact of child with justice system and charged with a sexual offence.

Scope for Reform, Rehabilitation and Restoration

Satya was not hopeful about getting out of the juvenile justice system. He believed that he would also be put in jail just like his father. He did not have anyone in his life who would be willing to help him. The victim was the only relative and relationship he had and he felt now even that was gone. Satya knew to do farm work and road tar-laying work. He used to think if he worked hard and didn't trouble anyone, he could still lead a happy life. But after being in custody, he felt quite hopeless, helpless and scared.

Positive Impact of JJ system

Satya was not able to recount any positive impact of the system.

Focus Points for Counselling Satya :

The themes sought to be highlighted in Satya's case were a lack of clear understanding about clear understanding of what constituted a sexual offence and constituted sexual abuse, consensual sex amongst adolescents resulting in legal conflicts, family violence, severe violence in school leading him to drop out which created the environment which most likely brought Satya into conflict with the law.

For Satya, the main psychological points to be focused on by the counsellor are:

1. **Personal Counselling to create awareness on sexuality, personal safety and boundaries** – The Counsellor would need to enable Satya to understand biological, psychological, emotional and relational aspects of his own sexuality and that of others. The consequences counsellor would also need to enable Subash to understand the legal and social of his sexual behaviour as an adolescent.

2. **Life skills education –** The counselor could enable Subash to develop life skills in the area of interpersonal communication, relationship boundaries, problem solving and future planning skills, decision making in terms of behaviour and consequences, and so on.
3. **Reform and restorative based approaches –** The counsellor could explore reconciliation with the villagers and the victim and victim's family given their past good relations and Satya's prosocial behaviours.
4. **Referral to JJB to consider Satya as a child in need of care and protection.** Given that Satya was under 16 years and that his cousin was technically an adult, at some point though counselling, he was bound to realize that technically this could be legally understood as she being the óffender' and he being the 'victim' The counselor would need to help in working through the emotions that Satya might go through when he arrived at this insight.

CHAPTER 6

VI DISCUSSION

The Mental Health Status of child in conflict with the law was analyzed in depth in terms of its prevalence and magnitude and presented in Chapter V. It was evident from the Tables that majority of the children who come in conflict with the law suffered from mental health problems on account of various psychosocial, economic and familial constraints. Further, when these children were exposed to law enforcement and custodial settings, they developed other mental health problems due to prolonged incarceration and lack of mental health services.

NCRB Report on Crimes in India (2016), reported that a majority of children in conflict with law (73.8%) apprehended were in the age group of 16 years to 18 years, which was confirmed by the present study that boys in conflict with the law in the age group of **16-18 years are most likely** or most vulnerable to come into conflict with the law. Studies have consistently shown that criminal activity and rates of offending begin increasing in preadolescence of early adolescence, reach a peak in late adolescence and then drop though young adulthood. (Farrington, 2001).

The results suggested that boys were most vulnerable at the High School level (9th and 10th standard) to come into conflict with the law. The findings were found to be consistent with the NCRB (Crime in India Report, 2016) finding for Karnataka where the highest level of education of children in conflict with the law was High School at 58.85% and the all-India data where the highest level of education was High school with 46.55%. However, while the findings of the present study indicated that PUC or 12th standard was the second highest level of education for 21.43 % of CICL, the NCRB data suggested that the Primary level was the second highest level of education of CICL in Karnataka at 25.99% and 32.26 % at the all – India level.

The obtained results suggested that the major reason for **disruption in education** of children in conflict with the law was their coming in into conflict with the law, compounded by difficulty in academics and death or absence of the father. The findings suggested that **due to the death of the father**, some children had to take up the financial responsibility of the entire family and, in search of money for livelihood, the education of these children had been disrupted.

The present study brought into sharp focus that the fathers of half of the children (50%) in conflict with law were in semiskilled or unskilled occupations, while a significant number of CICL (37.14%), had no father. The fathers in semiskilled occupations worked as construction labourer, painter, shop keeper's assistant, watchman and labour at garment factories while unskilled occupations included daily wagers and agriculture related jobs. More specifically, the obtained results suggested that the **absence of father** and occupation of father appeared to have a direct or indirect detrimental bearing on the education of their children; as due to the death of the father, the child had to give up his education, take up the financial responsibility of the entire family – and, in search of money for livelihood, knowingly or unknowingly, children may have got into conflict with the law. Therefore, this finding underlined the fact that children dropping out of school, having no father or parents working in semiskilled and unskilled occupations needed to be paid higher attention in order to prevent them from coming into conflict with the law.

One of the common and widespread myths in India is that working mothers did not or were not able to give time, supervise studies or monitor the activities of their children. However, the present study showed that there were an almost equal number of mothers who were working outside the home as the mothers who were housewives with no formal employment. Tripathi (1992) found that found that the children of working mothers were well nourished and had less behavioural disorders as compared to the children whose mothers were housewives.

The study found that clearly **only children from economically poor families are coming into conflict with the law**. Poverty is known to be a factor that can bring about many adverse childhood experiences in the lives of children. Poverty is a multi-dimensional phenomenon which affects health, education and quality of life in many ways. While poverty, in and of itself, might not necessarily cause a child to commit an illegal act, research has shown that there is a relationship between growing up in chronically poor household and impoverished surroundings and offences by children and adolescents. Factors like poor maternal health, prenatal and postnatal care, deficient nutrition, lack of education and employment opportunities which accompany poverty may also create a persistent disadvantage for the child which may lead to his coming into conflict with the law. (Jarjoura, Roger; Ruth Triplett, and Gregory Brinker; 2002).

The weak structure of the family in the life of the CICL was brought to the fore by the study, wherein a majority of the CICL were from a **single parent family, with either one or both parents dead**. This finding, along with the other finding in the same study that the fathers of almost 40% of the CICL were dead, which compelled the CICL to work and become the bread winners of the family at a young age, could be indicative that single parenthood placed an extra burden on the surviving parent which may be increasing the vulnerability of the child to come into conflict with the law.

Death of a parent or separation from a parent within the first 18 years of life is an adverse childhood experience that is known to have a negative impact on the mental health in later life. For children from lower socio-economic backgrounds, especially sons, the death or absence of a father often placed an extra burden on the son to now take on added responsibilities and become the breadwinner of the family. Upon the death of the father, many CICL were expected to give up their studies, take up a job, take responsibility for younger siblings, to provide financial as well as emotional support to the mother and other siblings and to act as the 'man of the house'.

Most mothers were found to be living with their children despite difficult circumstances. The mothers who were not living with their children were dead. It was very significant that such a large number of CICL did not have a parent. Death or separation from a parent was found to be an adverse childhood experience that has serious consequences for health and well-being in later life. (Felitti, Anda, Nordenberg, Williamson, Spitz, Edwards, Marks (1998). For a majority of the children in conflict with the law, the mother appeared to be the most significant person in their life even as the father appeared to be largely absent in the life of the child in conflict with the law.

Friends were the most important persons outside the family for a significant number of children in conflict with the law, reinforcing the fact that adolescents were most influenced by friends and peer pressure during this age and that friendship was the most significant relationship for adolescents during their teenage period. Further, the lack of strong support systems for the child within the family or school or community was highlighted. In the absence of such social support systems, adolescents turned to friends and other vulnerable youth for support. Interestingly, this finding also demonstrated that it was **possible for a state**

functionary to be a positive influence and role model for children in conflict with the law, as the superintendent of the SH appeared to have forged positive bonds with the children in his care to the extent that they considered him to be the only significant person in their lives (outside of their own families).

Most of the CICL appeared to have either a **troubled relationship with their fathers or the fathers were either dead or absent from their lives**. Reassuringly, many CICL described the relationship with their mothers as caring and loving, even as they often described her as 'helpless' and vulnerable herself. Hence, strengthening this parent-child bond by support for the mother through planned interventions might be one of the strategies to be explored.

Most of the children in the present study were found to have experienced some aspect of **neglect (physical or emotional**) from their families. This neglect was manifested as physical neglect like not having enough food, clothes or safety as well as emotional neglect including lack of affection, importance or protection. Several studies linking neglect with juvenile delinquency found that maltreatment of children has been known to cause chronic stress which can harm development of the brain, nervous system and immune systems resulting in health problems like depression, smoking, alcoholism, drug abuse, high-risk sexual behaviours, suicide and other chronic diseases. (NCIPC 2014).

A lack of emotional warmth towards each other and support for each other during times of crises was found to be a common characteristic of families where children were vulnerable to coming into conflict with the law. This lack of emotional warmth in the family, along with factors like neglect and the absence of supervision throughout childhood and adolescence, poor parenting practices with inconsistent and inappropriate discipline were found to be linked to delinquency among youth. (IMNRC 2001).

Parents of most of the children in conflict with the law were either **unable to understand and empathize with the child's problems** and worries or even worse, many children did not have parents, or families or anyone else who was able to understand their problem or worries. Setting clear expectations about children's behaviour, rewarding children for good behaviour, positive supervision, consistent disciplinary practices all form part of parenting competencies which have been found to have positive outcomes like decrease in substance use and antisocial conduct for children who have experienced abuse or neglect. (DSG, Inc. & CWIG 2015). Most parents of CICL were either not actively involved, or were involved only when there was a crisis or were not interested or involved at all in their children's lives. Other studies found that three indicators of parental monitoring, namely, knowledge of the child's whereabouts, active tracking and tracing of the child's whereabouts and child disclosure were linked to delinquency. (Hoeve, Dubas, Eicheisheim, et al 2009).

For most children in conflict with the law, **exposure to a doctor was rare** or happened only because of coming into conflict with the law when they were taken for a medical or psychiatric consultation as per legal requirements. Malnourishment, illness, injury, accident, substance abuse, violence, age determination procedures, medical check up to determine involvement in sexual offences were some of the reasons emerged, for visiting a doctor. Majority of the children had never been hospitalized, though some had undergone varying periods of hospitalization ranging from 3 days to 30 days. Disturbingly, the reasons for hospitalization stated by CICL included illness, injury, violence, accident, attempted suicide, police torture, substance abuse and addiction and mental illness. A ray of hope for the children at the SH was that most of them had received a general check-up and some had even undergone several health check-ups since their admission to the SH. However, the children at the OH had not received any health check up during their stay there indicating an urgent need for medical services for the children at the OH. Needless to say, the need for health care should be addressed by the institution meant for CICLs.

It is well known that alcoholism and substance use disorders are known to be risk factors for mental health conditions. (National Survey on Extent Pattern of Substance Use in India 2019). Not surprisingly, an **overwhelming majority of CICL were using a variety of substances** like cigarettes, beedis, marijuana, alcohol and inhalants, usually in combination with other substances and at a regular frequency of either daily, many times a week or weekly. Significantly, every single child at the SH had taken a substance at some point with some regularity. The reasons expressed by CICL for the consumption of these substances were that it made them forget reality for some time, they felt accepted by friends, felt grown up, felt smart and capable, it made them feel powerful and people were scared of them, made them feel sleepy. A few stated that reasons like working in a pub which exposed them to smoking and drinking, or demanding work conditions (like rag picking, scavenging, construction labor), and their poor social skills were the main reasons for them to get addicted to substances. Although more than half of the CICL had not received any treatment for their substance use, abuse or addiction or had taken some treatment but given up or relapsed, it was encouraging to note that most of them were willing to seek treatment if supported by their family or if the condition became serious and acknowledged that they needed help.

The findings brought into sharp focus the ominous presence of violence in the lives of CICL, as an **overwhelming majority were found to have a history of violence at home, with the violence directed at them as well as their mother and other family members.** The nature of violence directed at the child included pushing, shoving, pulling hair, slapping, kicking, hitting with object / household things, beating with hand, beating with stick, hitting on head with hand or object, burning, scalding or branding, stabbing with knife or sharp object, combination of multiple forms of violence. Further, more than half of the CICL had also watched violence on others in the family, extended family or community and had been subjected to violence by police. According to the Children in India report (2018), "Violence against children includes physical and mental abuse and injury, neglect or negligent treatment, exploitation and sexual abuse. Violence may take place in homes, schools, orphanages, residential care facilities, on the streets, in the workplace, in prisons and in places of detention. Such violence can affect the normal development of a child impairing their mental, physical and social being. Any form of abuse; physical, emotional, sexual, neglect, exploitation is potentially harmful to a child's health, survival, dignity and development." While it was not surprising that the all-pervasive nature of violence in the lives of the CICL had also led to them indulging in some acts of violence towards others, which included pushing, shoving, pulling hair, slapping, kicking, beating with hand, stabbing with knife or sharp object, breaking things but not hurting people. Significantly and disastrously, they also included a small but significant number of CICL who ended up being called upon to beat up others or in murder through violence. However, also equally significant to note was that the nature of violence shown by CICL did not include many of the types of violent acts that they themselves had experienced like hitting with objects or household things, beating with stick, hitting on head with hand or object, burning, scalding or branding. This was a very significant finding in terms of interventions that need to be designed to take advantage of the fact that **vulnerable youth who have undergone violence may not always indulge in violent acts of similar nature** and hence there is an immense opportunity for reform and inculcating non-violent forms of communication and problem resolution.

The four indicators used to check for concurrent risk of depression, namely, sadness and weepiness, energy and fatigue, changes in appetite and sleep disturbances over the last 4 to 6 week timeframe, revealed that CICL showed a **high risk on all four indicators.** An overwhelming majority of CICL had experienced deep sadness, weepiness, anger and an inability to cope over the last 4-6 weeks' time, had experienced low energy, fatigue and inability to cope and disturbances in appetite (including eating more or less than usual or having no interest in eating at all). Significantly, a majority of the children at the SH stated that their appetite was normal as usual. Very disturbingly, 100% of CICL experienced different levels of difficulty with sleep, ranging from difficulty in falling asleep, feeling sleepy all the time, staying awake almost all night, frequently disturbed sleep and having nightmares.

Disturbingly, a staggering number of CICL had thought about suicide at some point in their lives, as well as recently over the last 6-8 weeks and a significant number had a **history of attempted suicide** as well. The high level of risk as evidenced by suicidal ideation, history of attempted suicide as well persistence over prolonged period (6-8 weeks) was a very disturbing finding and a crisis interventional program as well as access to psychiatric services is required on an urgent basis to address this issue. A suicide helpline could be installed in every OH / SH with access to trained and expert suicide and crisis counselling in addition to psycho-education for the staff to identify children with a risk of suicide who could be referred to counselling is crucial.

The health status of both the parents of CICL was rather poor with both fathers and mothers suffering from communicable or non–communicable diseases (like cancer, diabetes, tuberculosis, etc.), alcoholism and mental illness. Further, the status of substance use in the family was high and more than half of the fathers were either presently alcoholic or had died of alcoholism and smoking. **A family history of mental illness w**ithin the immediate biological family and the extended family as well as a suspicion that there might be a possibility of some mental illness in their family even though no such diagnosis was made or treatment taken for the same, also seemed to be common. Additionally, a small but significant number of parents had also died due to illness, had committed suicide or had been murdered. Further, a disturbing number of CICL had a family history of **completed suicides** by immediate biological family members or had witnessed a suicide in their neighborhood.

The JJ Act mandates that children alleged to be in conflict with the law must be produced before the JJB within 24 hours. However, more than half of the CICL were not produced before the JJB within 24 hours and had been detained at the police station for more than 24 hours, with durations ranging from 4 days to up to a month and 1 boy at the OH shared that he had been detained on and off for over 3 months. Disturbingly, not a single child at the SH had been produced before the JJB within 12 hours. The JJ Act mandates that the police have to inform the parents and families of the children alleged to be in conflict with the law if and when they apprehend any such child. The JJB is also required to ask the child and police at the time of production whether the family was informed or not. Presence or absence of parents / guardian is to be noted in the JJB order. However, in many of the cases, police did not contact, or allowed only telephonic contact or contacted after a week. Sadly, a small but significant number of **children had no family and hence no one to contact** while they were in police custody. Fear and violence were the predominant emotions experienced by CICL in their contact with the police. Fear included a sense of helplessness and fear of sexual abuse, while violence also included experiences of violence and **violence to the extent that they felt the fear of death**, i.e., fear that they would die from the violence by the police. Shame, humiliation and anger were other significant emotions experienced by the CICL in their experience of the police.

Detention, institutionalization and incarceration must be measures of last resort as per the principles of the **juvenile justice legislation** as well as the UNCRC. However, **the average duration of detention at the OH was 22 days, while at the SH was 137 days.** Further research is needed to determine whether non-institutional measures and community-based methods of justice and rehabilitation were attempted before resorting to institutionalization.

The main categories of offences that CICL had been charged with were **petty, serious (nonsexual), heinous (non-sexual) and heinous (sexual).** Most of the children were charged with and found to be guilty of offences for the first time, with a very small percentage coming in conflict for the second time and very rarely for more than two times. Reasons for this could be that most of the CICL complete 18 years by the time their first case is completed. If at all they might have reoffended, they would more likely be found in the adult criminal justice system, which is not being currently tracked in India to check for individuals who have graduated from the juvenile justice system.

It was found that a majority of CICL were first time entrants to the system and also that an overwhelming majority of those that are 'found guilty' and placed at the SH were found so for the very first offence that they are charged with. This indicated that the **rate at which the JJBs were 'convicting' the CICL was very high**. While a small percentage of CICL were coming into the OH for the second time with petty offences (like petty theft, unlawful assembly, rioting, wrongful restraint, provoking breach of peace, voluntarily causing hurt, or serious(non-sexual offences) like theft in dwelling house, assembling for dacoity, lurking and trespass, etc., the CICL at the SH were entering the system the second or third time for heinous (sexual and non-sexual) offences like murder, attempt to murder, robbery, dacoity, kidnapping, rape and sexual assault of a minor. An important aspect to be considered was that CICL at the SH had been 'found guilty' of heinous sexual offences, despite the problematic interpretation of 'rape, sexual abuse / assault of minor' under the heinous sexual offences category wherein consensual sexual activity among teenagers is also considered statutory rape (under Section 376 of the IPC and child sexual abuse under POCSO Act).

A small but significant number of children admitted that one of their family members from their immediate biological family of origin was or had been arrested or convicted and was or had been in jail. Another significant number of children mentioned that they suspected that one of their families had been in jail but their family members were not talking about this openly. Some children also shared that the police had apprehended them as a means to get information about their family member who had come into contact or conflict with the justice system.

While there could be any number of adverse experiences that may have an impact on a person's mental health, a few have been shown and established through research to impact life-long mental health and wellbeing outcomes. The **disturbingly high number of CICL (77.14%) having ten or more ACEs** (out of the 20 ACEs listed for purposes of the study), must be read as a strong distress signal to the juvenile justice system. Describing the psychosocial and legal profile of children in conflict with the law in terms of the number and magnitude of ACEs that they have undergone within the first less-than-eighteen years of their lives, could be an important tool in understanding the complexity of their mental health needs and planning interventions on how to mitigate the effects of some of those ACEs.

Some of the ACEs that emerged strongly and were highlighted in the case studies were poverty, disruption in education, death of a parent, separation of parents (abandonment of mother and family by father), neglect, lack of parental involvement and poor family relationship, family history of poor health, child's history of prolonged illness/hospitalization, family history of alcoholism, child's history of substance abuse, family history of attempted suicide, family history of mental illness, child's history of attempted suicide, exposure to violence in the family, violence towards child, violence by police, involvement of family with justice system (family member convicted or in jail), incarceration of child, contact of child with justice system and being charged with a sexual offence (irrespective of whether the sexual encounter was with or without consent). Given the high number and variety of adverse experiences that children in conflict with the law have undergone, the **counsellor in the juvenile justice system must act as an early–warning system** to alert the mental health community to address the needs of this child, while he is still in the protective care and **custody of the juvenile justice system**.

The four key aspects of counselling examined to understand the status of counselling services being provided to CICL were; approachability of the counsellor, availability of the counsellor, frequency of the counselling provided and effects of the counselling reported by the child. Positive feedback about the counsellor at the MOH demonstrated that it was possible to provide competent and quality counselling despite the challenges in the work and the environment. However, the lack of referrals despite the availability of professional and specialized mental health services, the non-approachability of the counsellor, and feedback about the poor quality of counselling at the OH and SH at Bangalore reveal the **acute lack of professional mental health services in the JJ system.**

In a surprising finding, many children at the SH mentioned the superintendent as the person that they approach when in distress rather than the counsellor. Further, none of the CICL in either OH or SH ever approached the Probationary Officer, housefather or housemother, guard, cook or any other staff when in distress. In a situation where the Superintendent is perceived to be more approachable and child-friendly than the counsellor, it would be pertinent to investigate the reasons for such a situation. More importantly, this meant that many children at the SH and at the OH where the counsellor was unapproachable and unavailable, children did not talk to anyone at all and just remained silent even in extreme distress. One of the most valuable contributions a counsellor can make to the juvenile justice system is to **break this silence of the CICL through empathetic listening.**

A sense of momentary relief, a space to express emotions, an opportunity to reflect on mistakes, understanding right and wrong and understanding their own behaviour were some of the benefits of counselling listed by CICL. Sadly, a significant number of children stated that counselling did not help them at all or that the counsellor was indifferent and disinterested in them. Also, significantly, some children stated that they did not know **who was a counsellor**

or what was counselling indicating that the counsellor and the counselling services had not been effective at all in creating even **basic awareness about the counselling process**.

The top qualities expected in a counsellor by a CICL were that the **counsellor should be kind, should understand the child's feelings and should help the child in solving his problems**. Children also expected the counsellor to correct their mistakes and negative behaviour, to listen and to be able to speak the child's native language. Unfortunately, a significant number of children stated that they had no idea of who was a counsellor or what was counselling and hence they were unable to comment or respond to the question on the qualities of a counsellor. There is an urgent need to build some of the **core skills** needed for counselling CICLs – namely **empathy, non-judgmental acceptance and multicultural competency to communicate** to the diverse psychosocial backgrounds of the children. In addition, awareness of adolescence as a developmental phase, understanding the legal and custodial settings and the effect it has on growing adolescents and the rights that CICL are entitled to receive by law, are necessary qualities for a counsellor in the juvenile justice system.

It is well acknowledged that the relationship between the counsellor and the client is an important factor that influences the effectiveness of counselling. Studies have shown that a strong counsellor-client relationship was associated with positive outcomes and increased engagement of adolescents in therapy. (Bhola, Poornima & Kapur (2013). However, in the context of children in conflict with the law, the institutional settings and the fact that choice of counselling or counsellor was not a voluntary choice must be taken into consideration. Whether the feminine gender of the counsellors at the OH and SH had any bearing on counselling outcomes, whether these outcomes may have been any different if the counsellor had been male, needs further research. The SH counsellor was 70 years old, a religious nun, with little formal education or training in counselling in general, or with boys or with CICL in particular, who offered counselling based on religious beliefs of "sin, repentance and redemption" rather than evidence-based, professional counselling practice.

The complexity of the psychosocial problems faced by CICL in the face of the intersections of legal obligations, social norms, institutional rules that must be obeyed by the CICL call for a deep and nuanced understanding of this complex context from the counsellor. However, the lack of professional education, relevant work experience, role clarity as a counsellor, **job-specific training for CICL** and understanding the psychosocial context and background of CICL were starkly evident in the responses of the counsellors interviewed, which must be a cause of great concern and alarm for the JJ system in India.

Children in conflict with the law across the world are known to be suffering from a range of mental health problems. It was alarming that counsellor at the SH which housed children with some of the most severe kinds of mental health problems stated that these CICL had no mental health problems and only some anger issues and emotional problems. It is not surprising then that with this **lack of understanding of the mental health issues and absence of a developmentally -sensitive approach**, there have been no referrals either for psychiatric services or de-addiction programs or non-psychiatric rehabilitative services including educational, vocational or skill training programs, etc. Despite the presence of **NIMHANS** – a national, tertiary mental health care centre at Bangalore, children had not been referred for any specialized mental health services or programs merely because the counsellor at the SH was not aware of these facilities or that it was her job responsibility to make such referrals.

The counsellor's belief in the CICL's capacity to change his behaviour and be reformed should create motivation in the child to respond to such an expectation by behaving in positive ways. However, if the counsellor believed that the child had landed up in the juvenile justice system due to his 'sinful or criminal' mindset and felt either angry or self-righteous about his actions, the child might feel hesitant to confide thereby weakening the bond between counsellor and CICL. The fact that not a single child at the SH had ever disclosed sexual abuse to the SH counsellor over 7 years, underlined that not a single child felt encouraged to do so. Further by imagining CICL to be 'wounded sinners who needed to be saved', the belief in the unique agency and resourcefulness of the child to change or take responsibility for his **behaviour is seriously undermined**. Additionally, insisting that the CICL must 'repent' as a precondition for counselling goes **against the ethical tenets of non-judgmental, unconditional positive regard of counselling**.

Indisputably, children in conflict with the law require support for reform and rehabilitation from the counsellor, from their family and from the government. This support includes a range of factors like emotional and financial support from family, social acceptance from community, laws and law enforcement systems that do not penalize CICL even after they exit the system, government schemes that enable employment and income generating options for the CICL. The **counsellor is** thus **uniquely placed to identify these needs and capacities of the CICL** and contribute to building a support system for the CICL.

A counsellor working with CICL is expected to be aware of the reporting procedures to be followed if a child disclosed sexual abuse and also identify those children who might be showing signs of having gone through sexual abuse. While 'listening' and 'empathy' as the counsellor's response to disclosure of sexual abuse was a positive initial step, it would not be an adequate professional response in the context of mandatory reporting as required by law. Further, expressing anger at a child for an act of sexual abuse or having sexually abusive behaviour was certainly not the prescribed professional response for a counsellor. Having **clear and well-defined protocols on responding to disclosure and intensive training on counselling children with sex offence histories,** is a must for counsellors working with children in conflict with the law.

A **counsellor in the juvenile justice system is required to play a key role in the reform, rehabilitation and reintegration** of the CICL through professional inputs to the Social Investigation Report and Home Visit Report– which contain valuable information relating to the psychosocial circumstances of the child which may have contributed to bringing him into conflict with the law, the Individual Care Plan which contain detailed inputs on what the child needs and how he can be supported to be reformed and rehabilitated. These responsibilities are in addition to the primary role as a counsellor, providing individual, group and family counselling services, referrals for psychiatric and specialized services, non-psychiatric rehabilitative services like education, employment, life skills and vocational skill training and so on.

Emotional intensity of the work involved, stress and burn out were inherent challenges in the role of a counsellor of CICLs. Empathy, compassion and caring are qualities that are known to make a counsellor effective, but these qualities may also make them vulnerable to compassion fatigue, stress and burnout. (Thomson, Amatea & Thomson, 2014). Music, prayer, meditation and religion were some of the tools used by the counsellors at the SH and MOH to cope with these challenges. However, **safety measures, self-care, personal therapy and professional supervision of the counsellor by competent mental health professionals** needed to be built in as integral parts into the design of an effective counselling system for CICLs.

There was an urgent and critical need for a system to **protect the CICL from reprisals from the police for revealing violence or abuse by law enforcement officials as well as for the counsellor for reporting them.** Given the multi-linguistic and multi-cultural backgrounds of CICL who come into CCIs, it was important for counsellors to be able to understand the socio-cultural complexities and communicate with children in languages that they were familiar with. A competent counsellor can make a huge difference in the life of a CICL by teaching and modelling self-confidence, positive values and socially appropriate behaviour **and hence a need to appoint such counsellors for these particularly vulnerable children.**

According to the International Resilience Project (1995), "resilience is a universal capacity which allows a person, group or community to prevent, minimize or overcome the damaging effects of adversity". In the context of CICL, resilience could be described as the ability to cope with and bounce back from the adversities that brought the child into the justice system, to have belief in one's strengths, skills and potential and hence forms a key aspect in an individual's potential to reform. Three aspects of resilience were examined in terms of how the child described himself in terms of what he believed he was (strengths and positive qualities), what he could do (skills and talents) and what he had (potential and resources). (This description is based on the Language of Resilience: I HAVE, I AM, I CAN, by Dr. Edith Grotberg, (1995) A guide to promoting resilience in children: strengthening the human spirit, explained in the International Resilience Project).

CICL across institutions revealed **low resilience** in terms of their belief about their strengths and positive qualities, skills and talents and their potential and resources as most could only recognize one positive quality about each of these aspects of resilience. Further, the CICL at the OH were unable to recognize even one positive quality relating to their potential or resources. Surprisingly, CICL at the SH revealed relatively higher resilience with respect to skills and talents indicating that probably some of the skills development programs that they were attending (like training for the traffic police program, hotel management course, etc.) had perhaps given them some confidence to identify their skills.

While many CICL believed that they could change many aspects of their intrapersonal behaviour (like beliefs, thinking patterns, emotional expression, responding and coping styles, etc) by themselves, with or without support, the only aspect they believed they had no control over or could not change in their lives was **poverty and finance related aspects**. Many CICL were confused, uncertain and unable to think of what or how they could change any aspect of their lives. CICL at the SH were more willing to take accountability for their social behaviour indicating that they perhaps had greater awareness about themselves and their responsibility towards family and community. Future plans of most CICL were related to education and employment, many of them were afraid of the future and many others were unable to think about the future. Significantly, many at the SH wanted to care for their parents and give back to society in some way. This positive thinking needed to be channelized into concrete parts of intervention and care plans.

Most of the **CICL needed parental and family support, financial and social support to meet personal goals for rehabilitation.** Many were confused about what support they required or who could support them. While some CICL at the SH believed that the support of their families, especially that of their mother would be crucial to achieving their goals, some at the OH believed that their teachers and educational institutions could help them fulfil their goals. Very interestingly, almost half of the CICL at the SH stated that the Superintendent at the SH was that one person whose support could make their goals become reality, revealing the tremendous potential for positive influence that a functionary has over the rehabilitation of a CICL.

Revealingly, many CICL at the SH stated that they **needed social support in the form of community acceptance, jobs and moral support in order to achieve their goals.** Other types of support expressed also included support to stay away from crime, protection from police harassment, protection from the victim's family and mental health support like counselling, de-addition services etc. Very uniquely, one CICL at the SH stated that the support he needed was **forgiveness** and unless society and the victim could forgive him, he would not be able to achieve any goal for himself.

The juvenile justice system is not a place without opportunities for learning as expressed by a majority of CICL who shared that they had learnt something positive through their experience in the juvenile justice system. **The top four positive things learnt were self-awareness, learning right from wrong, learning a new skill and a new good habit.**

A majority of the children in conflict with the law expressed varying degrees of **remorse over the harm** caused. A small percentage who did not express remorse believed they were innocent or were confused about whether they were innocent or not. Majority of children in conflict with the law believed that the person(s) harmed most by their actions were their own parents and families and the victim and victim's family. The nature of harm caused by CICL was described as the loss of life of the victim, shame to their families and breaking of relationship with their own as well as the victim's family.

Almost all CICLs expressed some degree of empathy for the victim and / or their families. For a population that is often portrayed in popular media as cold, remorseless and without any feeling, **not a single child stated that they did not feel any empathy at all**. Some children did state that they and their families were the victims and hence they felt confused. An overwhelming majority of CICL expressed their desire to make amends in different ways like apologizing, begging forgiveness from the victim and/ or victim's family, meeting the victim's family and making amends, not causing any harm to anyone in the future, etc. However, some children also stated that they themselves were victims who needed help and had been falsely implicated. Some wanted to make amends and beg forgiveness but did not know how to go about doing it.

It was found that the **right to legal representation of the CICL was being upheld** with most children having a lawyer. However, there was a significant group of CICL who did not have a lawyer for a variety of reasons. Reasons for lack of access to a lawyer included poverty, lack of legal awareness, lack of faith in the justice system and not having any family to appoint a lawyer. It is possible that some of the children at the OH who stated that they did not have a lawyer, had been apprehended only a few days prior to data collection and therefore, their families might not have had the time, awareness or means to engage a lawyer. Most tragically, some of the children at the OH did not have a family or anyone who could or would engage a lawyer on their behalf. Despite free legal aid being a legal right and lawyers appointed at the JJBs (by the State / District Legal Services) to provide free legal services, poverty emerged as the main reason why CICL are unable to exercise the right to legal representation. Very disturbingly, one CICL at the SH stated that he and his family had not engaged a lawyer because they had no faith in the legal system and were very sure that they would not get any justice as they were Muslims. The CICL and his family being very poor, decided not to engage any lawyer as they did not have the means to pay for a lawyer and felt that despite having a lawyer, they were anyway bound to lose as they were Muslims.

Continued contact with family, and an active effort to build and repair broken relationships between CICL and their families was stated to be one of the core strategies in rehabilitation of the CICL at the Special Home, according to the Superintendent of the SH. Such a rehabilitation strategy could be strengthened with a more active and structured support from the counsellor.

All CICL, except one, given their **consent to talk about their family**. Many of the children specifically stated that they were happy to talk about themselves, their families and their lives. One child who initially said that he did not want to talk about his family, went on describe his father's alcoholism in great detail. When researcher cross checked and asked if it was alright to include the information thus given, child agreed and gave consent. All CICLs reported their experience of participation in the report as happy, that they had not experienced any distress on account of participation in the research study, that their participation in the research study was very useful to them and they would be willing to participate in similar research studies in the future. A "feelings check" process at the end as part of a closure process of the interview was done and almost all children reported feeling happy or relaxed at the end of the interview with the researcher.

CHAPTER 7

VII SUMMARY AND CONCLUSION

7.1 Introduction

The Juvenile Justice (Care and Protection of Children) Act, 2015, defines a "child in conflict with law" as "a child who is alleged or found to have committed an offence and who has not completed eighteen years of age on the date of commission of such offence".

The mental health status of a child in conflict with the law most often includes a history of physical and / or sexual abuse, neglect, impoverishment, poor health conditions, poor parenting, substance abuse, unstable or dysfunctional families, emotional deprivation, limited or no education and low socio-economic status. This psycho-social profile of children in conflict with law puts them at risk of developing mental health problems, deviant behaviours and coming into conflict with the law. Unfortunately, children in conflict with the law are often identified solely on the basis of the offences they have been charged with and their history of adversities and vulnerability is completely ignored. In such a context, attempting justice without ensuring psychosocial health is empty, ineffective and futile. Therefore, the present study hopes to contribute to a better understanding of the mental health status of children in conflict with the law and the measures that are required in terms of the mental health services (including counselling) to address and improve the mental health status of this particularly vulnerable and disadvantaged population.

7.2 Objectives of the Study

7.2.1 To study the mental health status of 'children in conflict with law'

7.2.2 To study the status of counselling provided to 'children in conflict with the law'

7.3 Major Findings of the Study

7.3.1 **AGE**: A majority of the children **(74.29%)** who come into conflict with the law were in the age group of 16 to 18 years.

7.3.2 EDUCATION:

7.3.2.1 Boys were most vulnerable at the High School level (9th and 10th standard) to come into conflict with the law. (41%)

7.3.2.2 The main reasons for disruption in education were failure in exams, death of a parent, compulsion to go to work and coming into conflict with the law.

7.3.3 FINANCIAL STATUS: An overwhelming majority (77.15%) of the children in conflict with the law were from very poor families (Monthly family income less than Rs. 10,000/-) while remaining 22.86% were from poor families. (Monthly family income less than Rs. 30,000/-)

7.3.4 **FAMILY:**

7.3.4.1 **Dead parent** (s): Majority of the children in conflict with the law (52.85%) were from a single parent family, father dead (37.14%), mother dead (15.71%), or both parents dead. (17.15%).

7.3.4.2 **Separated, absent parent** : A total of 74.28% (52.85% absence of father) + (21.43% absence of mother) of CICL did not have a parent in their lives on account of death or separation, remarriage, being in jail or refusal to parent.

7.3.4.3 **Father's occupation** : The fathers of half of the children (50%) in conflict with law were in skilled or unskilled occupations, while a significant number (37.14%), had no father.

7.3.4.4 **Mother's Occupation** : There were an almost equal number of mothers who were working outside the home (51.43%) and mothers (48.47%) who were housewives (32.85) and who were dead (15.71%).

7.3.4.5 **Significant family member** : Mother was the most significant person for an overwhelming majority (61.43%) of children in conflict with the law

7.3.4.6 **Father living with family** : Majority of the fathers (55.71%) of children in conflict with the law were either dead (35.71%) or did not live with them (20%)

7.3.4.7 **Mother living with family** : A majority of the mothers (75.71%) of children in conflict with the law lived with their children.

7.3.4.8 Neglect by family : Half of the children (49.99%) in conflict with the law experienced some aspect of neglect (physical or emotional) from their families.

7.3.4.9 Quality of relationship with family : Majority of the children (75.72%) in conflict with the law experienced poor quality of relationship of family members towards each other.

7.3.4.9.1 Understanding from parents : Almost half (48.57%) of the children in conflict with the law feel that they were not understood by parents or did not have any family who could understand them.

7.3.4.9.2 Involvement and Supervision : Majority of the children (88.58%) in conflict with the law felt their parents were not very involved or interested in their children's lives.

7.3.4.9.3 Relationship with father : Majority of the children (80.01%) in conflict with the law did not have a positive relationship with their fathers because their father was dead or not supportive.

7.3.4.9.4 Relationship with mother : Almost half (47.14%) of the children in conflict with the law described their relationship with their mother as caring and loving.

7.3.4.9.5 SOCIAL FACTORS : Peer Influence : Friends were the most important persons outside of family, for a significant number of children in conflict with the law. (42.86%)

7.3.5 Health Status:

7.3.5.1 Medical Services:

7.3.5.1.1 Access to medical services: Majority 74.29% (20% never + 54.29% once or twice) of children in conflict with law did not have adequate exposure or access to medical services

7.3.5.1.2 Reasons for seeking medical services: Main reasons for a child in conflict with the law for visiting a doctor or a hospital were illness (30%) or accident. (24.28%)

7.3.5.1.3 Hospitalization: A significant number (58.57%) of the children in conflict with the law had been hospitalized at some point in their lives. The main reasons for hospitalization includde illness, injury, violence, accident, attempted suicide, police torture, drugs and mental illness.

7.3.5.1.4 Status of general health check up in CCIs: A significant number (37.4%) of children in conflict with the law had a general check up at the CCI while another almost equal number (38.57%) had not undergone any check up at the CCI.

7.3.5.2 Status of substance use

7.3.5.2.1 Usage : An overwhelming majority (71.43%) of CICL reported to be using some substance.

7.3.5.2.2 Type of substance use : Almost half (48.57%) of the children in conflict with the law used a combination of substances (which included cigarettes, marijuana, alcohol and inhalants), while a significant number (20%) of others used cigarettes / tobacco based substances.

7.3.5.2.3 **Frequency of substance use** : Majority of children in conflict with the law took substances on a daily (35.72%) or weekly (21.42%) basis.

7.3.5.2.4 **Reason (s) for substance use** : The reasons given by children in conflict with the law for consumption of substances were that it made them forget reality for some time, made them feel accepted by friends, or made them feel grown up.

7.3.5.2.5 **Treatment for substance use** : Almost half of the children (44.28%) in conflict with the law did not receive any treatment or did not have access to any treatment despite being addicted to some substance.

7.3.5.2.6 **Willingness to receive treatment** : Half of the children (50%) in conflict with the law were willing to receive treatment for their substance addiction / dependence.

7.3.5.3 Exposure to Violence :

7.3.5.3.1 **History of violence** : An overwhelming majority (71.43%) of children in conflict with the law had a history of violence at home.

7.3.5.3.2 **Child-directed violence :** Majority of children (74.29%) in conflict with the law had violence specifically directed at them at home.

7.3.5.3.3 **Nature of child-directed violence :** The nature of violence experienced by children in conflict with the law included pushing, shoving, pulling hair, slapping, kicking, hitting with object / household things, beating with stick, hitting on head with hand or object, combination of multiple forms of violence, child having watched violence on others in the family, extended family or community, subjected to violence by police.

7.3.5.3.4 **Violence towards other children in the home** : A majority of children (69.99%) in conflict with the law had experienced violence towards other children in the home, including or excluding himself

7.3.5.3.5 **Violence by child towards others** : Half of the children (51.43%) in conflict with the law had shown violence towards others while the other half had not shown any violence towards others.

7.3.5.3.6 **Nature of enacted violence** : The nature of violence shown by children in conflict with the law was mostly slapping and beating with the hand (20%)

7.3.5.4 Risk of Depression and Suicide

7.3.5.4.1 Sadness and weepiness: More than half (52.85%) of children in conflict with the law had experienced deep sadness and weepiness and an inability to cope during the last 4-6 weeks.

7.3.5.4.2 Energy and Fatigue: A significant number (45.71%) of children in conflict with the law had experienced low energy and fatigue and an inability to cope during the last 4-6 weeks.

7.3.5.4.3 Appetite : A majority (72.86%) of children in conflict with the law had experienced disturbance in appetite (eating more or less than usual or having no interest in eating at all) during the last 4-6 weeks. However, significantly, 61.90% at the SH stated that their appetite was normal as usual.

7.3.5.4.4 Sleep : 100% of the children in conflict with the law had different levels of difficulty with sleep, ranging from difficulty in falling asleep, feeling sleepy all the time, staying awake almost all night, frequently disturbed sleep and having nightmares.

7.3.5.4.5 Suicidal ideation: An overwhelming majority (77.14%) of children in conflict with the law had thought about suicide at some point in their lives.

7.3.5.4.6 Concurrent risk of suicide: An overwhelming majority (71.42%) of the children in conflict with the law had thought about suicide over the last 6-8 weeks.

7.3.5.4.7 Attempt to commit suicide: A significant number (37.69%) of children in conflict with the law had a history of attempted suicide.

7.3.5.5 Family Health History

7.3.5.5.1 Father's health history : The health status of fathers of CICL was poor; a total of 82.87% fathers of CICL were either ill or dead.

7.3.5.5.2 Mother's health history : The health status of mothers of CICL was poor; a total of 88.57 % mothers of CICL were either ill or dead.

7.3.5.5.3 Status of substance use among parents : The status of substance use among the parents of children in conflict with the law was high; a majority (70.01%) had a history of using some substance. (smoking, drinking or drugs).

7.3.5.5.4 History of suicide in the family : A significant number (34.29%) of families of children in conflict with the law had a history of suicide.

7.3.5.5.5 History of mental illness in the family : A significant number (25.72%) of families of children in conflict with the law had a history of some mental illness.

7.3.6 Experience with police :

7.3.6.1 Detention by police : Slightly over half (51.43%) of the children in conflict with the law were detained in the police for more than what was permitted under the law.

7.3.6.2 Contact with parents while in police custody : A significant number (40%) of children in conflict with the law did not have contact with parents while in police custody.

7.3.6.3 Emotional impact of contact with police : An overwhelming majority (82.86%) of children in conflict with the law had a negative emotional impact of their experience with the police.

7.3.6.4 Prior contact with the justice system : An overwhelming majority (85.71%) of children in conflict had no prior contact with the justice system and were coming into conflict with the law for the first time.

7.3.6.5 Prior contact of family with justice system : Majority (64.29%) of the families of children in conflict with the law had no contact with the justice system.

7.3.7 Adverse Childhood Experiences: Majority of children in conflict with the law (77.14%) had 10 or more ACEs in their life.

7.3.8 Counsellor and Counselling Process :

7.3.8.1 Approachability of counsellor : The approachability of the counsellor at the OH Bangalore and SH Bangalore was very low (0%) compared to that of the counsellor at the OH at Mysore (40%). More than half of the children (51.43%) did not speak to anyone about their problems. A significant number (28.57%) of children at the OH approached the superintendent instead of the counsellor. An equally significant number (30%) spoke to their friends within the OH /SH rather than the counsellor.

7.3.8.2 Availability of counsellor : The availability of the counsellor at the OH Bangalore was very low compared to that of the counsellor at the OH at Mysore and the SH at Bangalore.

7.3.8.3 Frequency of counselling : The frequency of counselling offered by the counsellor at the OH was very low compared to that of the counsellor at the OH at Mysore and the SH at Bangalore.

7.3.8.4 Effectiveness of counselling : Children in conflict with the law found the counselling offered at the OH to be low in effectiveness when compared to that offered at the OH at Mysore and the SH at Bangalore.

7.3.8.5 Qualities of counsellor : The top three qualities in a counsellor expected by children in conflict with the law were that the counsellor should be kind, should understand the child's feelings and should help the child in solving their problems.

7.3.8.6 STATUS OF COUNSELLING SERVICES: COUNSELOR'S

7.3.8.6.1 Profile of Counsellor : Counsellors were both female. While the MOH counsellor was 30 years old, the SH counsellor was almost 70 years old. Education profile and work profile of SH Counsellor was not adequate or appropriate for CICL.

7.3.8.6.2 Training Status of counsellors at OH and SH: Both the counsellors (at SH and OH) were not adequately or specifically trained for their role as counsellors for CICL.

7.3.8.6.3 Counsellor's understanding of psychosocial context of CICL: Counsellor at SH had a poor understanding of the psychosocial context of CICLs, while the counsellor at MOH had some understanding of the psychosocial context of CICL.

7.3.8.6.4 Referral services by Counsellor: Referrals for either medical or psychiatric services or rehabilitative services by the counsellors at MOH and SH were very poor, with both counsellors being unaware of their role or responsibilities with regard to referral.

7.3.8.6.5 Counsellor's Perspective on CICL's capacity for reform and rehabilitation : The MOH counsellor believed that CICL had the potential for change and reform, while the SH counsellor believed that CICL were wounded children in need of healing and sinners who needed to be reformed and saved.

7.3.8.6.6 Support required by child for reform and rehabilitation : The support factors required by CICL for reform and rehabilitation, according to the counsellors were acceptance by family and community, financial support, less punitive laws and government schemes for employment.

7.3.8.6.7 Counselling Competence of counsellor at OH and SH: Both the counsellors (at SH and MOH) had poor awareness about due process, protocols and counselling practices to be followed for CICL.

7.3.8.6.7.1 Role Performance of the counsellor: Both the counsellors (At SH and MOH) had not prepared or contributed to SIR, ICP or Home Visit, and had conducted some unstructured group activities from time to time.

7.3.8.6.7.2 Factors influencing role performance of the counsellor: Both counsellors experienced stress and burn out due to the emotional intensity and demanding nature of work.

7.3.8.6.7.3 Coping strategies of counsellor : Coping strategies of counsellors included music, prayer, meditation and religion.

7.3.8.6.7.4 Support received and required by counsellor : Both counsellors received inadequate support for their work and required personal safety at the workplace. One counsellor required support in terms of professional supervision from a mental health professional, training for personal growth from the staff, government and a cordial work atmosphere, while other counsellor felt her religion equipped her in all ways for the role.

7.3.8.6.7.5 Impact of counselling services : Both counsellors believed that counsellors could make an impact in the life of a CICL and positively influence reform and rehabilitation.

7.3.9 Reform, rehabilitation and reintegration

7.3.9.1 Resilience

7.3.9.2 Belief in change by own effort: A significant number of children in conflict with the law believed that they could change aspects of their behaviour by themselves – with or without support.

7.3.9.3 Belief in what cannot be changed: The only aspect that children in law believed they had no control over or could not change in their lives was poverty and financial related aspects.

7.3.9.4 Future plans: A majority of the children in conflict with the law wished to pursue education or employment once they were out of the juvenile justice system. However, a quarter of them had no plans for the future.

7.3.9.5 Support required for reform and rehabilitation: Majority of the children in conflict with the law needed parental and family support, financial support and social support to meet personal goals and rehabilitation.

7.3.9.6 Deciding factor for reform and rehabilitation: Support of parents and family was the deciding factor in the reform and rehabilitation for a significant number of children in conflict with the law.

7.3.9.7 Remorse:

7.3.9.7.1 Remorse about harm caused : A majority of the children in conflict with the law expressed remorse over the harm caused. Those who did not express remorse believed they were innocent or confused about their innocence.

7.3.9.7.2 Remorse about person harmed: Majority of children in conflict with the law believed that the person(s) harmed most by their actions were their own parents and families and the victim and victim's family.

7.3.9.7.3 Remorse about nature of harm caused : The kind of harm caused by children in conflict with law was loss of life of the victim, shame to their families and breaking of relationship with their own as well as the victim's family.

7.3.9.8 Empathy for victim : A majority of the children in conflict with the law felt empathy for their victims.

7.3.9.9 Desire to make amends : An overwhelming majority of CICL (78.58) expressed their desire to make amends in different ways.

7.3.9.10 Positive experiential learning in the juvenile justice system :

7.3.9.10.1 Positive Experience of the juvenile justice system : Majority of the children in conflict with the law stated that they had learnt something positive through their experience in the juvenile justice system.

7.3.9.10.2 Nature of positive experiences in the juvenile justice system: The top four positive things reported to have been learnt were self awareness, learning right from wrong, learning a new skill and a new good habit

7.3.10 Rights of children in conflict with the law while in custody:

7.3.10.1 Right to legal representation: An overwhelming majority of the children in conflict with the law had legal representation.

7.3.10.2 Reasons for lack of legal representation: The main reason for lack of legal representation was poverty.

7.3.10.3 Right to family contact while in custody: Almost half of the children in conflict with the law had contact with the family while in custody.

7.3.10.4 Rights during participation in research study :

7.3.10.4.1 Consent to participate in study and talk about family : 100% of the children in the study gave their consent and showed willingness to talk about their family.

7.3.10.4.2 Experience of participation in research study : 100% of the children in conflict with the law reported their experience of participation in the study as happy.

7.3.10.4.3 Distress due to participation in study : 100% of the children in conflict with the law stated that they did not experience any distress on account of participation in the research study.

7.3.10.4.4 Usefulness of participation in study : An overwhelming majority of the children in conflict with the law felt that their participation in the research study was very useful to them.

7.3.10.4.5 Willingness to participate in future : An overwhelming majority of the children in conflict with the law expressed willingness to participate in similar research studies in the future.

7.3.10.4.6 Experience of interview process : An overwhelming majority of children in conflict with the law reported feeling happy at the end of the interview with the researcher.

7.4 Limitations of the Study

7.4.1 Limited coverage in terms of geographical locations across States and Union Territories: The study was limited to only 1 state of Karnataka due to difficulty in obtaining government permission to access children in conflict with the law in different states/UTs, on account of children at the Observation Home(s) and Special Home being in judicial custody.

7.4.2 Limited coverage in terms of geographical locations across districts within the State of Karnataka : The study was limited to only 2 Observation Homes (one in Bangalore and another in Mysore) and 1 Special Home (in Bangalore) as covering all districts would not have been feasible as there were very few number of children available in rest of the Observations Homes situated in Karnataka during the research period.

7.4.3 Non – inclusion of girls in conflict with the law from the study : There were less than 5 girls in conflict with the law in Bangalore at the time of data collection; hence this group was not interviewed.

7.4.4 Non-inclusion of children on bail : Scope was limited to studying mental health status of children in conflict with the law only while in the child care institution – and not while out on bail (though they would still be in the juvenile justice system even while on bail).

7.4.5 Focus on mental health status only : Scope was limited to studying present mental health status and risks to mental health and not screening, assessment or diagnosis of mental illness of children in conflict with the law.

7.4.6 Non-inclusion of Post-Traumatic Stress : Scope did not include Post Traumatic Stress which is one of the significant mental health conditions seen in children in the justice system. (For the child in conflict with the law, traumatic events like being apprehended by the police, possible violent encounter(s) with the police, being a witness, participant or initiator in the incident / legal violation that brought him in conflict with the law, separation from family, being placed in institutional settings – are all significant traumatic events – some of which may even have been life-threatening in nature. However, the complexity of screening, assessing and arriving at a diagnosis for Post-Traumatic Stress Disorder made it beyond the scope of this study.

7.4.7 Non-inclusion of verbal violence: Scope of the study only explored physical violence and did not explore verbal violence. It is possible that many of the children in conflict with the law may have come from socio-cultural backgrounds where use of street language, slang, etc, is seen as 'normal' and adults often casually address children and each other using caste-based slurs, gender-based slangs and language that may appear 'abusive' to individuals from a different socio-economic class or caste but not to members of that community. Therefore, what constitutes verbal violence or arriving at a common, universal definition of verbal violence in this context would have been difficult. Hence, verbal violence was not included in the scope of the study.

7.4.8 Non-inclusion of child sexual violence: Scope of the study did not explore child sexual abuse, (despite a strong likelihood of a history of child sexual abuse among this vulnerable population) on account of the ethical dilemmas and legal challenges that may have arisen on account of legal reporting of any sexual abuse to law enforcement agencies. The Protection of Children from Sexual Offences Act, 2012, mandates reporting of child sexual abuse by any professional. In the absence of access to a safe space, lack of mental health services, risk of another legal case prolonging the contact with the law, fear of reprisal by the abuser, social stigma and fear, children and families are known to resist reporting of child sexual abuse in the Indian context.

7.4.9 Focus only on 'counselling' in enabling reform and rehabilitation and not the range of other facilitating measures : Scope was limited to studying the status of counselling services received by the CICL and not all the other elements of services required to ensure mental health in order to enable reform, rehabilitation, restoration of the child back to community as envisaged by the Juvenile Justice Act.

7.4.10 Limited number of counsellors interviewed: The study is limited to interviewing only 2 counsellors – one from OH Mysore and one from Special Home, Bangalore. The Counsellor from OH Bangalore had just resigned from service at the time of data collection and hence could not be interviewed. This meant that the study did not have a large number of responses or diverse perspectives and experiences from counsellors working with children in conflict with the law. However, this study could be used as a starting point to undertake more detailed and in-depth study with a large number of counsellors across the State as well as country to get a clearer picture of the role of counsellors in enabling reform and rehabilitation of children in conflict with the law in India.

7.4.11 Study based on self–report only: The information given by each of the study respondents – both children in conflict with the law as well as counsellors have been taken at face value. There was a cross verification of data with regard to age, type, frequency and nature of offence, income and occupation of parents, educational background, etc from the official records available and maintained at the OH and SH for legal purposes. However, personal histories relating to medical and mental health, family, description of experiences with the justice system have been taken entirely on the basis of self-report only with no cross verification from any other sources like family, medical records, etc., since it was not available and contact with families was not permitted by the authorities.

7.4.12 Specific nature of settings : The present study was confined to study of mental health of children residing in OH and SH. Hence the, findings cannot be generalized for the children living in other types of child-care institutions

7.5 Recommendation to review impact of amendment to JJ Act, 2015 in light of finding

The JJ Act (Care and Protection) of Children Act, 2015 underwent an amendment in 2015 lowering the age of the child from 18 to 16 years, for those children who were in the 16-18-year group and who had been charged with a heinous offence. The present study found that a large majority of the children who had come into conflict with the law were in the age group of 16 to 18 years. Hence, lowering of age from 18 years to 16 years (Section 15 of JJ Act, 2015) in the case of children charged with heinous offences is not in the interest of children – as 75 % of the children are in this age group only, which means that when it is known that neuro-developmentally adolescents in the age group of 16 to 18 years are most likely to come into conflict with the law on account of neuro biological changes in the brain, peer pressure, poor impulse control and lack of future orientation (Laurence Steinberg), and the statistical data also shows that this is the age group that is coming into conflict with the law, then this is the age group that must be focused on for providing support for reform and not selection for punishment. Therefore, programs for prevention, reform and rehabilitation have to focus on the developmental needs of this specific age group of adolescents of 16 to 18 years.

This finding also has serious implications for the law and Section 15 needs to be interpreted to allow for children in the age group of 16 to 18 years to be "tried and sentenced" in the juvenile justice system rather than the adult criminal justice system. ('Tried and sentenced' – are words that are not recommended to be used in the context of children in conflict with the law as they are believed to be part of the stigmatizing semantics used. Instead, the terms 'inquiry' instead of 'trial' and 'found guilty or not guilty' are recommended to be used while referring in the context of children).

7.6 Suggestions for future research

7.6.1 Large scale and in-depth research studies into the prevalence and nature of mental health problems of children in conflict with the law in India could be taken up by the Government across different districts in Karnataka, as well as across other States in India.

7.6.2 Research into the link between exposure to adverse childhood experiences like child sexual abuse, violence, mental illness, poor parenting and poverty and offending by children in India.

7.6.3 Research into existing models of counselling and other mental health services being provided in other parts of the world that have been known to contribute to the reform, rehabilitation and reintegration of children in conflict with the law.

7.6.4 Research into whether extending the age of coverage of the Right to Education up to 18 years under the Right of Children to Free and Compulsory Education (RTE) Act,

2009, would result in lowering the incidence of children coming into conflict with the law.

7.6.5 Research into whether prohibiting all and any form of child labour till the age of 18 years, under The Child Labour (Prohibition and Regulation) Amendment Act, 2016, would result in lowering the incidence of children coming into conflict with the law.

7.7 Conclusion

The present study was an attempt to study the mental health status and counselling of children in conflict with the law. Children in conflict with the law almost always have a history of several mental health problems and psychosocial adversities which places them at risk for coming into conflict with the law. So, treating them for their mental health problems and helping them build 'psychological immunity' is one of the effective ways of preventing crime rather than trying to punish them ***after*** they have committed the offence.

Providing mental health services for children in conflict with the law is the responsibility of the State as laid down by the law. The Mental Health Care Act as well as the Juvenile Justice (Care and Protection of Children) Act, 2015 clearly lays down that mental health is the right of the citizen, including children in conflict with the law. Which means that all the functionaries responsible for providing these services have to look at this from a rights-based perspective and not as a 'service 'or as 'welfare' or 'charity'. Mental health is the ***right*** of the children in conflict with the law. Children in conflict with the law are also "children" first. Which means they are vulnerable and that we, as a State and as a society have a responsibility to care, protect and nurture them. This study is an attempt to encourage and remind the juvenile justice system and policy makers to make justice meaningful by recognizing that mental health is a right of every child in the juvenile justice system, including those in conflict with the law.

CHAPTER 8

VIII MENTAL HEALTH SERVICES FOR CICL: AN ALTERNATIVE MODEL

8.1 Legal and State mandate for the Model for Mental health Service for CICL pilot program

As a result of the disturbing findings of the present study highlighting the critical need for mental health services for CICL, the researcher proposed a model of mental health services for CICL to the Department of Women and Child, Government of Karnataka, in her capacity as a Member, Juvenile Justice Board, Bangalore (Urban). The proposed model was approved by the Honorable Karnataka High Court Committee on Juvenile Justice and the Karnataka State Legal Services Authority, which are responsible for monitoring the effective implementation of the Juvenile Justice Act, 2015 in the State of Karnataka. This model is being implemented since July 20th, 2019, as a pilot program at the Observation home Madivala, Bangalore, through the District Child Protection Unit, Bangalore Urban, with funding from private organizations who support the strengthening of community resources through corporate social responsibility funding.

8.2 Objectives of the Mental Health Services for CICL Model:

A first of its-kind holistic psychosocial health project for children (and families) in conflict with the law, the pilot model has the following objectives:

1. Provision of holistic health services – including physical, medical, social and psychological health services for children in conflict with the law and their families as envisaged under the JJ Act, 2015.
2. Creating an institutional and community ecosystem of services and support systems that enable reform, rehabilitation and reintegration of the child into the community.
3. Capacity building, awareness creation and sensitization of families, functionaries and institutional caregivers towards children in conflict with the law

8.3 Salient features of the Mental Health Services for CICL Model

1. **Infrastructure:** Establishing a physical space to ensure that professionals like counselor, doctor, psychologist, psychiatrist, social worker, etc. can provide services to the children at the OH. This has been done through establishing the Maanasa Wellness Centre at the OH, Bangalore which has a medical room, counseling room, family room, open learning space with library, indoor basketball court with space for music, dance, drama and other art-based therapies.

2. **Counselling Services:** Individual counseling services through experienced and trained counselors from academic institutions in the neighborhood, structured and customized group counseling programs through NGOs specialized to provide such services, family counseling program from the Department of Psychiatric Social Work, NIMHANS,

3. **Specialized Services:** Medical and Health camps from medical colleges in the neighborhood, Deaddiction program from the Department of Addiction Medicine, NIMHANS, Capacity building of mental health service providers by Department of Child and Adolescent Psychiatry, NIMHANS, Life Skills through Sports Coaching by an experienced Sports Coach.

4. **Institutional Services:** Induction program for children when they enter the OH, capacity building for caregivers to ensure mental health services entitled by law.

5. **Community based services:** Awareness creation and psychoeducation of stakeholder communities, employee engagement programs, mentoring programs, reading and remedial education programs.

6. **State and Civil Society Partnership and Joint Ownership Model:** The Model is a unique initiative that has brought together Civil society and the State in a collaborative manner. Each partner bringing the best of their resources to address a common social, legal and health problem. The Corporates from civil society contributes monetary resources through corporate social responsibility funds, the Government contributes infrastructure and administrative personnel for monitoring and management, while NGOs bring their experience and expertise of working in areas related to health of disadvantaged and at-risk communities, academic

institutions (offering post graduate courses in medicine, psychiatry, psychology, counselling and social work) and mental health professionals contribute their professional expertise and provide the services required.

CPSIA information can be obtained
at www.ICGtesting.com
Printed in the USA
BVHW060850140123
656278BV00010B/1181

9 781805 454441